Learn To Cook

ISBN: 978-0-9886736-0-1

Second Edition Published December 2012
First Edition Published June 2011

Dedicated to James Devery

Designed by Christopher Sharpe
Illustrations by Craig Matthew Staggs
Photos of Hilah by Nadia Caffesse

Special Thanks To:

Bruce Alter
Kirby Conn
Jill Hoefling
Jenny Lin
Laurel Kinney
Adriene Mishler
Diane Morrison
Billy O'Leary
Jessie Tilton
John Traigis
Natalie Vallot
Sam Weber
Dustin Wills

For over 170 video recipes, visit HilahCooking.com!

LEARN

to

COOK

A Down and Dirty Guide to Cooking
(for People Who Never Learned How)

by Hilah Johnson

Contents

How to Use This Book

If you're thinking, "Read it," you are correct.

I recommend you read it from the beginning to the end.

Don't worry about stopping to highlight or make flashcards or give yourself little vocabulary quizzes. I think you will recall enough information by the end of part one to actually start cooking some simple things. Do not be intimidated. Cooking is not rocket science. Cooking is for everyone.

Hopefully, the anecdotes and silly stories and jokes will do enough to hold your interest through the book, even if you don't really want to learn to cook but feel like you should learn to cook. Of course, for those who are really excited about learning to cook, and maybe even already know a little, this book has a lot of useful, real information for you, too.

In **Part One**, we deal with terminology of cooking, as well as how to plan meals, grocery shop, and prepare foods for cooking. This is by no means a comprehensive dissertation on the culinary arts, but it covers all the big subjects—the fundamentals that form the basis for all the other crazy things people do in the kitchen.

You may feel overwhelmed because it is a lot of information. Let me assure you again, you do not need to memorize the book or even understand everything in it before you begin your new cooking lifestyle. You will learn as you go, and with each success you will be more confident in your ability.

Part Two is where you'll find the recipes. Tucked into the sidebars of this section you'll also find more in-depth explanations of cooking techniques, choosing and prepping produce, unusual ingredients, and helpful tips. There's so much information crammed in there, you probably will find it useful just to read over all the recipes, even the ones you may not be interested in at first glance.

Some of the recipes have accompanying video demonstrations on-line. Just look for this symbol and it will tell you what to type into your doohickey!

Hi, I'm Hilah! Who Are You?

Welcome to this book. This book will teach you how to cook food you like to eat. Food that will make you popular with friends. Food that won't cost you a million dollars. Food that is healthier than what you are probably eating now, as a person who does not know how to cook.

So you don't get the wrong idea, I'm going to take a a few pages here to explain a little bit about my experiences and philosophy of food. That way, you'll understand where I'm coming from and what you can expect to get out of this book. Hopefully, this will all sound reasonable enough to you that we can be friends.

First, I'll state for the record that I am not a trained chef. But I have long been interested in food. Over the last twenty years, I have probably read more than a hundred books on cooking and nutrition and have been making cooking tutorial videos since 2010 at **HilahCooking.com**. The first cookbook I had was called *Who Is That Short Chef?* I think we picked it up one day at some kind of county fair or something — I remember a turkey leg and a lot of dust in the air. It was a good little book for kids; there was even a page for kids to draw on! FUN!

A Note On "Organic"

. . . .

This label has become very annoying to me, as ubiquitous as it is. Don't get me wrong, I believe organic farming is the way to go for the planet and for our bodies as well, but I will never, EVER list "organic" *anything* in any of my recipes. I think it's obnoxious, in the same way that specifying "good quality" anything is obnoxious. Yes, I do buy organically grown (and local when I can) produce and meat when I'm feeling rich. But I don't beat myself up over it when I can't afford it, and I don't think you should, either. Inform yourself and do your best, but don't go broke over it. That said, these are the "Dirty Dozen," meaning the most worth it to buy organically: apples, celery, bell peppers, peaches, strawberries, nectarines, grapes, spinach, lettuce, cucumbers, blueberries, and potatoes.

You were supposed to draw what you (the short chef) looked like, but since my brother and I were sharing the book, the drawing (done by me, the elder) was a weird mish-mash of what my brother looked like and what I looked like, down to what we were wearing that day.

Anyway, I think I was about seven, and that's pretty much when I started cooking. From there on out, I loved reading cookbooks. Seriously. I mean, I already really liked reading and eating, so once I discovered cookbooks, I couldn't get enough.

As I got older, I got more interested in the chemistry of cooking, too—not just how to make brownies, which were my specialty for many years.

Also, my parents cooked. Nothing fancy or elaborate, but we definitely weren't eating out all the time. My dad's specialties were chili, chicken fried steak, and cream gravy. My mom's specialty was using cookies to distract my brother and me from being annoying. She would put butter and sugar in a big bowl and tell us to go outside with it and sit in the sun until the butter was soft. Usually we would end up eating about half of the delicious butter-sugar mess before we went back inside.

My interest in nutrition specifically started when I was in high school and one day, like many "alternative" kids, decided that I was going to be A Vegetarian. Fortunately, I had hippie parents who were familiar with this "alternative" choice, and my mom gave me a book to read—*Diet for a Small Planet* by Frances Moore Lappe, which is a great book that I recommend to anyone who is considering adopting a dead-animal-free diet. Its original premise was the theory of protein complementing (combining foods to create a full complement of amino acids and thus a "full protein"). The practice has since been rebuffed as unnecessary by the American Dietetic Association and the author herself, but it still makes sense to me in an intuitive way and in a delicious meal way.

NEwayz, the vegetarianism lasted about eight years and included a short-lived stint with veganism, but the fascination with nutrition and vitamins and junk has stuck with me.

With all that in mind, this is still my cookbook, and these are all things I eat. For the most part they are fairly well-balanced and healthy recipes. What I mean by "healthy" is: I keep a loose leash on my calorie and fat intake and include lots of vegetables and fruit. I'm not a nutritionist but I'm no dumbass, either. You won't find anything in here that calls for a stick of butter (well, except cookies) or a pound of bacon. What you might find is "half a stick of butter" and "half a pound of bacon." To me, that's reasonable…sometimes.

Anyway, you've heard it before: moderation. That's my basic rule. But I also measure my moderation in forty-eight hour chunks. For example: On Monday, maybe all I will eat is Triscuits, coffee, and pimiento cheese; but on Tuesday, I will moderate by eating only romaine lettuce, roasted chicken, and apples. See what I did? In forty-eight hours, I got all my food groups. That is how old I am: I still think about food groups instead of the stupid pyramid.

Now let's talk about you. Why do you want to learn to cook? You know the answer to this. The most common answers are:

So you can eat better.
So you can save money.
So you can impress people.

These are all great reasons to learn to cook. But you're not going to eat better unless you like the food you cook; you're not going to save money unless you buy and cook food you want to eat; and you're not going to impress anyone by making crap. These are all facts.

This book can help you avoid all those possible outcomes and get the results you want by starting from the beginning and having reasonable goals. I'm not going to tell you what kind of food you should be buying, cooking, or eating. I'm not going to tell you to eat healthier, or organically, or free-range, or to quit using sugar or salt or wheat or lard or vodka. I'm not going to tell you to be a vegetarian or not be a vegetarian; to eat breakfast or to blow it off. You can put whatever you want to into your body, whenever you want to put it in. I'm going to help you make that happen.

PART ONE

Learn to Cook

CHAPTER 1

What Do You Like To Eat?

I had this roommate once who asked me to teach him how to go to the grocery store.

Sadly, I told him, "Just buy food you want to eat," then laughed in his face.

But that was many years ago and I have since come to realize that there are hundreds of smart, capable people out there who would ask the same question. (In my defense, that guy was a dillrod in a myriad of other ways, and I was about to kick him out of the house at that point. Still, I guess I'm sorry, dude, for laughing at you.)

Anyway, I should thank him now because I have thought back to that conversation many times while writing this book. I think the problem wasn't that he couldn't figure out how to get to the store, put groceries in a cart, and then purchase them–rather, the problem was that he had no clue what to buy. The guy was used to eating his meals in restaurants, where he was presented with a limited number of options. A grocery store offers unlimited options, as long as you know how to cook. Of course he didn't know how to cook, so how would he know what to buy in order to cook? Who's the dillrod now, Hilah?

So think about that little anecdote that makes me look like a mean old butthole. If you are in his boat, I think I can help you now that I have had many years to gather wisdom and magical tips. Give me a chance, huh?

First, I think it's important to differentiate between what you actually like to eat and what you think you should like to eat (i.e., breakfast, salad, oatmeal, tofu). Now is not the time to try and completely overhaul your eating habits (well, except in the case where you're eating chicken nuggets thrice daily). If you really want to learn to cook, learn to cook some things you know you already like.

This will help you learn in two ways: by cooking something that is familiar, you will be better able to judge your relative success at making it good; making something that you like will give you great satisfaction instead of great disappointment.

I mean, say you try out some Oyster'n'Eggplant Surprise (thinking that you would like to be the kind of person who eats crap like that) and the "surprise" is that it is revolting. Now, an experienced cook would blame the recipe and move on, but a new cook will likely blame themselves, causing a downward spiral of frustration, at the bottom of which lies a pile of garbage and strong urge to give up and never cook again. I don't want you to end up there.

4

What Kind of Person Are You?

How do you categorize your eating choices now?

This is not about judgment. This is about honesty. Think about me as you would a food therapist. I can only help if you are honest with yourself and me about your attitude toward food.

The following categories are all perfectly fine approaches to food and eating. As long as you understand what type of eater you are, you can figure out what kind of cook you should aim to be, and you will be a happier cook for having done so.

You likely will cross boundaries into more than one category, depending on your mood, the time of day, or whether or not those chocolate chip cookies on the reception desk at your grandma's nursing home are free. But generally speaking, what would you say about yourself?

I hope you don't have the idea that I am trying to "label" you or put you in a box of my own design. I'm not. But, here's an analogy for you: say you wanted to learn to play guitar. Say you also really loved Slayer. Doesn't it stand to reason that the first style you would attempt to master would be metal?

The point is not to fit you into one of my categories, though, it is to get you to clearly consider who you are, why you want to learn to cook, and what you want to learn to cook.

These are just categories that I came up with on my own, based on my experiences and the people I know. If you feel that you belong in a new and unmentioned category, please write to me about it. I'd like to know more about you.

5

Health Nut

Do you study nutrition labels and try to make conscious decisions to choose one thing over another? Do you believe in food as medicine and get joy from providing your body the best? Is your desire to cook driven by having more control over what you ingest?

Convenience Matters

Will you eat almost anything as long as it's fast and easy to obtain? Do you think of eating just as something you have to do in order to not die? If you could just take a pill instead of eat dinner, would you? Maybe you are interested in learning to cook so you can save money or time by not having to leave the house whenever you are hungry.

Adventurous

Are you up for anything and love to try new cuisines? Do you dream of taking food vacations to far-away lands and eating things that have no English translation? Want to be able to recreate fancy or weird food at home for way less than a restaurant while at the same time impressing the shit out of your BF or GF?

Close To Home

Do you patronize the same three restaurants? Do you always order one of the same three dishes? Are you reluctant to try new foods? Have a long list of "dislikes"? Feel a burning desire for mom's meatloaf every night of the week?

6

The next step on a successful journey to being able to cook: come up with a short list of maybe three dishes you would like to know how to make. This may seem silly or overly simple, but think about the following questions and write down some ideas if you want, or save paper and just keep them in your head.

* What are your favorite fruits and vegetables?

* What are your comfort foods? Dishes made by your parents or grandparents?

* What are your favorite restaurants and what do you order?

* Think about "meal parts" you are fond of. Do you love breakfast foods? Do you like soups? Sandwiches? Salads? Are you someone who likes "anything with cheese" for example, or "anything with noodles"?

* Think about things like that. Knowing the answers to those questions will help you cook things you like to eat.

Wonderful!

Now that you've got a neat little cheat sheet with some dishes you'd like to be able to make for yourself, let's talk about the recipes you'll use.

CHAPTER 2

How to Read a Recipe

If you can read, you can cook.

This may sound patronizing or trite, but I believe it with conviction.

Recipes are like road maps, and once you learn to read one, you can read them all. Of course it may be daunting at first with unfamiliar abbreviations and terminology and not enough pictures or explanations. But we can get through that.

I promise.

Numero Uno

It is very important to read the entire recipe before you begin. Often, even experienced cooks will get halfway through and realize they are out of milk or sugar or dog pee (probably shouldn't be making that recipe anyway) and then it's a real downer to have to run out to the store or, worse, decide to scrap the whole project and order pizza again. Seriously, I cannot stress this part enough.

By reading the recipe through, you also get a big picture idea of what has to happen. Invariably, there will be down time in the preparation: waiting for potatoes to boil, waiting for meat to sear. That time won't be wasted if you've read the recipe first and know that you could be mincing the onions during that time. When you're cooking, there will often be several things going on at once and it makes for a smoother ride if you can anticipate what is coming up next.

Numero Dos

Get all ingredients out before you start cooking so everything is on hand when you need it. This is especially important when trying out a new recipe to ensure that no steps are skipped and no ingredient left behind.

Numero Tres

Don't be afraid of the new words you encounter! Most of them are friendly. Many of their meanings are pretty obvious. Some maybe not so much.

To cover all our bases, here comes an exhaustive glossary of cooking terms to delight and inform you. This may indeed be the least fun and scariest-looking part of the book, but don't get freaked out. The good news is that only a few of these words will come into play in the recipes in this book. The rest is for reference and to get you familiarized with the concepts. So don't try to memorize it: just read through it once and get on with your life. I'll get into more detail on some of the more important ones later in Chapter Six.

The Strange and Wonderful Vocabulary of Cooking

Bain-Marie – A French term. *See Water Bath.*

Bake – To cook surrounded by dry heat, as in an oven. Unless specified otherwise, the oven should be preheated to the correct temperature before you put your stuff in it.

Baste – To periodically coat a food with liquid while cooking; liquid could be pan-drippings, fat, or a sauce. You can buy natural bristle or silicon basting brushes. Silicon may be preferred for their ease of cleaning. A turkey baster is another easy-to-clean option that works like a giant eyedropper.

Batter – The semi-liquid substance that results from the thorough mixing of dry ingredients (flour, sugar, etc.) with wet (eggs, milk, etc.). Batters are thinner (more liquid) than doughs. Examples: cake batter, pancake batter.

Beat – To mix at high speed with the purpose(s) of combining completely and/or incorporating air into the mixture.

Blanch – To cook a food briefly in boiling water. The purpose for blanching varies but it can be used to remove skins from nuts, tomatoes, and peaches; to partially cook something that is to be cooked further; or to remove salt or strong flavors from cured meats or even strong-flavored vegetables like onions. To properly count the time, put the vegetables in a large pot of boiling water, put a lid on the pot, and start your timer. When the timer rings, you need to stop the cooking process immediately by removing the thing from the boiling water and dropping into an ice bath to shock it. *See Ice Bath.*

Blend – This may mean to combine in a blender and whiz around until everything is smooth or pureed; it could also mean the same thing as stir or mix.

11

Boil – To cook in boiling water (temperature at or above 212° F). A full boil or a rolling boil are the same thing, and they mean that the liquid is boiling so furiously that it keeps boiling even when you stir it. Foods for which boiling is the best cooking method are few: pasta, some grains. A recipe for "Boiled Beef" for example, would be more accurately described as "Simmered Beef"; literally boiling beef can make it tough.

Braise – To cook over low heat for an hour or more, with a relatively small amount of liquid and covered with a tight-fitting lid. The cooking liquid is used as the sauce or gravy. Meats are usually browned or seared before the braising step begins.

Bread – The verb, means to coat a food in either crumbs or flour before cooking. *See Dredge.*

Broil – To cook by means of a heat element placed above the food. This is what a broiler is for. Your oven's broiler may have a High and Low setting, but on older ovens it's probably just On or Off. Check food frequently to prevent a fire. It takes only seconds to go from "toasted" to "in flames."

Brown – With ground meat, "brown" really just means "cook"; when a recipe calls on you to "brown ground meat," you should stir the meat as it cooks to break it up into chunks and allow it to cook evenly. With roasts and whole pieces of meat, brown may be used to mean sear. *See Sear.*

Brush – Kind of like baste, but you do it once before cooking. With pie crusts or bread, you may brush them with butter or egg-wash before baking to add color and a shiny look.

Butterfly – To cut a piece of meat almost all the way across, parallel to the cutting board on which it sits, and then open the meat like a butterfly or a "meat book." The purpose is to create a thinner cut that will cook faster or to create a larger surface to facilitate rolling or stuffing the meat with a filling. *See p. 86.*

Chop – To cut into near-uniform pieces.

Coat – To cover with something, be it flour, bread crumbs, egg, cornmeal, batter, whatever.

Combine – Combine means mix together. Something that is "combined well" is uniform in color and texture.

Core – To remove the core from fruits such as apples, pears, etc.

Cream – To beat fat (eggs, butter) with sugar (usually) until it is all light and airy. The color will lighten, as well. The purpose is to incorporate air into the mixture which makes a lighter, more delicate final product.

Cube – To cut into uniform chunks. Though there's no particular size designated by this word, ½" to ¼" cubes are a good rule of thumb. *See Dice.*

Cut-In – In baking, this is a way of combining solid fats (butter, lard) with flours. To do it, cut your cold fat into small pieces with a knife and add to your flour. Use your fingertips or a fork to mix, breaking the fat up into smaller and smaller pieces that are each coated in the flour. When you are done, there should be no dry flour left.

Dash – Just a shake's worth from a shaker of salt or spice, about ¹⁄₁₆ of a teaspoon.

Deep Fry – To fry in oil or fat that is deep enough to submerge the food completely. This means at least three inches deep usually. Be sure to use a deep enough pot so that you leave at least two inches of headspace between the oil level and the lip of the pot to avoid overflow when you put the food in. *See p. 93.*

Deglaze – To add liquid to a hot pan to remove and dissolve caramelized bits of food in order to make a sauce with them. *See Sauteed Steaks p. 172.*

Dice – To cut into small cubes: ¼" (small dice) to ¾" (large dice).

Dot – To top something with small bits of butter. This makes a crispy topping when baked or adds moisture to a dish.

Double – To double the yield of a recipe by doubling all the ingredient amounts. Cooking time is not necessarily doubled. Most recipes can be successfully doubled but, for reasons known only to the Great One, things start to go a little wonky when you try to triple, quadruple, quintuple, etc.

Double Boiler – The purpose of using a double boiler is to protect your food from heating up too fast, which, when cooking delicate things like custards and candies, may cause curdling or crystallizing. To rig up a double boiler, get a two to three quart pot and put a little water in the bottom. Find a heat-proof bowl that will fit into the pot, without touching the bottom of the pot (sort of hanging from the rim). Cook your food in the bowl, which sits over the water, which sits in the pot, which sits on the fire. Talk about putting some distance between your food and the heat element!

Dough – The moist, semi-solid substance that results from mixing dry ingredients with wet. As in bread or pizza dough, it is much firmer than batter.

13

Drain – To remove liquid after cooking (water from pasta or rendered fat from meat).

Dredge – To coat with crumbs or flour. *See Bread and Coat.*

Drippings – The liquid left in the bottom of a skillet or roasting pan after cooking meat. Usually made into a sauce or gravy. *See Pan Sauce.*

Drizzle – To pour a small amount of liquid over something.

Dry Heat Cooking – Includes grilling, sauteing, pan frying, deep frying, stir frying, baking, and roasting. Dry heat means the food is cooked without adding moisture (water). It usually requires high temperatures (over 300° F) and is the only way to achieve browning and crispiness.

Dust – To lightly coat with flour (some food item before cooking or the inside of a cake pan before filling with batter) or powdered sugar (some desserts after cooking).

Egg Wash – A well-beaten egg (plus water perhaps) that is brushed on baked goods before baking to make them shiny. *See Brush.*

Emulsify – To force two things that normally do not mix (e.g., oil and water) into an agreement in which one substance is broken into teeny droplets that are suspended within the other substance. With vinaigrettes, this means combining an acid (vinegar or juice) with oil until it turns "creamy" and uniform. An emulsion is the end product. Emulsifiers are additional ingredients that help hold the oil and liquid together in a stable relationship: egg yolks, mustard, and corn starch.

Entree – In English usage, this means the "main dish." In French, entrée means the thing that precedes the main dish.

Fold – To combine carefully so as not to break up trapped air bubbles. A way of using gentle, long strokes to combine something fluffy like beaten egg whites with something denser, like egg yolks.

Fry – This might mean deep fry, but can also mean pan fry, in which you only have a half inch or so of oil in a skillet and are browning thin cuts of meat, tofu, or vegetables (such as breaded eggplant).

Grate – This means using a grater to make tiny shreds of something, like carrots or cheese.

Grease – When greasing a cookie sheet, use just a tiny amount of oil (⅛ teaspoon or less), smeared in a very thin layer all over. A piece of wadded up waxed paper works well to spread it. Or you can just use some spray oil.

Grill – Cooking by putting a heat source under the food, usually done outdoors on a charcoal or gas grill.

14

Halve – To reduce all ingredients by half (50%) in order to lessen the final yield. Read the recipe carefully before attempting this; recipes calling for three eggs are tricky to cut in half. *See Double.*

Ice Bath – A large filled bowl filled with ice and cold water into which you drop blanched or parboiled foods to stop their cooking and cool them immediately. Dropping something into an ice bath is called "shocking."

Julienne – To cut something (usually vegetables) into long, thin, evenly sized strips.

Knead – When making bread, this is the activity that helps gluten form and results in a nice, chewy loaf. To knead bread dough, put it on a floured surface (clean countertop sprinkled with flour), pat or stretch it out. Using your palms, fold the dough over onto itself and press. Continue stretching, folding and pressing for however long the recipe says to do so.

Leavener (or Leavening Agent) – A general term for one of several ingredients that create gas bubbles and make baked goods rise. Leavening agents can be yeast, baking powder, or baking soda. Before the advent of those three, eggs and fats provided the only leavening for many baked things.

Line – Someday you may need to line a cake pan with parchment paper before filling with cake batter. To do so, lay out a large sheet of paper and put your pan(s) on top of it. Trace around with a pencil and cut out the shape. Lay it in the bottom of your pan. The recipe may further specify oiling the paper. This is a good idea when baking soft, high-sugar content cakes that have a tendency to stick to the pan. *See Vegan Chocolate Cake, p. 238.*

Marinate – To soak food in a flavorful marinade. Marinades are mixtures of liquid and spices that have an acid component, such as citrus juice or vinegar, that help tenderize meats. Be careful not to marinate longer than the recipe dictates as this can cause mushiness and no one likes mushiness.

Mince – Mincing is like chopping, but smaller. As small as you can get it. To mince something, start with a fine chop, and then run your big knife through the pile of chop several times until you have a pile of mince!

Mix – To stir things together.

Moist Heat Cooking – As opposed to dry heat, this means foods are cooked in the presence of added moisture, such as boiling, simmering, stewing, braising, steaming, or poaching. While you don't get browning or caramelization with these methods, they are generally much more forgiving (i.e. harder to screw up) than dry heat methods.

Learn to Cook

Pan Fry – To fry in oil in a skillet. Generally more oil than when sauteing and stir frying, but the food should not be submerged in oil. A half-inch is the maximum. *See Fry.*

Pan Sauce (or Pan Gravy) – A sauce made from the drippings left in a pan after cooking is complete.

Parboil (or Parcook) – To partially cook by boiling. Foods that have been parboiled may be further cooked by some other method afterwards or served in their partially cooked state (such as green beans served in a cold salad). *See Blanch.*

Pare (or Peel) – To remove the skin. You can use a paring knife (a small knife with a blade about 3" long) or a vegetable peeler.

Pinch – The amount you can pick up with your index, middle finger, and thumb, about ⅛ teaspoon.

Pit – To remove the pit or hard stone from the center of fruits such as peaches, cherries, or avocados

Pith — The bitter white part of citrus rinds, just below the colorful exterior zest. *See Zest.*

Poach – To cook food by immersing in barely simmering liquid (160° F-185° F); often used for fish or chicken. *See Chicken Salad, p. 130.*

Pressure Cook – Wet heat method of cooking under pressure that allows foods to reach temperatures above the boiling temperature of water. You need a pressure cooker for this. Refer to the manual for instructions.

Proof – Something done with yeast to activate it and to make sure it is still alive and viable before you waste a bunch of time making bread with dead yeast and end up with a hard, flat brick. To proof yeast, add it to a ¼ cup of warm water (110-115F) with ½ teaspoon of sugar and stir to dissolve. Set aside for five minutes, at which point it should look foamy. If it doesn't, get you some new yeast! Proof also refers to the second rising of a bread dough, after it's been shaped but before baking.

Punch Down – The funnest part of bread making. After the initial rise of the bread dough, it will be double its original size (so start with a BIG bowl). Then, you get your hand and make a fist and literally punch the dough in its dough-face and watch it collapse. Then you usually form it into a loaf at this point and let it rise once more (proof) before baking

Puree – To make into a smooth, lump-free substance. A blender or an immersion blender is good for this job. *See Blend.*

Reconstitute – To rehydrate a dried food, like raisins or chilies, by soaking in warm or hot water.

Reduce – To thicken and concentrate flavors in a liquid by boiling the water away into steam. Simmer or boil with the lid off.

Refresh – To soak in ice cold water for a few minutes to crisp up vegetables like wilty lettuce or celery.

Render – To melt the fat from meats by cooking. You can save it for a gravy or pan sauce or throw it away. If you decide to toss it, let it cool and then scrape it into the trash because it could stop up your Insinkerator and then your land lord will be PO'ed.

Rest – To leave alone for a few minutes. Rest meats after cooking and before carving to allow juices to redistribute. You may want to cover loosely with aluminum foil to keep warm. *See sidebar, p. 198.*

Rise – To set a yeast dough aside, covered, in a warm place so that the yeast can go forth and multiply and create bubbles and make the dough rise. *See Proof.*

Roast – To cook in an oven at a fairly high temperature. *See Roasted Chicken, p. 200.*

Roux – A mixture or flour and fat, cooked together and used to thicken gravies, sauces, and stews. Pronounced "roo."

Saute – To cook quickly, over high heat, in a shallow pan with a small amount of oil.

Scald – With milk, to heat to just before the boiling point. Sometimes necessary when baking to break up proteins.

Score – To make shallow cuts across a food, such as bread before baking or through fat on meat before roasting, to ensure even cooking.

Sear – To brown the outside of a food (usually meat) in a very hot pan before finishing cooking by another method (braising or roasting). Searing develops flavor and texture through the Maillard Reaction, which is fancy-talk for the browning reaction of the proteins and carbohydrates in the meat. Chemically, it's not the same reaction as caramelization but the word caramelized is often used to describe well-seared meat.

Season – When a recipe reads "season to taste," it means with salt and pepper, to your liking. You literally have to taste it and then season accordingly, in small increments, then taste it again. Repeat until you think it tastes good. I suggest using ¼ teaspoon as a starting point for a dish that serves 4 people and has no other sources of sodium (i.e. canned tomatoes, pre made sauces, or spice mixes) and adding more salt in dashes after that.

Shock – What you do when you drop something hot into an ice bath to stop its cooking and cool it.

Shred – Same as grate, but could also mean to cut into very thin strips with a knife, like cabbage for coleslaw.

17

Sift – To put through a sieve for the purpose of removing lumps and "fluffing up," as in flour.

Simmer – To cook just below boiling (185° F–200° F) so that small bubbles come up around the edges. May require adjusting the heat source to keep it from boiling.

Skim – To remove something from the top of something else. You might skim fat from stock or skim foam from boiling jelly. The easiest way to skim fat from liquid (if you have the time) is to refrigerate it until it's cold; the fat will solidify on the top, and you can lift it off.

Steam – To cook foods by surrounding with steam. You can use a perforated steamer basket inside a pot. *See Sweat.*

Steep – To soak in very hot liquid for the purpose of flavoring the liquid (e.g., making herb-infused oils and vinegars).

Stew – To cook in liquid, over a low heat for a long period of time, resulting in a thick, delicious gravy-like broth. A great way to cook tough cuts of meat and also beans. Like braising, but with smaller pieces of meat and more liquid. *See Beef Vegetable Stew, p. 157.*

Stir Fry – To cook quickly over a high heat in a small amount of oil, stirring constantly. *See Saute. See Tofu Stir Fry, p. 176.*

Strain – To remove particles by pouring through a sieve or a strainer. You might strain stock to get bits of herbs out of it or you might strain a lumpy gravy (oops!).

Sweat – To cook, covered, in a small amount of oil or water over a low to medium heat so that the vegetables (often onions) cook in their own liquid and soften but do not brown. This is a type of steaming.

Thin – To add liquid to something for the purpose of thinning its consistency (e.g., gravy, batter)

Toss – To casually throw around with abandon, and with joy in your heart, as in "toss the salad" or "toss your cookies."

Truss – To tie tightly. Roasts and whole birds will usually benefit from trussing so that they keep a compact shape while cooking, thereby looking better at the end. Trussing helps roasts cook more evenly.

Unleavened – Baked goods that do not use yeast, baking powder, or baking soda to make them rise. *See Chapatis, Flour Tortillas, Chapter 12.*

Water Bath, a.k.a. Bain Marie – This is kind of like a double boiler set-up, but you do it in the oven. To make a water bath, put the dish holding the food to be cooked (usually a custard or cheesecake or similarly delicate thing) into another, larger dish, and add enough water to the larger dish to bring the water level an inch or two up the side of the smaller dish. The water should not be more than halfway up the side of the smaller dish. Bake the whole contraption at once. The water serves as a cushion against the heat, so that the food heats up slower and cooks more gently and evenly.

Wet Heat Cooking – *See Moist Heat Cooking.*

Whip – Beat really fast with a whisk or an electric mixer so that air gets incorporated and makes the thing fluffy. You may be asked to whip to "soft peaks," which means whip it to the point at which, when you lift the whisk up, a bit of fluff follows it and then slumps over. "Stiff peaks" means that when you lift the whisk out a tiny, strong mountain of fluff stands up without slumping.

Whisk – This just means to use a whisk to mix something. That's all. A fork will often do as a whisk.

Zest – As a noun, the zest is the part of the citrus rind that is brightly colored and full of flavor and essential oils, and not the white part under that (the pith). As a verb, zest means to remove the zest. You can use a zester, a microplane, the tiny hole side of your box grater, or a vegetable peeler to remove ribbons of zest and then mince that up. Avoid getting the pith since that is bitter. *See Pith.*

Okay, are you asleep now? Or are you DEAD? Did I bore you to death?! I hope not, because now comes the fun part!

Just kidding.

There's still some more boring stuff to go over first.

Learn to Cook

MEASURING CRAP

I personally hate measuring crap. But sometimes it must be done. And sometimes it must be you who does it. Here are some tips on that business.

You will notice that I only instruct on how to measure by volume. You are very clever! In the U.S., most ingredients are quantified by volume (cups or fluid ounces); recipes written by "foreigners," however, will often use weight (grams or ounces). While it is true that weight is a more exact way to measure (and especially in baking, exactness is important), volume is simply more convenient, and that's what I will use in my recipes.

Possibly you already understand that a "cup" is equal to eight fluid ounces. Fluid ounces measure in volume as opposed to regular ounces, which measure in weight (or mass, as in, 16 ounces in a pound). It's kind of confusing. But if you remember that one fluid ounce is equal to one shot of tequila and that eight shots of tequila is equal to a cup of tequila… well, then I think you got it.

When purchasing measuring cups, you will find two distinct types. The first is a set of four in incremental sizes: 1 cup, ½ cup, ⅓ cup, ¼ cup. These are for measuring dry ingredients like flour, sugar, bread crumbs and the like. They must be filled and leveled with the top for accuracy. The other type is shaped more like a pitcher with a spout and usually made of glass or clear plastic. This type is designed for measuring liquids. The spout makes it easy to pour and the markings don't go all the way to the top of the cup to minimize spill-risk. (It is possible to interchange these two types of measuring devices; I do it. Might not turn out as perfectly as it could, but then, I don't care about things being perfect.) Measuring spoons come in increments of 1 tablespoon, 1 teaspoon, ½ teaspoon, ¼ teaspoon and sometimes ⅛ teaspoon. These are used for wet or dry ingredients.

When measuring dry ingredients like flour and sugar, fill the cup up overflowing, give it a gently tap on the side to settle it lightly, then use a knife or your finger to level it off. Just let the excess fall back into the storage container, unless your knife or finger is very dirty. In that case, see ***Chapter Six: Hygiene!***

Measuring spoons used for dry ingredients like spices, baking soda, and salt should be used the same way: over fill, gentle tap, level off. It's also a good idea to measure your spices and seasonings (including salt) AWAY from the pot. Trying to scoop or pour out "just the right amount" while holding the entire jar of pepper in one hand and a tiny metal spoon in the other is practically begging someone to come along and jangle your elbow or step on your foot and, whoopsie! Four ounces of pepper along with the pepper jar are now freestyling through your chili.

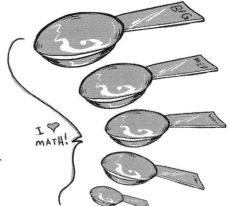

The proper way to measure liquids in a liquid cup is to set the cup on your counter, put yourself at eye-level with it, and pour in the liquid until it reaches the appropriate measure line. This is why a transparent material is important.

For the most accuracy, prepare ingredients before measuring. "Minced onion" should be minced before measuring; sifted flour should be sifted before measuring.

One of the trickiest things to figure out can be cheese measurements. Some recipes (even in the U.S.!) measure cheese by weight; others by volume of grated cheese. But eight ounces of cheese by weight (one half pound) once grated measures approximately 16 fluid ounces (two cups) of cheese by volume. When in doubt, remember the order of operations from algebra class. If the recipe reads "4 ounces of cheese, grated," you should probably weigh it and then grate it. If the recipe reads "4 ounce of grated cheese," it most likely means one half of a cup. Why they wouldn't just say "half a cup" I don't know; I won't do that to you, though. Volume all the way, baby!

For a table of measurement abbreviations and equivalencies, check the appendix. I think I put one back there. (I kid. Of course I did!) You shouldn't need it to make any of the recipes in this book, since I tried so very hard to not use abbreviations and to offer the equivalencies within the ingredients list. But if ever you find yourself with a cookbook that is less friendly than this one, you may need a chart.

Aside from that, there are certain assumptions that can be made when reading recipes. These assumptions hold true for recipes in this book and in most well-written cookbooks.

1) Spices are assumed to be ground unless otherwise stated. More on that in the next chapter, but for now just remember that if you like buy whole spices and grind them yourself, you must grind them before measuring, not afterwards.

2) Things like garlic, onions, oranges, bell peppers, and nuts: you can safely assume that the recipe requires that these be peeled, seeded, or shelled before chopping and measuring out. In other words, if it's inedible, you don't need to wait for me to tell you to remove it before proceeding.

3) If not otherwise specified, edible peels like those on potatoes and apples can be left on or pared off according to your preference. A rule of thumb is that skins which can easily be pierced with your fingernail are fine to eat.

4) Citrus juices are assumed to be fresh unless otherwise stated. Of course, nothing will 'splode if you use bottled juices, but most things taste a little nicer if you can use fresh juice, especially in uncooked recipes such as salad dressings.

5) Herbs are assumed to be dried unless otherwise stated. I have tried to offer equivalencies for fresh herbs if you happen to be so lucky as to have them. If you want to substitute fresh for dried or vice-versa, use this ratio: 1 unit dried herbs = 2 units fresh herbs. Most dried herbs have more concentrated flavor that their fresh counterparts. Parsley and cilantro are notable exceptions in that they are almost always meant to be used fresh because dried parsley and cilantro have virtually no flavor.

How to Choose a Recipe

Think back to *Chapter One* and what kind of eater you are. Choose something appropriate. For example, if you are a "convenience matters" type of person, pick a simple recipe the first time out; less than five ingredients or no more than two techniques (i.e., mix and bake) is advisable. If you are "close to home," choose something familiar like macaroni and cheese, or even better, a recipe from a family member (preferably one who is still alive and you can call for help if necessary). Now that you have put some thought into food, it should be fairly easy to choose something you will enjoy eating.

Also, it seems like beginning cooks are often turned off by long recipes with lots of steps. But in many cases, these are the exact recipes you want. A really short recipe is likely to be so short because it assumes that the reader knows a certain amount of "obvious" information. A long recipe is probably long because it offers very detailed instructions. I like detailed instructions when I'm learning something new.

Cooking For Your Tastes

Most recipes are malleable, meaning you can and should adjust them to suit your palate. Don't hesitate to taste as you go. Add more pepper, salt, lemon, whatever you think it needs more of. Go slow, adding just a little at a time and pay attention to how the flavor changes with each addition. This is how you learn how much is enough. Hopefully you'll stop before enough becomes too much! As I mentioned in the previous vocabulary section, when a recipe states "season to taste," a) it means with salt and pepper, and b) assuming there are no other sources of sodium in the dish (e.g., canned products or spice mixes) it's safe to start with a ¼ teaspoon of salt for a recipe that serves four people. Always add judiciously and err on the side of not salty enough. You can always add more at the table if you think it needs it.

As you become more comfortable cooking, you will gain confidence in being able to spot a good substitution opportunity when it comes up: swapping out onions for more celery, or ground turkey for ground beef, or cheddar for swiss. Changes like that are easy ways to make the recipe "your own." I'll point out good substitutions in my recipes to help you learn, and pretty soon you'll be changing things up like crazy!

That's when cooking *really* gets fun.

Eyeballing Measurements

"Eyeballing it" is a great skill to teach yourself. You can easily train your eye by measuring different amounts of salt with a measuring spoon, then pouring it into the palm of your hand. Memorize what 1 teaspoon, ½ teaspoon and ¼ teaspoon look like in your hand. Practice a little. Get good at it. Now you can also eyeball spice measurements! It will save you a little time and washing measuring spoons, but it's also an easy way to suddenly feel a lot more confident in the kitchen. I don't recommend beginners eyeballing anything larger than a teaspoon. You could really screw something up. No offense.

CHAPTER 3

Equipment

I read somewhere that one of the top five reasons people don't cook is because they don't have a properly equipped kitchen.

I think what this really means is that lots of people have been tricked by Crate and Barrel catalogs into thinking that they need a bunch of junk in their kitchen to make it work.

Not true.

Yes, you do need a few items unless you're into cooking squirrels on sticks with your hobo buddies. But for under $50 you can get enough tools to make at least a few different meals.

The bare minimum I'd say:

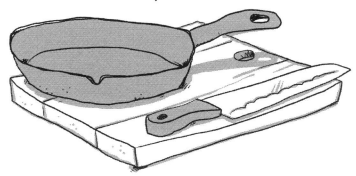

8" – 10" Cast Iron Skillet

Cast iron is my absolute favorite material to use for just about everything, but particularly high-heat cooking like stir frying, sauteeing, deep frying and searing. It transfers heat evenly and can go from stovetop to oven to outdoor grill to trashcan fire without a hitch. It is nearly indestructible as well as very affordable. Once well-seasoned, your cast iron skillet will work almost as well as any non-stick skillet on the market.

I recommend you season a new pan, even if it says "pre-seasoned." Here's how:

1. Take off all the packaging and labels, duh.
2. Wash the skillet. Use a plastic scrubbie or brush and clean all the surfaces of the skillet with hot water. Don't use a wire brush or anything that might scrape the surface.
3. Preheat your oven to 350° F.

Nonstick Cookware

If you'd rather try nonstick cookware, you should understand its limitations. For one thing, nonstick surfacing (Teflon) is poisonous and can flake off into your food if you aren't careful not to scratch it. Don't use metal utensils or abrasive cleaners on nonstick cookware. Ever.

Also be VERY sure you never heat it empty. There should always be some water or oil in the pan while it heats to prevent overheating which makes the nonstick molecules fly out of the pan and into your nose and give you brain cancer. Just sayin'.

4. Put some shortening, cooking oil, or lard in the skillet. (If you're using a solid fat, heat it up in the skillet on the stove to melt it before spreading.) Then smear a thin layer of your chosen substance all over your skillet, inside and out. Get nasty with it. Wipe off any excess pools or puddles.

5. Put the skillet in the oven upside down so that as the skillet heats up, any excess lube will drain away from the cooking surface. If you want to save yourself some trouble, put a cookie sheet or some foil on the lower rack so you don't have to clean your oven after this.

6. Cook your skillet! Don't freak out if it starts to smoke. This means the oil or grease is filling up the pores in the cast iron and making it nice and smooth. Just open a window and flip on a fan. Let it cook for an hour. Then turn off the oven and leave it in there for another hour.

7. Carefully remove the skillet. Use oven mitts because it's still gonna be hot. Put it on a heat resistant trivet or something. Let it cool completely. Repeat steps 3-7 if the surface doesn't feel smooth.

8. Start cooking with it! Don't attempt delicate things like fried eggs at first, but start using it to saute, stir-fry, pan-fry, for steaks, bacon, even cornbread. Every time you use it, it gets better.

9. Cleaning a cast iron skillet is best done using only hot water and a plastic scrubber. Soap, detergents, and copper or steel scrubbers will damage the seasoning. If there is something really stuck, you can use a couple spoonfuls of salt or baking powder in the skillet for extra scrubbing action. Once the skillet is cleaned, dry it well either with a towel or on the stove. When it's dry, put a few drops of any oil you have close-by in the skillet and wipe it around. Drying it well prevents rust and the extra oil helps the seasoning. Treat your skillet like this after every meal you cook and it will continue to get smoother and slicker and even easier to use and clean.

10. Cast iron is not without limitations, though. I gotta be real with you. It's not the best choice for cooking acidic foods for long periods of time because it can impart a metallic taste. Long-simmered tomato sauces are the best example of a food that's probably not going to fare well in cast iron. You wouldn't want to use cast iron to make a balsamic reduction, either. Times like those is when stainless steel pots and pans will come into play, but I can honestly say that I do 90% of my cooking in cast iron.

Chef's Knife

Get one with a blade between 8-12" long, a riveted handle, and a tang that runs all the way down the length of the handle. The tang is the continuation of the blade that extends down the handle. That will be a sturdy knife. High-carbon stainless steel is what most commercial knives are made from and it's a great choice. Prices range from $15 to well over $100, but you should be able to find a decent one for between $30-50. Knives should be hand-washed and dried after each use to prolong their lives. I'll talk more about knife use and care in Chapter Six.

Large Cutting Board

Get one that's at least 12" x 10" to give you plenty of room to work and make little piles of all your chopped up stuff. I strongly recommend wooden cutting boards. Wood is easiest on your knives and no matter what you've heard, it does not "harbor" bacteria from food prep. Plastic ones are fine and inexpensive, but they start to look ugly quickly. Glass cutting boards wreak havoc on your knife edge and are dangerously slick. Sorry. Wooden cutting boards should be washed with hot water and dried with a dish towel after each use to keep from warping. Plastic ones can be washed by hand and many are also dishwasher-safe.

Stainless Steel Pot with Lid

If you're cooking for a family, I suggest making your first pot purchase a big one. A large 6-8 quart stock pot will make family-size batches of chili, stew, and pasta a breeze to handle. If you're cooking for one or two most of the time, a 2-3 quart sauce pot will do for you. Whatever size, look for stainless steel pots with tri-ply aluminum or copper bottoms.

Utensils

Those I use most are a large metal spatula (pancake turner) and a set of wooden spoons. Of course, metal utensils can not be used on nonstick coated pans, but wooden spoons are safe for all!

28

With only these fairly inexpensive items (okay, assuming you have a working stove and oven), you could make a badass stir fry; some wicked steaks and potatoes; a frittata for breakfast, lunch, or dinner; fancy shrimp scampi; juicy-ass hamburgers; shoot, you could even make enough spicy chili for you and a loved one. Trust me, you'll figure out lots of other one-pot meals, too, if that's all you got.

But far be it from me to keep your kitchen miserly and bare! Here are some other useful tools you may find you need as you expand your repertoire.

Cutting

Honing Steel – This is literally a piece of steel with a handle. Regular, proper use realigns the microscopic edge on your blade and keeps it sharp without having to resort to a sharpening stone. Use this on your knife about very 50 cuts to maintain the edge. *See instructions in box to right.*

Knife Sharpener – I used to recommend using a sharpening stone, but I started using a precision-angled sharpener instead and found it much better on my knives. Look for one that has two grits (coarse and fine) and rubber feet for stability. *See instructions in box on next page.*

Paring Knife – A small knife with a blade 3-4" long. It makes peeling vegetables and coring fruit a lot easier and safer than using a big chef's knife.

Vegetable Peeler, a.k.a. Swivel-Blade Peeler – This little gadget is an extremely efficient and safe way to remove the thin skin from carrots, potatoes and apples. You can also use it to shave off pretty ribbons of hard cheese like parmesan and even make chocolate curls.

Steels

Keeping your knives sharp will make cooking faster and less frustrating, not to mention safer. Use a steel between sharpenings and also right after sharpening to remove tiny nicks and smooth the edge. Hold the steel by the handle, upright, with the point on the countertop. In the same way you sharpened the knife, now run it from the butt to the point along the steel, towards you, at about a 20 degree angle. Use a light hand and about five strokes on each side. Rinse and dry both the knife and steel after use.

Grater, a.k.a. Box Grater, Cheese Grater – I'm pretty sure you know what this is. A box grater has 4 sides, each with a different size of grating holes. I prefer this style for its function and stability.

Stovetop Cooking

Sauce Pot – This is a pot with a handle and a lid. They come in sizes from 1.5 quarts (6 cups) to 3 quarts typically. The ones I use most are a 2 and 3 quart size.

Soup Pot, a.k.a. Stock Pot – This is a large pot, taller than it is wide, with handles and a lid. Mine holds 8 quarts, and that's big enough for boiling pasta and making popcorn!

Griddle – A large, flat pan with short or no sides to get in the way of flipping pancakes and whatnot.

Steamer Basket – The folding type is the most space-efficient. It folds and unfolds like a flower to fit any size pot. I've also seen flexible silicon steamers, but they seem tricky to use.

Splatter Screen — This is a round steel mesh screen with a handle. It's a wonderful tool to use when frying to block popping grease, keeping you safer from burns and keeping your stove and countertops and floors even from becoming coated in grease spots.

Knife Sharpeners

To use a sharpener: Place the sharpener on a flat surface. Hold it steady with your non-dominant hand. For regular sharpening, place the butt of the blade in the fine groove and pull the knife towards yourself. Repeat about five times. For very dull blades, start with the coarse groove, then the fine. Run the knife on a steel to smooth it, then wash and dry.

Oven Cooking

Baking Dish, a.k.a. Casserole Dish – These can be glass or ceramic and come in a variety of sizes and shapes; the ones I use most are the round 1.5 quart and 2.5 quart sizes. If you can get some with heat-proof glass lids, they will come in handy when cooking in the oven or microwave. No lid? Use some aluminum foil (don't microwave it) or microwave-safe plate. Problem solved.

Cookie Sheet, a.k.a. Baking Sheet, Sheet Pan – These can be aluminum, steel or insulated aluminum. Dark-coated pans (like some non-stick pans) may cause cookies to get too brown on the bottom (or burn). Insulated pans take longer to heat up so things will usually need a few minutes more to cook.

Muffin Tin, a.k.a Cupcake Pan – Get a standard, 12-hole muffin pan. It can be used for cupcakes, muffins, rolls, mini-meatloaf, and even mini quiche. Make somebody a special birthday breakfast.

Cake Pan – Straight-sided pans, usually of metal. Standard sizes are the 9" x 13" rectangular, 8" x 8" or 9" x 9" square, and 8" diameter round. Dark-coated pans may cause excessive browning.

Roasting Pan – This is a large (around 16" x 12"), deep-sided pan with a domed lid that allows you to fit big hunks of meat in it and cover it. Some come with a roasting rack that goes in the bottom. Get that one if it's not much more expensive. You can use this for your Thanksgiving turkey! Aluminum roasters are available, but they are very flimsy so I don't recommend using them for anything heavy.

Loaf Pan – Deep, rectangular pan used for breads and meatloaf. Many bread and meatloaf recipes can also be formed by hand on a cookie sheet, so a loaf pan may not be a necessity for you.

Pie Pan – Round, flare-sided pans for pies and quiche, often made of glass. Disposable aluminum pans can be found, too, and come in handy for potlucks and other events where you'd rather not worry about losing your good pan.

Hot Mitts – Necessary equipment for safely removing hot pans from the oven or handling a cast iron skillet on the stove if you don't have big, tough calloused man-hands like I do. You can use folded up dish towels, but be warned of the risk of those suddenly coming unfolded and either catching on fire or causing you to drop whatever you were holding like your hands were made of silly putty. Hot mitts are cheap. You can get them at the dollar store. You should.

Trivet – Use this to protect your counter tops from being burned by setting hot pans on them. I often use my wooden cutting board or an extra hot mitt instead.

Cooling Racks – These are racks made of skinny metal bars that you can set hot cookies and cakes on to cool faster. They are also good to drain and cool deep-fried things on to avoid the sog-factor.

Mixing and Measuring

Bowls – Stainless steel or glass are best; one big bowl is good to start with.

Liquid Measuring Cups – Shaped like small pitchers with graduating sizes. A 2-cup capacity is very versatile. You can also use these to neatly pour pancake batter. *See Chapter Two: Measuring Crap.*

Dry Measuring Cups – When you grow up, you can invest five dollars and make a cake for your grandma. *See Chapter Two: Measuring Crap.*

Measuring Spoons – These come in sets: tablespoon, teaspoon, ½ teaspoon, ¼ teaspoon. You should get a set if you have no idea how much a teaspoon is. If you have some idea, you can probably estimate well enough with an eating spoon, until you start baking. That's when you need some exacting science and shit. *See Chapter Two: Measuring Crap.*

Thermometer – An instant-read thermometer is good to measure the temperature of meats to prevent food poisoning and experience the joys of eating a perfectly medium-rare steak. You might also use a thermometer for deep frying.

Utensils, Etc.

Spatula – I mean a "pancake turner," not a rubber spatula. Ugh, if you insist on using a non stick pan, make sure your spatula is plastic so it won't scratch the non stick surface.

Tongs – 12" tongs are good and easy to maneuver. Use for flipping all kinda things.

Wooden Spoons – I prefer using wooden spoons to cook because I dislike the cling-clang of metal on metal and the handles don't get hot. Ha, but they do catch on fire if they fall out of the pot and next to the gas flame the second you leave the room so be careful of that.

Big Spoons – A slotted (holey) one and a non slotted are both helpful in serving vegetables, soups, and sauces.

Whisk, a.k.a. Balloon Whisk – This is the one that has six or eight loops of wire arranged in a balloon shape for beating eggs and cream into a tizzy.

Rubber Spatula – Great for scraping every last bit of batter or dough from a bowl so you can eat it. A silicone one holds up to high temperatures so it can also be used to scrape hot sauces from pots.

Ladle – For serving soup and gravy and portioning out pancake batter. Get a ½ cup or 1 cup size.

Colander – This is great for draining pasta quickly and safely. If space is an issue, you can find collapsible colanders now.

Mortar and Pestle – This is the bowl-and-stick thing that I use all the time at home and on the show to grind up spices. I think it's fun to use, and I enjoy the muscle required to get my spices ground up. You really only need this if you want to use whole spices. And believe me, sometimes it's kind of a pain. I like pain. If you don't, but you still want to grind your own spices invest in a coffee grinder that you use only for spices.

Small Appliances

Blender – Blenders are great for making smoothies and piña coladas and will serve as a decent stand-in for a food processor if you need to grind nuts or make bread crumbs. For pureeing hot soups or sauces, I recommend the...

Immersion Blender, a.k.a. stick blender – It's like a blender at the end of a heat-proof stick so you can put it right into a pot of hot something-or-other and puree it right where it sits.

Electric Mixer – You can get a "hand mixer", which is just the mixer part with no way to attach a mixing bowl (so you have to hold it with your hand); this is fine if you'll just use it occasionally for cakes and whipping cream or don't have much counter space to store a stand mixer.. A stand mixer is a heavier-duty machine that the bowl clamps or screws onto so you don't have to hold anything; many models are strong enough to knead bread, but they are also priced accordingly (read: expensive).

Crock Pot, a.k.a. slow cooker – Pretty awesome thing if you like one-pot meals and want to come home and have dinner be ready already. Get one with a removable insert (most new models have them) for easier clean-up.

Learn to Cook

CHAPTER 4

Pantry

This past August I was at the grocery store.

The end of August is a fun time to go to the grocery store because all the college kids are coming back and they're at the grocery store with their parents, stocking up on Totino's, breaded chicken patties, Ramen noodles, and cereal. It's pretty clear those kids don't know how to cook, but they are surviving on "beige food."

The saddest thing I saw, though, was this dude plodding around with his mom and dad and he had big ol' bags of flour and sugar and baking soda and shit in his cart. And I was like, "Either that dude's in pastry school, or his mom made his grocery list." I figured it was the latter. So, now, while all the other kids were getting food they knew how to prepare (microwave!), this poor sap was getting stuck with a bunch of food that he probably had no idea what to do with.

And I was like, "Hey, that's funny. But also sad."

Blargh. I guess there's a lesson in that crappy story somewhere. I think it is that when you're starting out, you don't need to stock up on the pantry staples of the pioneer days. You need food that you can make meals out of, not just fried pies and corn pone.

THE BASICS

What I've tried to do here is come up with a list of the most versatile and inexpensive ingredients that you can keep on hand to make several different meals out of through the power of recombination. These are also shelf-stable things that will keep a while, since you might not yet be cooking every day and I don't want you to waste a bunch of food or money. Frozen fruits and vegetables are great for beginner cooks because they keep longer than fresh so you don't have to worry about feeling sad when that organic baby spinach that you paid eight dollars for gets all slimy and stinky in the crisper drawer.

Now, I am not saying you should go out and buy all this stuff at once! Get the spices and oils but then pick and choose among the other suggestions according to your habits and taste. With these basic ingredients on hand, you could make pasta salad; peanut noodles; spaghetti and marinara; beans and rice; veggie tacos; rice, corn, and cheese casserole; tuna or chicken salad; peanut soup; rice pilaf; ramen noodle casserole; quesadillas; omelets; frittatas; french toast; egg and cheese breakfast tacos; grilled cheese; vegetable soup; tuna patties; pan-fried fish; and succotash. All recipes are in this book.

Spices and Oils

» Multipurpose oil like canola or light olive oil (see the next section on Oils for more information)

» Salt and pepper

» Apple cider vinegar

» Garlic powder, fresh, or jarred minced garlic (I much prefer the flavor of fresh garlic but it should be used within a week. Garlic powder will last indefinitely and jarred garlic for a month refrigerated.)

Pantry Shelf

» Dry pasta and/or ramen noodles

» White or brown rice (depending on what you like: white rice cooks faster, but brown rice has more minerals and fiber)

» Beans and lentils

» Jarred tomatoes

» Canned tuna and/or chicken

» Peanut butter

» Bread and tortillas (refrigerate if not used within a week)

Refrigerator/Freezer

» Eggs (will keep for at least a month)

» Milk or fake milk

» Butter or margarine

» Cheese

» Mayonnaise, mustard, salsa, pickles, jelly

» Onions, celery, and carrots (will keep 2 weeks or more refrigerated)

» Apples, oranges, and lemons/limes (keep a week or more)

» Frozen chicken breasts, fish fillets, ground meat

» Frozen vegetables and fruits: greens, corn, peas, lima beans, green beans, squash, okra, berries all take well to being frozen. These are not so delicious: Brussels sprouts, snow peas, carrots, peppers.

EXTENDED BASICS

Okay now, say you're ready for more options. You're into it and ready to commit to a nicely stocked pantry and spice cabinet. You're also cooking more often now and don't have to worry so much about things going afoul before you use them. And maybe you're ready to try some more worldly dishes that require more than salt and pepper. I'm not saying you should go out and blow your wad on all this stuff at once by any means. Please don't blow your wad. You will slowly and eventually amass all this and more if you keep cooking. These are just some ideas to get you off. Ahem.

Spices and Oils

» Oregano, basil, cumin, curry powder, cinnamon, red chili flakes, chili powder (see Spice Chart for more information)

» Toasted sesame oil (see the next section on Oils for more information)

» Red wine vinegar and/or balsamic vinegar

» Soy sauce (refrigerate if you don't use it often)

» Fresh or powdered ginger

» Honey

Pantry Shelf

» More grains: sushi rice, quinoa, oatmeal, and bulgur

» Flours: white and/or whole wheat; corn meal (keep these in the fridge for longer storage)

» Potatoes and sweet potatoes (keep them in a dark, dry place to keep them from sprouting baby potato plants from their insides)

» More types of beans and lentils

» Sugar and/or brown sugar

» Baking powder/ baking soda

Refrigerator/Freezer

» Nuts (add to salads and casseroles)

» Yogurt (plain yogurt can sub for sour cream in many recipes or can be used in breakfast smoothies)

» Lettuce, parsley, chilies and bell peppers (will keep a week or so)

» Tomatoes, avocados (keep them on the counter until ripe; you can hold them in the fridge for a couple more days after that)

» Firm tofu

» Fresh or frozen meats and fish

With all that plus the basic-basics, you can expand your repertoire to include things like chili; corn fritters; taco salad; macaroni and cheese; chicken divan; fish tacos; roasted chicken; meatloaf; vegetable curry; shepherd's pie; lentil soup; chapatis; tortillas; spinach dip; cobbler; tabouli; hummus; cornbread; cinnamon apples; pancakes; cinnamon toast; bean burgers; berry muffins; sushi bowls; stir fry!

Some other things I like to keep on hand, and hopefully you too will some-day find nice to have around: canned coconut milk (for curries and soups), artichoke hearts and soba noodles (for fancy salads), fish sauce, bacon, parmesan cheese, rice noodles, rice wine vinegar, capers (for fancy sauces and salads), and about 300 different hot sauces.

ALL ABOUT OILS

The smoke point of an oil is the temperature at which an oil begins to smoke, although it's more useful to think of it as a range than a specific temperature. Understanding an oil's smoke point is the best way to determine its safest and most delicious applications. Before an oil reaches its smoke point, some molecules have already begun to break down into their fatty acid and glycerol parts; once the oil begins to smoke, much of the nutritive qualities and flavor are destroyed and free radicals have begun to form. This is why it's very important to use oils with a high smoke point for high-heat frying like stir frying and deep-frying. The more refined an oil is, the higher its smoke point; the less refined, the lower the smoke point (think about how quickly butter burns with all of its protein and sugar "impurities"). The smoke point of any oil will decrease after its been used so be careful when reusing oil (as you might in a deep-fryer) and limit it to no more than once or twice.

Here is a general guide to safe temperature ranges and best uses of oils. Because the smoke point can vary even from brand to brand depending on the cultivar it was extracted from and how it was processed and refined, it's a good idea to check the label. It will usually offer the recommended (safe) uses, if not exact temperatures. The asterisks (*) indicate my personal preferences for health, tastiness, and affordability (not necessarily in that order).

Raw in Salads, Uncooked Sauces & Garnishes: Oils with smoke points under 300° F/150° C. This is the time to use cold-pressed, unrefined and unfiltered oils to their best advantage. Unrefined almond, avocado, flax, hazelnut, sesame, walnut, and extra-virgin olive oil are all good to use uncooked. Heat destroys many of the subtle flavors in seed and nut oils so use them uncooked and appreciate the nuances they

Multi-Purpose Oils

Beginning cooks of course have no need to stock 10 different oils in their kitchen. I don't even keep more than four different oils around at any one time. My favorite multi-purpose oils that can be used for everything from salad dressings to frying are refined canola, refined safflower, light olive oil (not extra-virgin) and grapeseed oil.

add to recipes. While refined almond, sesame, and avocado oils are safe to use at high temperatures, their flavors are better appreciated if added at the end of cooking. Some oils that are safe to use at high temperatures also make a good base oil for salad dressings and vinaigrettes because of their mild flavor; these include canola, corn, safflower, and sunflower.

- » Almond
- » Avocado
- » Extra-virgin olive
- » Flax seed
- » Hazelnut
- » Sesame
- » Walnut

Baking, Cakes & Cookies: Oils with smoke points between 300–375° F/ 150–190° C. Of course butter is popular, but lard is also great for baking. Vegetable oils appropriate for baking include almond, canola, olive, safflower, and sunflower. Extra-virgin olive oil also works well in baked goods, but its flavor might overwhelm some recipes. Virgin coconut oil makes great lightly-coconut flavored pie crust and pastry. Margarine and shortening are options, too.

- » Almond
- » Butter
- » Canola
- » Coconut (virgin or refined)
- » Lard
- » Margarine
- » Olive (virgin or extra-virgin)
- » Safflower
- » Shortening
- » Sunflower

Medium-heat Sauteeing & Sweating: Oils with smoke points between 300–400° F/150–204° C. In addition to the oils suitable for baking, I'll add ghee (clarified butter), grapeseed oil, virgin olive oil, peanut oil.

- » Bacon fat
- » Canola (refined)
- » Corn
- » Ghee (clarified butter)
- » Grapeseed
- » Peanut
- » Refined coconut
- » Refined sesame
- » Virgin olive

High-Heat Stir Frying & Deep Frying: Oils with smoke points above 400° F/204° C. Almost any refined oil will work for frying, but the most common are canola, corn, grapeseed, peanut, safflower, extra-light olive oil, and "vegetable oil," which is a marketing term for a blend of oils (or sometimes just soybean oil) designed to have a mild flavor and high smoke point. Avocado oil has a remarkably high smoke point, but its expense might make it unfeasible to use for deep frying. High-oleic oils come from plants that have been bred to be extra-high in monounsaturated fats, making them good choices for high-heat frying. You can find canola, safflower, and sunflower oils in the high-oleic form. Deep frying is one time I use vegetable shortening; because it reverts back to a solid when cool, it is easy to dispose of in the trash.

- » Almond
- » Avocado
- » Canola
- » Corn
- » Grapeseed
- » High-oleic canola, safflower, sunflower
- » Lard
- » Light olive oil
- » Peanut
- » Safflower
- » Shortening
- » Vegetable oil

How to Store Oils

To maintain freshness and protect them from going rancid, store oils away from heat and light. Unrefined nut and seed oils are especially prone to going rancid so it's best to store them in the refrigerator. Olive oil may turn solid in the refrigerator, but will liquify after several minutes at room temperature. This is the reason many salad dressing recipes will use both extra-virgin olive oil (for flavor) in combination with a refined oil (to keep it fluid).

Discarding Leftover Oil

To help your city's water company, please do not dispose of oil down the drain (or the toilet)! Not only can it cause blocked pipes, oil is problematic to water treatment plants.

The best way to dispose of large amounts of oil (more than a spoonful) is through the solid waste department. If you're dealing with shortening, lard, bacon fat, or other saturated fats, allow them to cool until they solidify, then scrape into the trash can. (Though, like many a grandma, I keep leftover bacon fat in a jar in the refrigerator to use for cooking.) Smaller amounts can even be wiped out with a paper towel or a napkin from Chipotle (of which I have hundreds) and tossed before washing the pan.

Liquid oils should be allowed to cool and then poured back into their bottles or any disposable container and thrown away. You can also double up some plastic grocery bags, pour the cooled oil in that, then tie it shut and put it in your regular trash. Some cities may offer oil recycling or you could contact a nearby restaurant that recycles their cooking oil and ask if you can add yours to their bucket. If you don't do a whole helluva lot of frying, you might want to find a large gallon jug or pickle jar, keep it under your sink or in the garage and pour your used oil into that until it's full, then drop off the whole lot at once.

I'm not sure if it's exactly right or not, but if I'm dealing with the small (tablespoon) amounts of oil (not solid fat) left in a pan after sauteing and such, I don't bother with any of the above, and I just wash the damn thing.

Learn to Cook

WILD & CRAZY GRAINS

Barley

You're probably familiar with barley only in terms of beef-barley or mushroom-barley soup and that's because it does really well in long-cooked soups and stews. Barley grains are pretty large and even when cooked for a long time, they hold up in shape and texture. I really like barley as an alternative to rice as well, just cooked and buttered and served along side any kind of saucy meat. It takes about 45 minutes to cook and it's pretty inexpensive.

Rice

Rice is categorized by the length of the grains: short grain, medium grain and long grain.

Short Grain Rice Varieties include sushi rice (aka Japanese rice), Calrose (a Japanese hybrid grown in California), Arborio rice (used in risotto), Bomba (used in paella), and glutinous rice (used for sweets mostly, such as mochi). Short grain rices are sticky and tend to clump together when cooked. (No rice actually contains wheat gluten protein, however.) *See Sushi Bowl, p. 178.*

Medium Grain Varieties are sold as medium grain rice (true story) and are a good all-purpose rice for pilaf, plain old rice, or Spanish rice. Often, they are just labeled "medium grain rice" with no fancy name or specific purpose given. They are the in-between rice — not as sticky as short grain, but not as fluffy as long grain rice. *See Spanish Rice, p. 214.*

Long Grain Rice Varieties are Basmati (typical of Indian cuisine), Jasmine (very fragrant, typical in Southeast Asian cuisine), and Texmati (a basmati hybrid grown in Texas). Long grain rices cook up fluffy, and the grains remain separate unless the rice is terribly overcooked. *See Fried Rice, p. 139.*

Rice also comes either milled or unmilled; that's "white" or "brown" in layman's terms. Almost any of the varieties mentioned above can be found in both white and brown forms, the former having been stripped of the husk, bran, and germ; the latter having only been husked, leaving the bran and germ. You will see claims of the health benefits of both white and brown rice, but it is a fact that brown rice retains more fiber and nutrients (although the calories are about the same as white rice). To make things more confusing, "red rice" is another long-grain variety that, when sold unmilled, is reddish instead of brown, and "black rice" is an heirloom variety that is deep purple all the way through, even after it's been milled.

Wild Rice

Wild rice isn't actually related to rice, but it looks like rice. It takes a long time to cook and it's quite expensive, but it's got a great chewy texture and a striking black appearance so it's fun for special occasions. It cooks in 45-50 minutes, about the same time as brown rice, making it a good pilaf-partner since you can cook them together in the same pot.

Polenta and Grits

These are both made from corn that's been dried and ground. Either can be cooked into a hot cereal or cooked and then refrigerated to cool into a firm dough that may be fried. Cooking times vary, but can be anywhere from "instant" for instant grits to 20 minutes for coarse polenta. Check the package directions to be sure. *See Baked Grits, p. 209.*

Millet

Millet is kind of old-fashioned and hard to find anywhere but the bulk section of natural food stores anymore, but it's a mild grain that actually makes a nice hot cereal when sweetened with maple syrup or brown sugar. It looks like little yellow balls, and I think it's attractive. It cooks in about 20 minutes.

Bulgur Wheat

This is made from whole wheat berries that have been cooked, then dried, then crushed (or cracked). It reconstitutes quickly in boiling water making it a great thing to keep on hand for fast meals and side dishes. It's used in tabouli *(p. 125)* , but can also be added to white rice when making pilaf.

Couscous

Alert! Alert! This isn't really a grain! It's a teeny tiny pasta made from wheat that is often mistaken for a grain. Quick-cooking couscous is super tiny, like smaller than a grain of rice. Israeli couscous is larger and round, maybe about the size of a grain of rice if a grain of rice was smashed into a spherical shape. Quick couscous just needs to be reconstituted with boiling water (like bulgur) but Israeli couscous is boiled like pasta.

Quinoa

Botanically-speaking quinoa isn't a grain, either; it's a seed. But for culinary purposes, it is cooked and served as such. It looks like little round snail shells to me. It's a high-protein food that cooks relatively quickly, making it a great choice for vegetarians or anyone who wants to get more protein in their diet. It comes in three varieties: white, black, and red but they all cook the same and taste pretty much the same, too—kind of nutty and earthy. It's pretty easy to find these days in the bulk section of most large stores, but it costs quite a bit more than many other grains. It cooks in about 20 minutes, but does require a quick rinse or soak in water before cooking to remove a slightly bitter resin that coats each seed. *See Quinoa Salad, p. 244.*

PICKIN' OUT PRODUCE

Generally speaking, when you're picking produce at the store the first things to look out for are bruises— identified by dark or soft areas, and punctures —identified by holes or sticky spots. Fortunately, those things are easy to notice with even a half-assed inspection. Generally you don't want any produce that looks wilted or shriveled, but that should be common sense I'd think. For fruits, to really speed up ripening, put it in a bag with an apple or a tomato; those fruits release ethylene gas that naturally hastens ripening (this has the same effect on all fruits, excepting citrus).

Here are some more specific things to keep in mind for some certain items.

Apples

There are many varieties of apples but the best ones in my opinion for eating are Gala, Fuji, Pink Lady, Honeycrisp, and Braeburn. Apples good for cooking are Granny Smith, Golden Delicious, and Rome. Apples are at their best in the fall months. Check carefully for soft spots (bruises). Keep apples in the refrigerator for longest storage.

Asparagus

When you're looking to buy asparagus, check the tips. They should be firm and tight, not soft or wet-looking, and the little "scales" should be tightly closed, not flopping all open for the world to see underneath their skivvies. The diameter of the stalks —thick or thin, fat or not—matters little. I prefer the thicker stalks because I think they taste better. You may like the skinny ones because they are cuter, and that is okay with me. You buy whatever size asparagus stalks you like. Store like cut flowers in a jar with a little water in it in the fridge. Use it within a few days of purchase, or it will get soft and yucky.

Avocados

It can be tricky to tell when they are ripe. The best thing to do to is buy them when they are green and hard and ripen them at home using the old "in a bag with a fruit" trick described above. I find that if I buy the ones that are ripe at the store, they are often bruised inside. Anyway, when ripe, avocados should be slightly soft around the stem. Ripe avocados may be held for up to 3 days in the refrigerator to avoid over-ripening. Hass avocados are the smallish, bumpy, black ones you see around; Fuerte are the large, smooth, green ones. I like the flavor and texture of Hass better.

Berries

Check for mildew and wetness on the bottom of the box. If that's all clear, give the box of berries a sniff. If they smell like berries and aren't mushy or moldy, buy them! If they don't smell like berries, leave them be. They won't taste very good and probably aren't worth the high price tag. Store berries in the refrigerator and eat within a few days; berries are "berry" perishable! (Sorry about that.) Don't wash them until right before you eat them. If you can't resist a great sale and end up with WAY too many berries, you can freeze them in plastic bags to use in smoothies later (cut the stems off strawberries first).

Broccoli

The heads of broccoli should be tightly formed and dark green (sometimes even purple). Don't buy broccoli with yellowish heads or actual flowers opening because that broccoli is overly mature and will probably be tough and bitter.

Cabbage, Carrots, and Celery

These should all be heavy for their size and not soft or floppy. Store in the refrigerator and they'll keep fine for a couple of weeks.

Citrus

This includes lemons, limes, oranges, grapefruits, and the like. Get the heaviest, smoothest ones you can to ensure lots of juice. Store them at room temperature for a week or refrigerate up to three weeks. Citrus fruits for eating, like oranges and tangerines, are at their peak in winter through spring months; tangerines were a Christmas stocking staple when I was growing up. Grapefruits are best from January to June.

Cucumbers

Choose the firmest, heaviest cucumbers in the pile. I also try to pick out the smaller ones because the seeds will be softer and fewer usually. Refrigerate up to a week to ten days.

Eggplant

Get one that is heavy for its size (that's a pretty good general rule for everything actually) and has smooth, non wrinkly skin. Take a look at the blossom end—that's the end opposite the stem end—and see that little brown patch? I've heard that if you find the eggplant with the smallest and roundest brown patch possible, that eggplant will have fewer seeds, which is good. I don't know if it's true, but I still use that to help me decide which one I'm going to take home. Globe eggplants are most common (the big, purple balloons), but long, skinny Japanese eggplants are becoming more common.

Garlic

Look for heads (bulbs) of garlic with intact papery skin, firm cloves, and no sprouts sticking out the top or powdery mildew stuff. Store at room temperature in a darkish place.

Mangoes

Inspect your mango. Make sure it is slightly soft and smells strongly of a mango. If it doesn't, let it sit out on the counter for another day or do the "fruit in a bag" trick. If you find Ataulfo mangoes (smallish, yellow, and kidney-shaped), get them! They are so sweet and delicious when ripe, you'll fall in love.

Melons

When you are picking out a melon, check out the stem end; there shouldn't be any stem left (stem indicates it was picked too early). What you want is a stem end that looks like a little divot and when you sniff it around there it should smell like melon. If the stem check is good but it doesn't smell like melon, leave it on the counter for a day or two. Ripe melons can be refrigerated for a few days to prevent over-ripening, which results in a mushy melon.

Mushrooms

I mush prefer to buy mushrooms in bulk so I can inspect them individually, rather than in the styrofoam packs. I also buy whole mushrooms rather than pre-sliced because they last longer. Looks for firm, dry, non-shriveled, non-slimy mushrooms. They should be stored in a paper bag in the fridge if you can. Plastic retains moisture, and mushrooms go squishy on you. Wipe mushrooms with a damp cloth to remove dirt or if they are very dirty, give them a rinse and a dry. White button mushrooms are common and inexpensive; cremini (aka baby portobella) are the little brown caps and those are pretty cheap, too.

Onions

I'm talking about "dry" onions here or "round" onions, as opposed to green onions (scallions). Look for heavy onions with an intact papery skin, no mildew spots or soft spots, and no green sprouts poppin' out the top. Yellow and white onions are best for cooking. Red onions and sweet onions like Vidalia and Walla Walla are good for eating raw. I've heard that sweeter onions of all varieties are more flattened like a UFO than globe-shaped. No idea if that's true, but I adhere to it. Keep your onions in the fridge, and they will make you cry less when you cut them.

Pears

Pears are best in the fall and winter months. Ripe pears should be very slightly soft and very fragrant. If you have time, I really recommend buying pears unripe and letting them ripen at home to avoid accidentally buying bruised fruit disguised as ripe fruit (much like with avocados). There's not much better thing to eat than a sweet, juicy Anjou or Bartlett pear. The brown skinned Bosc pears are best for cooking.

Peppers

Fresh peppers should be smooth, firm, and shiny. While the seeds of bell peppers and other mild peppers should be removed because they are bitter, the seeds and membranes of hot chilies might be removed because that's where most of the heat lies. If you like spicy foods, by all means leave the seeds and membranes in there! Store peppers in the refrigerator for longest keeping.

Pineapple

To pick out a pineapple, first look at it; it should be a little yellowish at the base and all the "scales" should be around the same size. Smell it; it should smell like pineapple, but not like a fermenting pineapple (it's over-ripe if it smells like booze). Pull out a leaf; the leaves from the center of the crown should pop out with a gentle tug when it's ripe. Like most other fruits, pineapples continue to ripen after they've been picked so it's okay to get one that isn't completely ripe; just leave it on the counter for a few days until it passes the leaf and smell test.

Potatoes

For easiest cleaning and scrubbing, choose potatoes that are smooth, without a lot of crevices. Don't buy them if they've got any green color on them or if they've started to sprout and, once home, store in a dark, dry place. Two main varieties are waxy boiling potatoes (red skinned, good for potato salads) and the starchy baking potatoes (Russet), which are also good for mashing. Yukon Gold are an in-between potato. Fingerling potatoes are small and good for roasting whole. Potatoes can keep up to a month under the right conditions, but in my slightly warm and bright kitchen, it's more like a couple weeks max.

Summer Squash

The summer squashes include zucchini, yellow squash, pattypan squash, and other varieties with a thin, edible skin. Looks for shiny, smooth, heavy squash, and your life might be easier if you pick out ones that are all about the same size because they will cook more evenly. Smaller squashes will have smaller and fewer seeds and that's nice. Store them in the refrigerator for up to a few days; they'll start to wither around day five so try to use them soon after purchase.

Sweet Potatoes

Follow the instructions for potatoes to find a good one and store the same way, though sweet potatoes don't last quite as long as regular potatoes.

Learn to Cook

Tomatillos

Depending on where you live, fresh tomatillos may be hard to find but if they are there, they are easy to spot because they look kind of weird like pale green Chinese paper lanterns. Pick out firm ones that just fill their husks or are barely breaking through. You might notice the skin of the fruit under the husk is slightly sticky but that is okay. Store them, in their husks, in the refrigerator for up to two weeks.

Tomatoes

Tomatoes are one of the most abused fruits. They are almost always picked green, then shipped a long ways, turning red on the way but without developing much sugar or flavor. Summertime is the best time for good tomatoes at the store. Look for ones that are evenly colored, bright, and heavy for their size. If there are leaves and stem attached, they should look fresh and green. And by all means, if you find a tomato that actually smells like a tomato, take that one home and never let it go. Or at least eat it in a fresh salad where you can best appreciate its flavor. Roma or plum tomatoes are great for sauces and nothing beats a ripe beefsteak tomato slice on a burger. Cherry tomatoes are generally very sweet all year round, which makes them a good choice for winter cooking and salads.

Winter Squash

These are the hard squashes—the ones with thick skins that must be peeled off before eating. They store well, two weeks or more, at room temperature. Some popular types are butternut squash, acorn squash, spaghetti squash, and pumpkin. Winter squashes are mostly densely textured and lightly sweet (spaghetti squash is a notable exception with its stringy noodle-like texture and bland taste). They can keep out on the counter for a few weeks.

HERBS & SPICES

What's the difference between herbs and spices? Herbs are the leaves and stems of plants. Spices include all the other parts: bark, fruit, buds, seeds, roots. That's the difference! That's it! While fresh herbs of all sorts are just about as easy to find as dried herbs these days, the only fresh spices I've ever seen for sale are ginger and turmeric root. So for practical purposes, I'll be referencing dried spices and both dried and fresh herbs in this section.

I have created a chart here that lists common herbs and spices and what they taste like, what they go with, and what's a good substitute. Man, that was really hard. Much like describing what a wine tastes like, describing what an herb tastes like is necessarily subjective and poetic. I realize that words like "woodsy," "grassy," and "resinous" might not tell you much but it's the best I can do, short of making a scratch-and-sniff page, which I would have done if that were possible. Willy Wonka, where are you when we need you?!

You will observe that many of my descriptive words show up again and again. Interestingly, this is not due to a poor vocabulary, but rather to the fact that many of the herbs we use regularly do have similar fragrances and flavors. It's pretty neat, really. Let's look at: anise, caraway, coriander, cumin, dill and fennel (All members of the carrot family! Wow!). When you check out the chart, you see that four out of six of those have "licorice" or "fennel" flavors. Fascinating. When you really pay attention to what various herbs smell like you will notice lots of similarities, too. In fact, if you are really interested cooking, I recommend you take a trip to a spice shop and smell all the jars to your heart's content. Or until you get a rash in your nose.

Substitutions

Please take note that while I have offered you substitutions, I make no promises. There are some cases, such as a roasted chicken, where a teaspoon of rosemary makes a fine substitute for a teaspoon of thyme. In other cases, such as a salad dressing, rosemary would overpower if substituted in the same quantity as thyme. For that reason, I have included only the vaguest ideas for equivalencies but generally, the exchange rate must be left up to your discretion.

And, obviously, there are no perfect substitutes. For example, just because I listed nutmeg as a possible substitute for cardamom doesn't mean the recipe will taste the same at the end. But I bet it will still taste pretty good. And just because something is different doesn't mean it's not good!

A couple of words you'll find in the chart that may need some explaining.

Crucifers – Crucifers are a large group of vegetables. They are members of the cabbage family and include: broccoli, cauliflower, cabbage, Brussels sprouts, rutabaga, and mustard greens. They all share a characteristic "vegetable" taste and smell. Brassica is the genus and another nickname for the gang.

Solanaceae – These are another large gang of vegetables: the nightshades. The genus Solanum includes potatoes, tomatoes, eggplant, chili peppers, sweet peppers, and tomatillos. (And tobacco!)

If you see either of these words in the ***"Goes in/with"*** column of the chart, you know that you can put that herb or spice with any one of the vegetables in that group and it will work. The amounts you use will vary, but if you know what to use, that's half the battle. Also, if you find on your own a seasoning that complements one of those vegetables, you have most likely found a seasoning that complements all the vegetables in its same group. Viola! You're on your way to creating recipes!

Storing Herbs and Spices

Finally, since you'll be using more herbs and spices now, here are some tips on proper storage to maintain optimum flavor. Don't worry. It's not hard.

Using spices – If you can, buy seed spices (cumin, coriander, mustard) in their whole form and grind them yourself as needed. If that is not possible (you have no mortar and pestle; you have no coffee grinder; you have no patience; you have no arms), then store ground herbs in as dark and cool an area of your kitchen as you can find, while still keeping them handy, or else you will just forget about them and they will turn to dust.

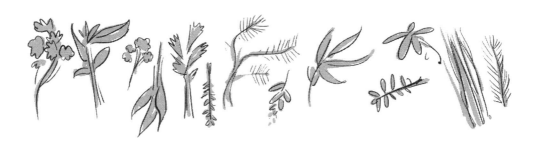

Learn to Cook

Using dried herbs — Similarly, there is no call to buy herbs that have been already "rubbed" or "ground" or "crumbled." Jesus, those things are easy as hell to do on your own when you're good and ready. Dried herbs lose their flavor quick enough; having them pre-mashed and mangled is just going to make their flavor evaporate that much faster. Have a little respect for the herbs and spices, please!

Using fresh herbs – It's a good idea to wash fresh herbs before using them to remove dirt, sand, and poison. If the herbs are fairly clean already, you can just hold them by their stems under running water for a few seconds; give them a shake off in the sink and you're ready to chop 'em. Dirty-bird-herbs might do better with a soak in a bowl of water. Cover with water and use your hands to delicately swish them around then lift out into a colander; you should see lots of dirt left behind in the bowl. Give them one more rinse off to make sure you got it all, then shake to dry and go on with your bad self.

To completely dry washed herbs, gently fold them up in a clean towel and squeeze lightly. You would definitely want to do this before trying anything fancy like deep frying herbs and before drying to preserve herbs (see below).

Preserving fresh herbs — Fresh herbs are best stored, short term, in a glass of water as you would keep cut flowers. Put a plastic produce bag around the glass and herb to keep a humid environment. Parsley and cilantro will keep a week or so like this, refrigerated. Basil and sage should be left out on the counter in their glass of water and will keep only a couple of days.

For longer term storage, chop the herbs and freeze them in ice cubes to be added to recipes later. Cilantro and parsley can both be treated this way. You can also store whole leaves covered in oil in a jar in the fridge for two to three weeks. Basil takes particularly well to the oil treatment.

To dry fresh herbs, get a paper lunch sack and put the cleaned and dried herbs inside, leaves pointing towards the bottom. Use a clothespin or binder clip to clamp the top of the bag closed around the stems. Hang in a dark place for about a week until dry. Remove the leaves from the stems and store in a tightly closed jar as you would any dried herb.

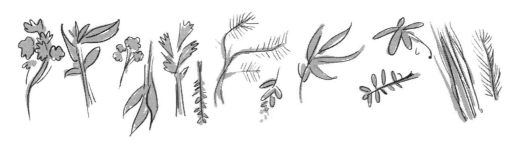

55

Spice World

SPICE/HERB	TASTES LIKE	GOES IN/WITH	SUBSTITUTE WITH	FUN FACT
Allspice (Jamaica pepper)	warm and sweet; like a mixture of nutmeg, cloves, cinnamon	Jamaican cooking, pickled vegetables and fish, pumpkin pie, meats, wild game, barbecue sauce, sausage	cloves; or a mixture of cloves, cinnamon, and nutmeg	It's grown exclusively in the Western hemisphere!
Anise (Aniseed)	fennel, licorice, tarragon	fish, shellfish, chicken, lamb, spice cookies, pickles, cakes, rye bread, asparagus	fennel seeds, tarragon	Mexico is the world's largest producer.
Annatto (Achiote)	not much, used for its bright yellow color	Spanish rice, Mexican and South American dishes, dry rubs, anything that would look better yellow	turmeric for color	The Mayans used it to make body paint and lipstick.
Basil (Sweet basil, Italian basil)	sweet-spicy, green, slight anise flavor	pesto, salads, solanaceae, fish, eggs, chicken, oranges, zucchini, oregano, garlic, cheese, melons	dry basil or oregano in cooked sauces; parsley in place of fresh basil	Add dried basil at the beginning of cooking to bring out the oils. Add fresh basil at the end of cooking to retain its flavor and color.

SPICE/HERB	TASTES LIKE	GOES IN/WITH	SUBSTITUTE WITH	FUN FACT
Basil, Thai (Spicy basil)	peppery, slight clove flavor	Vietnamese and Thai cooking, stir-fried dishes, seafood, chicken, coconut, salads, cilantro, solanaceae	Sweet basil, cilantro	Basil is related to mint!
Bay leaf (Two similar herbs: Bay laurel and California bay)	floral aroma, piney, woodsy; California bay is spicier	soups, pickles, pot roast, stock, poaching liquids, French and Mediterranean cooking	Interchange, keeping in mind California bay is stronger; thyme, rosemary	Drop whole leaves in soups and sauces then pull them out before serving so no one chokes.
Caraway	spicy, anise/ lemony flavor	rye bread, apples, sauerkraut, cabbage, turnips, pork, soft cheeses, German and North African cooking	anise, fennel, or coriander seeds	I've heard that you shouldn't cook caraway seeds for a long time or they may turn bitter.
Cardamom (Green cardamom)	sweet, ginger, black pepper, citrus	Creamy desserts, chai tea, spice cookies, Indian cooking, coffee	orange zest, nutmeg, ginger	Cardamom is related to ginger!
Cayenne (Red pepper, bird pepper)	hot	tomatoes, meats, hot sauces, seafood, eggs, fried foods, cheese	red pepper flakes, Tabasco sauce, pepper spray (kidding)	Cayenne pepper is good for your cardiovascular system.

SPICE/HERB	TASTES LIKE	GOES IN/WITH	SUBSTITUTE WITH	FUN FACT
Celery seed	super strong celery flavor, slightly bitter	seafood, chicken, tomatoes, cole slaw, salad dressings, potato salad, Bloody Marys	minced celery, celery leaves, celery salt	Celery seed is cultivated from wild celery, not the one grown for its stalks.
Chervil(Garden chervil)	mild parsley/ anise flavor	eggs, seafood, poultry, salads, French cooking, mild cheeses	parsley, dill	Use fresh chervil and add it at the end of cooking.
Chives	delicate onion or garlic	seafood, potatoes, cream soups, eggs, green salads, mayonnaise salads	minced green onion tops	Pretty puffy pink flowers can be eaten, too; put 'em in a salad
Cilantro (Fresh coriander, Coriander leaves, Chinese parsley)	green, slightly bitter (to some people, it tastes bad, like soap; it's genetic)	citrus, coconut, seafood, poultry, chili peppers, Indian, Asian and Mexican cooking, salsa, avocados, pineapple, papaya	sometimes can use fresh parsley or a squeeze of lime juice	Always use fresh cilantro and add leaves at the end of cooking to retain flavor.
Cinnamon	spicy and sweet	cooked fruits, oatmeal, chocolate, cinnamon rolls, cinnamon toast, hot toddy, mulled wine/ cider, stewed meat	smaller amount of ground cloves or allspice	Recently, cinnamon has been shown to reduce blood sugar in people with Type II diabetes.

SPICE/HERB	TASTES LIKE	GOES IN/WITH	SUBSTITUTE WITH	FUN FACT
Clove	peppery, warm, astringent, pungent	tomato sauces, beef stews, Indian curries, mulled wine/ cider, chai tea, spice cookies, chutney, pickles, ham	allspice, cinnamon	Cloves are the unopened flower buds of a tree. Those flowers never had a chance.
Coriander (Coriander seeds)	orange peel, faintly sweet	lamb, sausage, oranges, lemon, seafood, Indian curries, pickles, mushrooms, ham, pork, dry rubs, carrots, sweet potatoes, squash	lemon or orange zest, sometimes cumin	Coriander is a mild spice, well suited to dry toasting to bring out its flavor.
Cumin (Comino)	smoky, nutty, peppery	carrots, potatoes, Mexican and Indian cooking, cheese, beans, rice, chili, lime/ lemon, cilantro, squash, zucchini	commercial curry powder or chili powder, depending on the dish	Cumin benefits greatly from being toasted before adding to foods.
Dill seed	mild caraway, fennel/anise	potatoes, coleslaw, cabbage, carrots, dill pickles, fish, cottage cheese	dill weed, fennel seeds, anise seed, caraway	The seeds are small enough that they are usually sold and used whole.

Learn to Cook

SPICE/HERB	TASTES LIKE	GOES IN/WITH	SUBSTITUTE WITH	FUN FACT
Dill weed (Dill)	delicate fennel, licorice, parsley	fish, eggs, salad dressings, potatoes, carrots, asparagus, beets, crucifers, sour cream, Scandinavian and Russian cooking	dill seed, fennel, tarragon, parsley	Dill flowers are also edible and make a pretty yellow addition to salads.
Epazote	medicinal, camphor, mint	Mexican cooking, soups, posole, beans, cheese, corn, cilantro, lime	oregano, cilantro	It's hard to find, but easy to grow! Sorry that fact wasn't more fun.
Fennel (Fennel seed)	licorice	leaves: salads, citrus fruits, avocado, fish; seeds: tomato sauces, pickles, Italian sausage, beans/lentils, pork, olives, cheese	dill seed or leaves, anise seed	"Florence fennel" is a different plant, grown as a vegetable. Find it in the produce section and eat raw or steamed.
Fenugreek	maple syrup, celery	leaves: rice, potatoes; seeds: Indian pickles and curries, meats	substitute fenugreek leaves for seeds, or just leave it out	Fenugreek is used to make fake maple flavoring.
File (Gumbo file, file powder)	grassy, slightly bitter, lemony	used as a thickener for gumbo, stews, bisques	nothing	Pronounced "feel-ay," add it in at the end of cooking or it may turn stringy.

Learn to Cook

SPICE/HERB	TASTES LIKE	GOES IN/WITH	SUBSTITUTE WITH	FUN FACT
Garlic	spicy, oniony when raw; sweetens when cooked; garlic powder has a different flavor that does not sweeten with cooking	meat, fish, beans, onion, solanaceae, squash, ginger, salad dressings, aioli, just about anything benefits from a little garlic (or a lot)	1clove, minced = 1 teaspoon minced = 1/4 teaspoon garlic powder; add more onion, ginger, or cayenne when lacking garlic	Garlic powder's best use is in breadings and rubs and places like that where fresh garlic can't be used.
Ginger	hot, spicy; dried, ground ginger is earthier than fresh	Indian and Asian cooking, citrus, salad dressings, sweet potatoes, bananas, sushi, tofu, gingerbread, broccoli	1 tablespoon fresh minced ginger = 1 teaspoon dried, ground ginger	You may see a recipe that calls for "a 1 inch piece of ginger, minced" which is about 1 tablespoon, minced.
Horseradish	hot mustard or radish	fatty meats, potatoes, roast beef, seafood, ham, cocktail sauce, creamy sauces, solanaceae	wasabi, hot mustard	Prepared horseradish is pre-grated and mixed with vinegar; look in the refrigerated section.
Juniper berry	pine needles	game meats, fatty meats, thyme, sage, bay, onions	splash of gin	Used to flavor gin!
Kaffir lime (Keiffer lime)	extra fragrant, perfumey lime/ tangerine zest	coconut, chicken, fish, basil, Thai and Indonesian cooking, cilantro, cardamom, chiles	lime zest and juice; lemongrass	Look for it at Asian supermarkets; fresh is much preferred over dried.

SPICE/HERB	TASTES LIKE	GOES IN/WITH	SUBSTITUTE WITH	FUN FACT
Lavender	flowers, perfume	goat cheese, game meats, salads, chocolate, tea, candies, sugar syrups	rosemary	Shove it in a sock and make a sachet.
Lemon grass	lemon/ginger, floral	tofu, seafood, coconut, chicken, chilies, Southeast Asian cooking	lemon or lime zest and juice	Mince fresh lemongrass finely or leave it in large enough pieces to pick out. It's very fibrous.
Mace	sweeter, sharper, nutmeg	cream sauces, desserts, cooked fruit, sweet potatoes	slightly more nutmeg	Mace is the aril: the outer covering around a nutmeg seed shell.
Marjoram (Sweet marjoram)	spicy, sweet, camphor notes, like mild oregano	lamb, poultry, eggs, chilies, soft cheeses, tomato sauces, lemon, vinegar, crucifers, green beans, dill, basil, thyme	oregano, thyme, basil	Romans used marjoram as an aphrodisiac. Ooh la la.
Mint (several types: spearmint, peppermint, etc.)	sweet, spicy, cooling	lamb, zucchini, citrus, peas, solanaceae, salads, fruits, mojito, mint julep, Greek and Mediterranean cooking, yogurt	interchange different types of mint; basil	Of all the mints, peppermint keeps its flavor best when dried.

Learn to Cook

SPICE/HERB	TASTES LIKE	GOES IN/WITH	SUBSTITUTE WITH	FUN FACT
Mustard seeds (several types: black, brown, yellow)	sharp, pungent, mustard	dry rubs, cheese, chicken, roasts, dill pickles, salads, sauces, potatoes, Indian cooking, crucifers	interchangeable, keeping in mind that yellow is the mildest and black is the strongest; prepared mustard	Mustard seeds are available whole or ground. "Prepared mustard" refers to the mustard you put on a sandwich.
Nutmeg	spicy, cinnamony, perfumy	cream sauces, greens, spinach, crucifers, eggnog, spice cookies, cheese sauces, potatoes, lamb, eggs	smaller amounts of mace, cinnamon	Nutmeg is a bad-ass because it's delicious and poisonous. Use no more than 1/8 teaspoon per serving.
Oregano (Wild marjoram)	spicy, piney, thyme, lemony, slightly bitter	chili, beans, rice, tomatoes, capers, parsley, green beans, citrus, meats, eggplant, Greek and Italian cooking, Mexican cooking	marjoram, basil, small amounts of rosemary in Greek and Italian cooking	Oregano is considered best when dried! Win for the little guy with no garden!
Paprika (Pimenton)	sweet and hot varieties; also available smoked	meats, chili sauces, Eastern European and Creole cooking, goulash, sausage	cayenne (small amounts); annatto (for color only)	Avoid cooking over high heat with paprika; it burns easily.

Learn to Cook

SPICE/HERB	TASTES LIKE	GOES IN/WITH	SUBSTITUTE WITH	FUN FACT
Parsley (Types: Italian or flatleaf parsley; curly parsley)	grassy, fresh, green	practically anything	sometimes fresh basil or mint	Sprinkle chopped parsley on top of an otherwise ugly casserole to make it more attractive.
Pepper-corns (three types: black, white, green are all harvested from the same plant)	spicy, hot,	savory dishes, berries, citrus, butter, cheese, cinnamon, cloves, eggs, beef, everything!	interchange the three, keeping in mind their potency; sometimes also use cayenne	Green peppercorns are mildest. Fermented, they become black pepper, the most aromatic. White peppercorns are fully ripened berries with the hottest flavor. Add all at the end of cooking for best flavor.
Peppercorns, pink	spicy, fruity, floral	fish, citrus, fruits, salad dressings, ginger	lesser amounts of black pepper	These burn easily so avoid direct heat cooking.
Red Pepper Flakes (crushed red pepper)	spicy	pizza, italian food, sausage, meats, tomato sauce	lesser amounts of cayene pepper, black pepper or fresh chiles	Made from a variety of hot peppers.
Turmeric	earthly, slightly floral aroma	curry powders and pastes, coconut, chicken, rice, potatoes	annato (for color)	Related to ginger, turmeric gives bright yellow color to food.

Learn to Cook

NOTABLE SPICES

Here are some notable spices that weren't included in the chart. I separated them because they are blends, not individual spices.

Curry Powder – Curry powders vary quite a bit from brand to brand. Typically, though, they all include: turmeric, coriander, cumin, fenugreek, and cayenne; some may also have cinnamon, caraway, clove, mustard, cardamom, or any number of additional spices. Try one and then try another one. Find one you like.

Herbes de Provence – This is a mixture of dried herbs that are characteristic of Provencal cooking. It includes: thyme, savory, basil, fennel, and sometimes lavender. I seriously have never bought this, but the Barefoot Contessa uses it a lot.

Chili Powder – Pure chili powder can be made from any number of dried chiles: ancho, cayenne, chipotle, pasilla. It is just pulverized chiles and can be used to make sauces and as seasoning. Blended chili powder is a mixture of chiles, garlic, oregano, cumin, and often salt. Labels can be misleading; you will have to read the ingredients list to be sure. Pure and blended chili powders can be interchanged, but you might need to adjust salt in the recipe accordingly.

Chinese Five-Spice Powder – This is a sweet-hot blend used frequently in Chinese cooking. It always includes: star anise, cloves, cinnamon, Szechuan pepper, and fennel seeds. The ratios vary between brands but the five spices remain the same. I don't usually keep this one around, preferring to just add a dash of cinnamon, cloves, and anise seed instead. It's not exactly the same, but I don't make Chinese food often enough for that to matter to me.

Garlic Salt, Celery Salt — These, as you may have guessed, are garlic powder mixed with salt, and celery seed powder mixed with salt.

Lemon Pepper — A mix of lemon zest or lemon-flavored-particles, salt, and black pepper, this is good to use in a pinch on fish and chicken when you wish you had some fresh lemon juice to go over it but you just don't.

Grill Seasoning — This is a very generic term for any coarse-ground spice mix. They usually include salt, pepper, red pepper, onion and/or garlic, plus herbs. They're intended to be used on steaks and other cuts of meat or fish that will be grilled.

Seasoned Salt — An all-purpose blend of salt, spices, and herbs. Notable brands are Lawry's, Tony Chachere's, and Season-all. Lawry's was used on pretty much every meat I ever ate as a kid. And I admit to keeping some "Chach" around for times when I am too brain-tired to think about what spices to season my dinner with. The downside to these is that they are very high in sodium. I feel like I end up with saltier food using these seasoned salts than when I season with individual applications of spices, herbs, and salt.

CHAPTER 5

Conquering the Grocery Store

To begin, you should have a plan for what you're going to eat in the upcoming week. For a beginner cook, a good starting point would be just to pick some dinner options and make a list of what you need based on that. Breakfast can always be cereal when you're starting out, and lunch can be leftovers.

I know this might seem lame and boring, but even if you do it half-assed, it will make shopping and cooking easier. By half-assed, I mean figure out at least two things to make for dinner this week. Browse the recipe section and pick out a couple of recipes you'd like to try. Then buy what you need to make those two things, thus giving you a purpose while you're in the store and an answer later on in the week about "what's for dinner." (Of course, if you want to go whole-hog and plan some menus for breakfast and lunch, too, I won't stop you. But for our purposes, let's start with a dinner menu-creating exercise. Stop me if I talk too much. Just kidding. I'll never stop.)

HOW TO MAKE A
GROCERY LIST

Something you may want to keep in mind when you're planning meals and making a grocery list is what is on sale. Fortunately, what is on sale is often what is in season. So there's a win-win, for cost and flava! You probably get a weekly flyer in your mailbox from the grocery stores closest to you that has sale items listed next to their crappy clip-art pictures and in-store coupons. Sadly for me and you, the coupons are usually only good for people who don't cook.

A dramatic, but kind of funny, way of thinking about it is "coupons for food that will kill you." Of course, everything is killing us, but the point is that you won't need to buy most of the things that the store offers coupons for, because soon you will no longer be eating frozen pizza for every meal. Yay for you! But it is helpful to pay attention to the meat and produce sale items and base your menu ideas on those. It will save you some money and give you a starting point for planning your meals.

Here is an example of what a weekly menu plan might look like, given that green beans, broccoli, oranges and chicken are on sale:

> » Roasted chicken with steamed broccoli and rice *(p. 200)*
> » Chicken divan—made with leftover chicken and broccoli *(p. 166)*
> » Rice, corn, cheese casserole—made with leftover rice *(p. 156)*—with orange and spinach salad
> » Green beans Gianchi over spaghetti *(p. 158)*
> » Beans and Greens *(p. 156)* and garlic bread

Blam! Five nights of cheap, easy, and healthy dinners! And I'll have extra beans and casserole to take for lunch or even eat for breakfast!

Now that you have a list of meals to make this week, look at the ingredients lists on the recipes and compare those with what's in your cupboard and refrigerator/freezer. Write down everything you need to make your recipes that you don't already have. The first week, that may be everything. That is okay. Next week won't be as bad. And the week after that will be even better.

Based on the example above, I know I need to get chicken, broccoli, rice, milk, cheese, corn, spinach, green beans, spaghetti, beans, tomatoes, onions, bell peppers, and bread.

I'll check and make sure I have basic spices and seasonings like garlic, basil, oregano, curry powder, chili powder, and oil. Twenty things tops! It's not so much stuff to get.

Learn to Cook

ORGANIZING YOUR GROCERY LIST

One thing that will truly make your life easier (I swear) is organizing your shopping list. Not every store is laid out exactly the same way (duh), but there are certain things you can count on being grouped together nearly always. If you can write out your list so that your items are grouped likewise, you will get out of the store faster and forget fewer things. Here's a run-down on typical grocery store organization:

Produce Section — I'm sure you've seen this. It's colorful and sometimes you get sprayed with water. It is always on one end of the store or another.

Dairy — This section includes butter, milk, half-and-half, yogurt, cheese. It also, usually, houses eggs and somewhere nearby, lunch meat and bacon. It is often along the back wall of the store.

Bread, etc. — Bread, tortillas, bagels, peanut butter, jelly, and honey (and sometimes even mayo and salad dressing) are on the same aisle.

Canned Vegetables, Beans, Fruit — Together forever (or at least until the Apocalypse).

Baking and Spices — Flour, sugar, spices and oils (along with cake mixes and stuff) are gonna be in close proximity.

Frozen — This is easy to find because it's cold over there. Ice cream, pie crusts, and juice are probably close together. Then frozen vegetables, fruit, and meat. Your Red Barons and Hungry-Mans are still right where you left them. You won't need those anymore. Say goodbye.

Drinks — Coffee, tea, soda, juice—these are all gonna be near each other.

Learn to Cook

WHEN TO GO

The best times to AVOID the grocery store are the first and fifteenth of each month. That's when a lot of people get paid, and the stores are more crowded. But you might be one of those people, so here are some other things too keep in mind.

Avoid going on weekday evenings. Between about four and seven, stores are all a'bustle with suity-types picking up some vino verde and store-made sushi to eat while watching *Moonstruck* on cable; people that don't know how to cook getting frozen pizzas and three liters; and cranky kids that just got picked up from day-care and really want to just go home and watch TV, right after they knock over this whole display of creamed corn, pee their pants, and ram a cart into your elbow bones.

You should definitely avoid going Saturday and Sunday afternoons. That's when all the college kids rouse themselves from their hungover slumber to pick up Pringles, Oreos, Bud Light, Kraft singles, and a bunch of other stuff that starts with a capital letter and you probably shouldn't buy… and condoms. AND that's the day all the families come out to do their weekly shopping which means every aisle is blocked by at least two overflowing carts, parked side-by-side, one with a crying baby and the other with a surly preteen stealing that baby's candy — parents nowhere to be found. Also, Sunday especially sucks for shopping because the stores are pretty well run ragged by that point and you will see a lot of empty shelves. Wo-wo-wo—we're all out of raisin bran, sucker.

So basically, I'm saying avoid the grocery store most of the time. I know that isn't practical. But if you can shop early mornings (before eleven!) or weekdays, do it. It will make your first, tender trip to the grocer more pleasant. After nine p.m. is a good time to avoid crowds, too, but you will also find a serious dearth of employees, so if you need help finding prune juice it could take a while.

Eating by the Seasons

Seasonal eating is fun and pleasurable and good for the earth and your body. If you are an experimental type, I suggest perusing a farmers' market once a week and picking up some wacky new things you've never seen. Then Google them when you get home. Then make something with them. It's really fun, and it will probably turn out good. I hesitate to recommend this to all brand new cooks because depending on your personality there could be a very high risk of frustration and disappointment. Don't get frustrated! Take it easy now!

PRICE COMPARISONS

So, now you are at the store. And you are doing your best. And you have a handy list. And you are picking out olives. Which olives are the best deal? Twelve ounces for $2.49 or fifteen ounces for $3.59? A little thing called "Unit Price" is what you need to know about now. Of course, you could carry a calculator with you and divide the cost of the item by how many ounces it contains. Easy enough. But, did you know that the stores will usually give you that information on the label? That's cool. So, when you look at the price tag, you see the price in big font. Somewhere around that there will be a small box with a much smaller font that will tell you the unit price (per ounce or pound or whatever). This is very helpful for shoppers on a budget. Just pick the one with the lowest unit price. In the example above, the unit prices are $.21 per ounce and $.24 per ounce. So you see that the twelve ounce jar is a better deal! (Be wary that some stores try to trick you by using different units; always make sure the units you are comparing are the same.)

Grocery Store Etiquette

BE AWARE. Be aware of the people around you and where they are trying to go. Be considerate. For the love of God, don't leave your cart parked right in the middle of the damn aisle, hogging up all the space. Park it as close to one side of the aisle as you can and don't get huffy when someone has to move it a little. Don't block the entire display of lemons with your body or your cart or your giant bag while you pick out the perfect one. Be polite. Say "excuse me" when you need to get around someone who isn't following these rules of etiquette. Help out. If there's no one bagging your groceries, you are allowed to do it yourself. Waiting for someone else to bag your shit up just slows the line down for everyone—especially on a busy day. Bring bags. Either invest in some tote bags or, at least, bring in your old plastic or paper bags to reuse. I reuse produce bags all the time because I don't have any of those little mesh bags.

CHAPTER 6

Starting to Cook...

Finally!

You made it home, groceries in tow. Congratulations!

You have completed the most annoying and arduous part of the journey. It's all downhill from here! I mean that in the fun, good, bike-riding kind of way.

In this chapter, I'll be going over a lot of stuff you might remember from chapter two, if you didn't skip it, or Home Ec, if you had to take that class. I took it as an elective in seventh grade, and it was kind of fun. We made a pillow and ironed a shirt and learned to set a table.

Funny story about that:

One time, the teacher was going over what the various items on the table were called—plate, water glass, napkin, flatware—when she got to flatware, this mean dude yelled out, "Hilah is flatware!" and everybody laughed. It doesn't even make sense, but I knew what he meant, and clearly so did everyone else in that damn class. Stupidly, I still stood up for that same asshole once when the teach was giving him a hard time about his handwriting, which she claimed looked like "chicken scratch," and which I claimed to be able to read. What was I thinking?! That butt-brain should have gotten detention for all I care.

Anyway, we didn't much go over how to use a chef's knife, probably because we were all twelve and somebody would have gotten hurt. So, in case you had a class like mine, I'm going to teach you proper knife skills now.

HOW TO HOLD A CHEF'S KNIFE

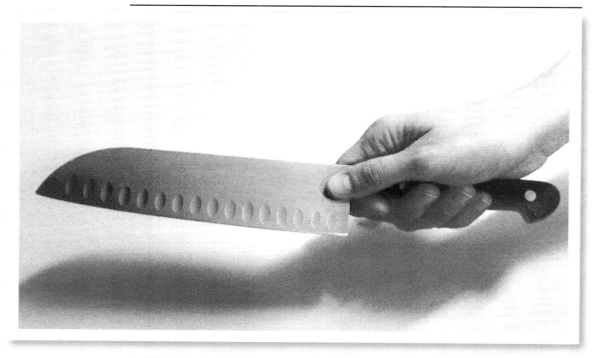

Hold the knife (by the handle!) in your dominant hand. The top of your hand should be facing up when the edge of the blade is on the cutting board. Inch your hand up the handle, towards the blade, until the side of your curled-up index finger rests on the outside of the blade and your thumb tip is pressed on the side of the blade that is facing you. Your middle, ring, and pinkie fingers should be wrapped tightly around the handle now.

By "choking up" on the knife as you would a baseball bat, you have more control over where the blade is going.

More control = Less missing fingers.

HOW TO
SLICE & DICE

When your knife is very sharp, as it should be, you will need to apply very little pressure to achieve slicing and dicing. A sharp knife will literally feel like it's gliding through the food, and you are really only directing it. If you find yourself having to press down with the knife, stop and sharpen it or switch knives. A dull knife is dangerous because while it may be too dull to cut that tomato skin, it's still plenty sharp to cut your hand and the harder you are pressing down, the more likely the blade is to slip off track and go right into some part of your body.

When cutting rounded objects like potatoes and onions, make a flat side to work from first thing. That means either cut it in half or just trim off a sliver, and lay it flat side down before you cut further. I'll talk more specifics in the next section.

What's Your Other Hand Doing?

Your guiding (non-dominant) hand should be holding the food steady and safe and helping to keep the knife going where you want it. Be sure to keep your fingers clear of the knife blade. Some recommend curling your fingertips under so that your second knuckles actually touch the flat side of the blade. I take that a little differently and instead think about using my fingernails to hold the food, but not allowing the blade to actually tough any part of my hand. Whether you have fingernails or you're a biter, I think my way is a good way to get your fingertips safely out of reach while still holding the food steady.

HOW TO MINCE

When you need to reduce a pile of chopped or diced something into a pile of minced something, your guiding hand will do something different. Use the palm or fingertips of your other hand to hold the tip of the knife against the board. Keeping it against the board, your other hand will raise and lower the knife, cutting into the the food, going back and forth, until the desired fineness is reached. The motion should resemble rocking back and forth. It will take practice to be able to do this quickly; don't rush yourself.

KNIFE CARE

Knives should be hand-washed and dried after each use. Dishwashers jostle them around too much and can cause chipped edges, not to mention the damage that detergents and immersion in water can do to the blade and the handle. If you have a honing steel, run the knife blade over that a few times on each side after about every 50 cuts or so. And don't use your knife as a scraper! I know I have a terrible habit of doing this — using the knife edge to help me pick up piles of chopped vegetables — but don't make it your habit! It's really hard on the knife edge and will dull it quickly. Instead, use a tool called a bench scraper, your hands, or just pick up the board and dump the stuff wherever it's supposed to be. Safe and protective storing of knives does not include shoving them into a drawer with a bunch of other junk. A knife block or a wall-mounted magnet bar are the best ways to store knives, protecting you and the knife from damage. If you can't do that, the next best thing is to sheath the knife in a heavy cardboard envelope. As mentioned in chapter three, cutting on hard surfaces like glass, metal, and marble will dull your knife quickly; always use a wood or plastic cutting board. And don't use knives for anything besides cutting. Trying to MacGyver a knife into a bottle opener, pry-bar, or can opener is inviting destruction into your home. You'll damage your knife and pieces of the blade might even snap off and fly into your face. Ouch. Srsly.

HOW TO CUT UP STUFF: PLANTS

Cutting up stuff is an inescapable part of cooking. The sooner you learn to cut onions, garlic, celery, and carrots, the sooner you will be making some bad ass soup, etc. Let us begin.

Onions

Onions make you cry. The only thing I have found that really helps minimize the effect is to store the onions in the refrigerator and cut them while they are cold. Being cold makes the tear-inducing sulphuric compounds chillax and not jump straight into your eyeballs. Some people say you should never refrigerate onions, but those people are cooking fearmongers; I do it all the time and my onions still taste like onions. That said, here is the fastest, easiest way to chop up an onion:

With the onion on the cutting board, hold it upright with your nondominant hand (upright means with the hairy root end down and the dry, leafy bits up). Cut down through the middle of the onion. Peel the paper off the onion halves and discard (in your compost bucket, if you have one). Lay the onion halves, cut side down, on the cutting board. Putting the flat side down stabilizes the onion and makes cutting safer. Cut off the dry, leafy bit at the end. Now you have three options on the shape of the onion pieces you want.

1. **Pretty Half-Circles** — nice for salads and sandwiches—Cut slices parallel to the end cut, any thickness you prefer, although thinner is nicer if you're eating them raw. Blammo. Onion rainbows.

2. **Neat Julienne** — nice for stir frying and stewing—Cut off the root end and discard. Slice the onion lengthwise, from root to top end, perpendicular to the end cuts you made. ¼" - ½" slices are perfect.

3. **Cool Cubes (Dice and Mince)** — With the onion flat on the board, make 3-5 cuts into it like you did in the julienne method, above. DO NOT cut all the way through the root end. Leave the roots intact so that your onion doesn't burst apart like a broke Rubik's cube. Now that you have those cuts made, you are ready to cut the onion like you did in style #1: half-circles. As you cut this way now, tiny cubes of diced onion will fall onto your cutting board. Pretty! It's like confetti! Have a party! (To mince onions, start with dice and then pile them up and rock your knife over the pile several times until they are all tiny and triangular; see previous section.)

Garlic

Yes, you can buy preminced garlic. No, I don't ever use preminced garlic. Yes, you can use pre-minced garlic. No, I don't care. But to me, garlic-in-a-jar has a weird smell that I don't like. So here's how to do it the old-fashioned way.

1. **Minced or Mashed Garlic** — Pull a clove off the garlic head and put it on the cutting board. Use the side of your knife to crush the garlic clove by pressing down slowly or by giving it a quick whack. Slowly is safer for beginners. The garlic clove will pop open and the guts will be splayed out all over. Pick the papery peel out and then just rock your knife over the mashed guts until they are pulverized guts.

2. **Sliced Garlic, For Fancy Times** — Pick off a clove. Slice off the end that connected it to the whole head. It's the little, hard, flat end. Just cut that off. Then use your fingernails, or a paring knife if you're a biter, to remove the papery peel. Then lay the clove on the board and slice thinly. This is a nice thing to do if you want to make fried garlic toasties for putting on top of salads or mashed potatoes. Fancy! Have a party!

3. **Garlic Press** — This is super easy. Just put the whole clove (no need to peel) into the basket part of the press, fold over the hammer part, and squeeze. Garlic squirts out the holes. Voila! The downside to this is it's a pain in the ass to clean and you lose some garlic, but it is easy and fast.

Celery

Sometimes you'll need diced celery for soups and sometimes you'll want sliced celery for salads. Celery sticks are eaten raw and are the easiest celery shape to cut. Let's start there.

1. **Celery Sticks** — Pull of some celery stalks and wash them. Duh. Trim off the fat white end and the leafy green end. Compost that or stick them back in the fridge to use in soups. Now cut the stalk crosswise into 2–3" lengths. Viola. You're done.

2. **Celery Slices** — Start with a clean stalk. Cut off the ends and lay it down so that it is flat and steady. Cut crosswise into slices between ½" and ¼" thick. If you want fancy Chinatown-style slices, cut them at a 45º angle.

3. **Celery Diced** — Same as before, clean and trim ends. Don't make me tell you again. Slice the stalk lengthwise in half. Now cut crosswise to make little cubes.

Carrots

If you want to know how to cut carrots into the perfect tiny cubes that you get in your frozen mixed vegetable bag, you're reading the wrong damn book, buddy. It is possible to cut carrots like that, but it requires forcing a round peg into a square hole and you end up wasting a lot of carrot. I will instead tell you how to cut up a carrot into imperfect tiny cubes.

1. **Carrot Sticks** — I usually would never suggest peeling a carrot, but if you are having the Pope over for crudités, it might be a good idea. Just use a vegetable peeler and go around it once, holding the stem end and peeling down and away from you in long, lengthwise strokes. Great. Now cut off the stem and tip. Great. Now cut it in half crosswise so that you have a fat half and a skinny half. Now cut each of those halves into two, lengthwise. The fat end halves can be cut lengthwise again. Perfect. You probably have six carrot sticks now. Or a bloody mess.

2. **Carrot Cubes** — Do like you just did for the carrot sticks and then cut the sticks crosswise into chunks. If you will be cooking with these cubes, don't bother peeling the carrots first. Save time and nutrients! Win-win!

Bell Peppers

This is also applicable to hot peppers. The first thing is to remove the seeds and stem. Cut the pepper in half lengthwise, from stem to butt. Break the seeds, membranes, and stem out and toss them. Now you have two hollow halves.

1. **Strips** – Cut lengthwise strips, ¼" to ½" wide for stir frying or eating raw

2. **Dice** – Cut strips first, then across into squares of any size you like for soups or sautees

Once you know how to cut up all those things, you can surely figure out how to cut up anything else: zucchini, potatoes, eggplant, apples. Just relax and don't be so worried about the shape, as long as your pieces are fairly evenly sized so that everything will cook at the same rate.

Avocados

Holding it in your palm, cut all around it from stem to end; you will feel your knife hit the big pit in the middle. Remove the knife and twist the two halves apart. One has the pit stuck in it. To remove: hold the avocado in your palm and strike the pit with the blade of your knife in a sharp, quick, but not too hard, motion. Lift the knife up and the pit comes with it. Now you can use a big spoon to scoop out the flesh from each half, then slice or cube. Sprinkle with lemon or lime juice or vinegar to keep it from turning brown. To unlodge the knife from the pit, scrape the blade against the edge of your sink or something to push the pit off. If, sadly, you find yourself half-cut into an avocado that isn't completely ripe, the best way to salvage it is to mash it up with some mayonnaise or sour cream and make guacamole. The mayo adds the creamy texture that an unripe avocado lacks.

Mangoes

Mangoes may be baffling to you but here's the easiest way to cut them up. You see that a mango is shaped like a flattened kidney bean or egg. What you don't see is that there is a large seed in the center, taking up almost the middle one-third of the fruit; we need to cut around that. Hold it so that it sits on one of the narrow sides and use a sharp knife to cut down, about ⅓ of the way from the outside. If you hit the seed, just wiggle your knife around it. Cut off the other mango "cheek" the same way.

Now you have two big pieces of mango with the skin still attached. Use a paring knife to score the fruit, being careful not to press so hard that you cut through the skin on the other side. You can cut it in just one direction for slices or cut it in two (like a tic-tac-toe game) for cubes. Once it's scored, pop it out so that you're looking at something kind of like a porcupine back. Then use the paring knife to carefully cut the slices or cubes away off the skin.

When you are making something that includes several different vegetables that are all to be cooked in the same vessel (eg, in a crock pot or a stir fry), take their relative densities into consideration when you cut them up. On Earth, dense = hard. It doesn't take a genius to realize that the harder something is, the longer it will take to cook. So in order to avoid undercooked carrots and overcooked zucchini, you need to cut the carrots into smaller pieces than the zucchini. There's an inverse ratio of density : size. Got that? Now you're a genius. Congratulations. And I know you can figure this out on your own, but here's a handy list of dense vegetable and nondense vegetables:

Real Dense — carrots, red and white potatoes, rutabagas, turnips

Kinda Dense — russet potatoes, sweet potatoes, winter squash, onions

Meh — broccoli, cauliflower, green beans

Softies — eggplant, summer squash (zucchini), asparagus, leafy greens, bell peppers, mushrooms

Melons and Winter Squash

Cut melons (and winter squashes) up into manageable pieces before trying to peel them. For example, first use a big knife to cut it into two symmetrical pieces. Scoop out the seeds with a spoon and toss them (in the compost, eh?). Cut each half in half again, then those into halves, all symmetrically, so you have eight slices. These are now easy to hold on to while you peel with a paring knife or vegetable peeler. Then cut the slices into cubes or whatever.

Pineapples

Lay it on its side and lop off the top and bottom. Set it upright on one of the flat ends and using straight, downward strokes, cut off the skin all the way around; it falls away in long, strips. Get them out of your way and cut down through the middle of the pineapple. Lay the halves down and use a paring knife to cut out any "eyes" that you missed. Cut each half lengthwise into half and half again so you have eight long pineapple wedges. Cut out the core from each wedge by laying it on a flat side and cutting off the inside area, a strip about a ½" wide. Then cut each wedge into cubes and remove any more bits of skin or "eyes" that you missed.

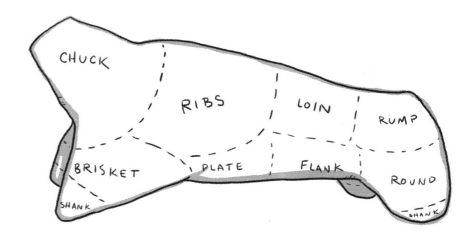

HOW TO CUT UP STUFF: ANIMALS

These days, it's so easy to buy dead animals that are already cut up, skinned, and prepped for you that it hardly seems worth it to include a diagram of a side of beef in here. So I wouldn't, except it is helpful to have some idea of what you're buying at the store, so I did.

Beef

Meat that comes from the center-ish part of the animal is going to be the most tender, and therefore most suited for the high-and-dry-heat cooking methods like grilling, broiling, and sauteeing. These cuts include ribs, short loin, and sirloin. The steak cuts you hear most about —Porterhouse and T-bone — both come from the short loin. Ribeye steaks come from the rib section while top sirloin and tri-tip steaks come from the sirloin section. Flank and skirt steak must also be cooked fast and hot.

Cuts that come from the shoulders, rump, or shanks have more connective tissue that can be tough if not allowed a long, slow cooking time. When properly done, however, these cuts are tender and delicious. Notable beef cuts good for braising include chuck and shoulder roasts, rump roast, and brisket. Good cuts for stewing include those plus bottom round, blade steak, and short ribs.

85

Pork

The tenderness or toughness of various pork cuts follow the same rules as for beef, but with different names. Pork loin, tenderloin, and chops are lean cuts and all do best cooked quickly via grilling, high-heat roasting, and stir fying. For best results, cook all lean cuts of pork to medium doneness; they will still have a faintly pink inside. Picnic shoulder and Boston butt roasts are great for braising and slow-cooking. You can also find legs, sometimes labeled "fresh ham," that do well braised, too. Spareribs, bacon, and pork belly come from the underside and are delicious in their fattiness.

Poultry

You can save money cutting up your own whole chicken, assuming you like dark and white meat. Quartering a chicken is the easiest way to get it separated into serving sizes. This method will give you two leg/thigh portions and two wing/breast portions that can be roasted, grilled, or braised. You will need a very sharp knife, and a pair of kitchen shears are helpful, too.

Begin by cutting down each side of the bird, from the tail to the back, through the skin and connective tissue. Then cut through on either side of the backbone, from tail to neck. You will need to apply some pressure to cut through the bones. Get rid of the backbone now.

Open the bird like a book. On the inside, you will see a diamond-shaped bit of white cartilage covering the breastbone. Use the tip of your knife to cut through the cartilage, then use your fingers to pry that bone out. It will take some muscle. Once the breastbone is out, it's easy to cut the bird into two symmetrical halves between the breasts.

Butterflying

Butterflying a boneless cut of meat or seafood is also good to know how to do. To butterfly, lay your meat hunk on the cutting board. Get a really, really sharp knife in your hand. Hunker down, eye-level, with the meat and, holding it steady with the palm of your other hand (fingers out of the way, please!), make a cut into the side of the meat as close to halfway as you can manage. Cut across, parallel to the cutting board, stopping about one inch from the other side. Unfold the meat slab like a book. Now you should have a piece of meat, wider and longer but thinner than the original. Pick it up and make it fly around like a butterfly. Or be an adult.

KITCHEN HYGIENE & SAFETY

I guess I should briefly go over some basic de-germing and non injuring yourself techniques for the kitchen before we get started.

Keep it Clean! Commercial and professional kitchens have much more stringent policies than are necessary in home kitchens. But there are still some rules that always apply.

» Wash your hands before you start cooking. Use soap (it doesn't have to be anti-bacterial) and warm water and dry them with a clean towel.

» If you're making things like bread or meatloaf where you'll be using your hands to get in there and mix stuff, remove your rings and bracelets first.

» Wash your hands after handling meat, poultry, or seafood. If you're in the thick of things and can't stop, I totally understand. That is why I (along with every chef everywhere) keep a clean towel nearby when cooking. Wipe your hands to at least keep them dry, if not decontaminated, so you're not pulling a Mr. Butterfingers with your knife.

» Wash cutting boards well with very hot water after using them, especially after using them for meat and poultry. While the idea that wooden cutting boards harbor bacteria has been shown to be false, you obviously don't want to leave residue sitting on your board.

» The idea of rinsing poultry before cooking is very outdated. You really don't need to do that for any reason. Any bacteria on the surface of the meat is going to be killed upon cooking, and rinsing it off just increases the bacterial "spread" to your sink, countertops, floor, yourself, and lots of other places where it's not going to be easy to clean up.

Learn to Cook

Safety First! Cuts and burns are the injuries most often sustained in the kitchen. Here's how you can avoid an injury, plus what to do if it happens anyway.

» Tie long hair back and don't wear loose-fitting clothes or sleeves when cooking. These are more a matter of safety than hygiene in a home kitchen. Don't want to catch yourself on fire.

» To avoid steam burns, always remove lids *away* from your face as if the lid were a shield, and don't hover right over the stove.

» Be extra careful carrying heavy pots of boiling liquid. Lifting a pot of cooked pasta to the sink and dumping it into the colander is dangerous enough without kids or animals running into the kitchen. Make sure the coast is clear before you go!

» Use hot mitts or hot pads to handle hot skillets, pots, and pans.

» Never put hot liquids in a blender. Hot liquids build up pressure and can blow the lid off, spraying hot stuff everywhere.

» Cover splattering frying pans with a splatter screen or stand back to avoid getting popped with hot oil.

» Keep handles of pots and pans turned inward, not sticking out past the edge of the stove, to avoid knocking them off.

» If you do burn yourself and it's minor (most kitchen burns) immediately run cool water over the burn for 10-15 minutes or until the pain subsides or immerse it in a bowl of cool water. Don't use ice or any other "home remedies" like butter or egg whites. Just cool it off, put a Band-aid over it and take some Advil or Tylenol. Don't pop the blister if you can help it. If your burn is bigger than 3 inches across or your skin has turned black or white, you need to see a doctor.

» Always hold knives by the handle and if you drop a knife, step back quickly. Do NOT try to catch the knife, even though your lizard brain will be screaming at you to grab it.

» Make sure your knives are sharp. Dull knives slip around more, making them harder to control and more likely to go where they aren't supposed to go.

» If you cut yourself, allow it to bleed for a few minutes to help wash out any contaminants. Then apply pressure to stop the bleeding. Gently wash with water, dry, and cover with a Band-aid. Antibiotic ointment may be applied first if you have some. If you can't get the bleeding to stop or the cut is deep or has something lodged inside, head to the ER, buddy.

No Fires. It's also important to not catch things on fire. Be careful around gas stovetops and broilers; don't wear loose long sleeves or fluffy frilly clothing and be sure to tie your hair back. Don't lean over a gas stove. Also pay attention when deep frying. I'll talk more about the specifics on safe frying later in this chapter, but for now remember:

NEVER PUT WATER ON A GREASE OR OIL FIRE. It will not put the fire out; it will only cause flaming oil to splatter all over the place.

NEVER TRY TO MOVE A POT OF FLAMING OIL. It may seem like a good idea to take the fire outside. After all, it's in a pot! With a handle! But you risk spilling boiling fire-oil on yourself or something else that may be even more flammable.

If the fire is contained in a pot or pan, smother it with a tight-fitting metal lid. Glass lids might break. If the fire has spread beyond the cooking area, smother it with baking soda (it will take a lot) or use a chemical fire extinguisher. Of course the fire extinguisher will ruin your food and be a bitch to clean up after but at least you are no longer in danger of burning your house down.

And don't hesitate to call 911 for the fire department. Grease fires can get out of hand quickly, and no one will fault you for being cautious. Plus, your tax dollars pay for the service so use it if you need it.

COOKING TECHNIQUES, REVISITED

So now you have a big pile of chopped up vegetables and/or meat in front of you. What are you going to do with them? Steam them? Saute them? Boil them? Roast them? Braise them? Chug a pint of whiskey and throw them against a wall in tearful frustration because you don't really know how to do any of that? STOP. Relax. I'll tell you. You can still have the whiskey if you want, though.

Moist Heat Methods

These are the cooking methods that rely on water (or another liquid) or steam to transfer heat and cook the food.

Steam — I know you know what this is. It's cooking with steam! FYI, it's about the most nutrient-conservative cooking method out there and it doesn't require any oil or fat. Foods keep their colors and don't have much, if any, "shrinkage." If you want to splurge on a three dollar steamer basket, that is the simplest way to do it. Get a pot, at least a 2 quart capacity. Put about an inch of water in the pot and then your basket, unfolded as far as it will go in the pot. The water should not come up over bottom of the basket. Put your vegetables in the basket. You can cook various vegetables at the same time: just put the densest ones on the bottom where they're closest to the heat. Put a lid on the pot and turn the heat on high. Listen and look for bubbling noises and steam; that's how you know it is boiling. Turn the heat down to medium and steam as long as the recipe dictates. Be careful not to let the water boil away completely. You can set up an "alarm" by putting a marble or penny in the bottom of the pot; when you no longer hear a jangling, it needs more water in the bottom. And be very careful when removing the lid to avoid a steam burn; tilt the lid off away from your face.

You can also steam foods without a basket, but instead using aromatic vegetables as a base. Layer an inch or so of onions, celery, carrots, fennel, peppers, tomatoes (cut into strips) in the bottom of a pot. Add just enough water or stock to barely cover. Place your main item (fish fillets, chicken tenders, etc.) on top of that. Cover and steam until cooked. The vegetables and stock in the pot can be served as a sauce over the meat.

Foods that take well to steaming are vegetables, poultry and seafood fillets, dumplings, and wontons. Any tender protein can be steamed as long as it's cut down to a size small enough so that it will cook quickly. Because steaming doesn't add any flavor on its own, it's a good technique to use when you want the distinct flavor of the ingredients to come through. If you like, though, you can also steam with wine, tea, or broth instead of water or add herbs and spices to the steaming water to impart a delicate aroma. *See Steamed Broccoli (p. 218)*.

Poach — Like steaming, poaching is most appropriate for vegetables and tender proteins like poultry and seafood. Unlike steaming, poaching offers an opportunity to use the poaching liquid to add flavor to the food. Poaching liquids are usually stocks or broths, fortified with aromatic vegetables, herbs, or spices, even wine, juice, vinegar, or tomato sauce. The poaching liquid can be reduced quickly, after the food is cooked and removed, and used as a sauce. I don't poach very often because I like to mess with my food while it cooks, and I am very impatient. Poaching takes a little more time than other methods, but for certain foods the results are unbeatable.

Shallow poaching is done in a covered skillet with only a small amount of liquid, resulting in a cooking method that combines poaching and steaming. *See Perfectly Good Fish (p. 162)*.

Deep poaching is well-suited to bone-in chicken pieces, meatballs, pork, or whole fish. It's similar to simmering, but done at a lower temperature. The poaching liquids used are the same as in shallow poaching, but you will need enough liquid to submerge the food. Use a big enough pot to allow the food plenty of room to move around and be completely surrounded by liquid. The temperature should be between 160-185° F. It's hot, and the water surface may move around, but there shouldn't be any bubbles around the edges. If there are bubbles, it's simmering and you may need to turn the heat down. *See Chicken Salad (p. 130)*.

Learn to Cook

Simmer — Simmering is like deep poaching done at a slightly higher temperature. I like to use this for beef and pork cuts and dried beans. The higher cooking temperature works well to make a thick sauce or gravy out of any liquid you might cook meat with. *See Chili (p. 152), Meaty Sauce (p. 187), and Baked Beans (p. 246).*

Boil — Like I said before, many things that you may think of as "boiling" should really be simmering, like soups and stews, braises, and sauces. Things that literally can be boiled are potatoes and other root vegetables and pasta. This is so easy even a stupid baby could do it (not recommended). Get your potatoes or other root vegetables. You will retain the most vitamins if you boil them whole (and in their peels), but they will cook a lot faster if you cut them into chunks. Your call. How much time do you have? Also, you get to decide if you will eat the peels or not. If you're going to eat them in the final dish, then scrub them well with water and a brush to remove the dirt. If you're going to peel them after cooking, then fuck it; save some water. So now, put your potatoes (whole or chunked, peeled or not, decisions, decisions) in a large pot and cover with water. Put a lid on the pot and put it over high heat. Bring to a boil and then turn the heat down to medium; a full boil will be too rough on your food and break it apart. Crack the lid a tidge to let steam escape so your pot don't boil over and make a big mess. Cook until a skewer or small knife easily pierces a potato. This might be ten minutes for small chunks or as long as thirty for whole potatoes. Beets and turnips take a little longer than potatoes; rutabaga and carrots don't take quite as long. *See Mashed Potatoes (p. 217).* Cooking pasta is covered later on in the pasta section.

Braise — Braising is done in a fairly low temperature oven (300°–350° F) or over low stovetop heat for a long time and always with a tight lid. Meats are seared first to give them some color and deepen the flavor, then a small amount of liquid (beer, wine, tomato sauce, broth, or even water) is added, the pot is covered, and a long, slow simmer happens. Sometimes meat may be lightly dusted with flour before searing; this adds body to the finished sauce. Both braising and stewing are best done with less tender cuts of meat because the long slow process breaks down collagen and connective tissue, creating a fall-apart tenderness and a rich, tasty sauce. Whole cuts of beef or pork work well braised. Root vegetables can also be braised, though of course they won't take near as long as meat. Crock pot cooking and pressure cooking are both forms of braising. *See Braised Pot Roast (p. 159) and Maple Glazed Sweet Potatoes (p. 223).*

Learn to Cook

Stewing — Stewing is like braising, except usually done stovetop and with smaller pieces of meat. Enough liquid is used so that the food is submerged, a lid placed on the pot, and simmering begun. The same tougher cuts that work well in braising also work great stewed. Many stews make a great one-dish meal. *See Beef Vegetable Stew (p. 157).*

Dry Heat Methods

These are the methods that use air or oil to transfer heat.

Saute — In French, sauté literally means "jump around" . . . or something like that. Basically, you are cooking food in a shallow pan over fairly high heat with a little bit of any heat-stable oil (see Chapter Four for more on which oils to use). It's pretty much like stir frying. Searing, pan searing, pan broiling, stir frying, and blackening are all techniques that are based on the saute. You want to use a big enough skillet so that all the food fits in a single layer so everything touches the hot oil and pan at once. Preheat your cast iron or stainless steel skillet on high for a minute, then add two teaspoons to a tablespoon of oil and let it heat for thirty seconds to a minute. If you are using a nonstick pan (and breaking my heart!), preheat the skillet with the oil already in it, then add the food. Meats should be turned when they easily release from the pan, which is a little bit after the juices start to come up to the surface of the raw side. *See Sauteed Steaks (p. 172), and Sauteed Collard Greens (p. 219).*

Pan Fry — Pan frying is similar to sautéing, but uses more fat and a slightly lower temperature for a longer time. There should be enough oil in the pan to come up half-way the height of the food being cooked. Meats are usually breaded, floured, or battered before pan frying, making the end result more similar to something that has been deep-fried rather than sauteed. Meat cutlets are cut into portion sizes and many times tenderizes with a mallet before breading and cooking. *See Fish Tacos (p. 183) and Pan-Fried Bean Burgers (p. 174).*

Deep Fry — Deep frying differs from pan frying in the amount of oil used. In deep frying, the oil should be deep enough that the food is completely submerged in oil. It produces a crispy, brown exterior while keeping the interior of the food juicy. Deep frying is done with the oil temperature between 325–375° F (165–190° C). A frying thermometer is the best, most reliable way to maintain an even temperature which is important for ensuring a crisp, non-greasy product. When your oil temperature is too low, your fried foods will have a greasy finish. This is why it's not a good idea to overload the oil — the temperature will drop as you add food and, the more added at once, the more the temperature drops and the longer it will take to come back up to the correct-temperature. The thermometer should not touch the bottom or sides of the pot or fryer for an accurate reading.

If you don't have a thermometer you can still estimate the temperature of the oil using the "Bread Cube Method." Drop a cube of bread into the oil and count how many seconds it takes to brown.

» 20 seconds: oil is between 385–395° F (196-201° C)

» 40 seconds: oil is between 375–385° F (190-196° C)

» 60 seconds: oil is between 360–375° F (182-190° C)

Choose an oil with a smoke point that is well above your target heat to minimize the danger of smoking and fire (see Chapter Four for more on oils and smoke points).

Fry oil may be reused, but I don't recommend you reuse it more than once. One reason is that it develops unpleasant flavors that may transfer to your food; another is that the smoke point of an oil decreases with each use. If you want to reuse it, allow it to cool then strain it to remove particles and keep cool and dark until next time.

To reduce the mess associated with deep frying and frying, I recommend using a splatter screen which will catch most of the popping oil while allowing steam to escape. Also make sure the that pot or fryer you are using isn't filled up too high; leave at least 2 inches of space between the oil level and the lip of the frying vessel. This helps prevent boiling over, which is not only dangerous, but also a pain in the ass to clean up.

Stir Fry — Traditionally done in a wok, but a large skillet will work as well. Do not use a non stick skillet because the coating cannot stand up to the high temperature required. Preheat the wok or skillet empty until it smokes. Add the oil. Then add meats and vegetables in stages of longest to shortest cooking time. Stir or shake the pan quickly, moving it constantly until everything is cooked. It happens quickly so make sure to have all your ingredients cut up and ready to go in before you begin. Add seasonings like fresh garlic, ginger, and soy sauce last to prevent their burning and mucking up all the flavors. *See Chicken Lo Mein (p. 175) and Tofu Stir Fry (p. 176).*

Bake — Baking is cooking food by way of indirect heat, as in an oven, where the food is cooked from contact with dry, hot air. Breads , cookies, and pies are baked. The terms "baking" and "roasting" can be used interchangeably when talking about meat cookery, though "baked" is more often used in recipes when the meat is cut up into portion sizes before cooking. *See Pineapple Lemon Chicken (p. 167), Potato Bake (p. 197), and Brownies (p. 237).*

Roast — Roasting in many ways is synonymous with baking in that it's done in an oven, uncovered, so that the hot air can circulate all around the pan. When meats are roasted, however, they are usually done so in large chunks (think of a roast beef or whole chicken), and the end result is a crusty exterior with a juicy interior. Often roasted meats are browned on the stovetop before baking to add depth of flavor. The juices rendered from the meat while cooking are usually incorporated into some kind of sauce or pan-gravy after the meat has cooked. Lean meats are best roasted with some fatty covering to protect from drying out in the oven; a few strips of bacon laid over the top works well. People usually think of roasting as something you do with big hunks of meat, but you can also roast vegetables. *See recipes for Roasted Chicken (p. 200), Roasted Asparagus (p. 202), and Oven Fries (p. 205).*

Broil — Best used for cuts of meat and vegetables that are naturally tender and quick-cooking, broiling is a form of direct-heat cookery like grilling. (Grilling is another matter for another book, preferably written by a boy, not a girl—*I kid!*—but really it's a whole different subject.) Use small cuts of tender meat or fish when broiling to ensure the food is cooked through by the time the outside is done. Most broiler racks or pans are adjustable so you can move the food nearer or farther from the heat, controlling how quickly it cooks. Obviously using an indoor gas or electric broiler won't give you the same smoky flavor of a charcoal or wood grill, but you will still get the similar benefit of a lovely charred exterior. You can also use the broiler to roast peppers, quickly add color to already-cooked meats, and make toast. Use caution when broiling; don't forget about your food or it could catch fire. *See Tiny Fake Pizzas (p. 137), Cinnamon Toast (p. 102), and Stuffed Peppers (p. 210).*

Microwave

I'm sure I don't need to tell you how to use a microwave, since if you don't know how to cook, you probably couldn't have lived this long without one. You might even be dead now if the microwave didn't exist! Think about that.

But, really, all I want to say here is that I love the microwave! I've got a few friends who are afraid microwaves are going to poison their food and give them brain cancer, and I have one thing to say to that: GET OVER IT, HIPPIES! (Insert winky-smiley emoticon here.)

Microwave ovens are way more energy efficient when compared to gas and electric ovens. Also, because they cook food quickly, you retain a shitload more nutrients as compared to boiling or something. Plus, in Texas it is over a hundred degrees (Celsius! JK) for most of the year, and I'll be damned if I'm going to turn on the oven every time I want to make some fuckin' enchiladas.

Couple things, though, and then I will STFU: Don't use plastic (Saran) wrap in the microwave—it can't stand the heat and spits out plastic molecules all over your food—I don't want to eat plastic; use a paper towel or a glass lid to save trees. Same thing goes for plastic containers; I mean . . . Fine, okay, I'm just saying that I don't usually reheat things in plastic containers unless I am particularly lazy and/or hung over. Also, the microwave is great for casseroles and other moist things that you might usually bake in the oven; it SUCKS for cooking any kind of bread or baked goods. Due to the science behind how it works, it's just impossible to get things delightfully browned in the microwave.

Bonus Tip: You can, however, cook eggs and bacon in the microwave. *See page 96.*

Learn to Cook

PART TWO

Recipes

Let's Get Cookin'!

For Serious, Y'all!

Now we get to the fun part.

Are you ready to rumble?

I am!

Here are some recipes, grouped by meal and loosely organized from super-duper easy to just easy. Nothing in here is very complicated because I want you to succeed. And please don't be turned off by the odd, long list of ingredients. None of them are expensive or hard to find. Pinky swear.

You may notice that a lot of these recipes don't call for much salt, if any. I believe that heavy-handed use of salt is dangerous to one's health (it can cause high blood pressure and water retention, which is hard on your kidneys) and have been accustoming my palate to using less. You may, of course, salt your food to your liking, but for health reasons, I recommend trying a few bites before you add salt at the table. I bet you will be surprised at how quickly your taste buds adjust.

That goes for canned food, too. Most canned vegetables are available with no added salt. Get that one and take control over your diet. Having said that, though, I must also include this caveat on canned foods generally, and particularly acidic foods like canned tomatoes. The chemical Bisphenol-A (BPA) is present in canned food, thanks to the plastic lining inside most cans. Acidic things like tomatoes cause it to leach out more. There is increasing evidence that BPA can fuck up your reproductive junk. I'm not going crazy here, but I just wanted to let you know in case you want babies someday. Might want to avoid canned foods altogether. Fortunately, tomato sauce is also in jars and boxes now. Maybe that's better for you. And pretty much any vegetable you can buy canned is also available frozen. It's up to you of course, but I'll tell you that I've pretty much given up all canned foods after reading some of the studies.

Onward. I have also given alternatives when possible; in case you don't have a particular ingredient or spice, there may still be hope for you and your supper. When you encounter something like this: "1 teaspoon oregano" and you are all out of oregano, please refer to **Spice World** in Chapter 4 to find a suitable substitution: e.g., if it's an Italiany dish, opt for basil; if it's a Mexicany dish, opt for cilantro. The measurements may not be exchangeable one-for-one but I've given tips on that, too, in the spice section.

Garlic measurements are given by number of fresh cloves and by teaspoons, minced, in case you use garlic in a jar or have some freakishly small or astoundingly large garlic cloves. I didn't offer equivalents for using garlic powder because I almost never use it and much prefer fresh garlic flavor, but if you must: 1 teaspoon of garlic = about ¼ teaspoon garlic powder (NOT garlic salt).

Further, when you encounter something like this: "1 cup minced red onion, white onion, or green onions", that means one cup of minced red onion (preferably). Lacking that, use white onion; lacking that, green onion. The order in which they are listed is the order of preference, but it's never terribly important to any of these recipes because they are meant to be easy and not stressful on you. If the recipe doesn't specify what type of onion or apple or whatever, then *it doesn't matter*.

So relax, follow the instructions, ***and it will be okay***. Really.

And that reminds me, too, that many recipes in here will just call for "oil." I've not specified because for any given purpose, there are many oils that will work, and I don't want you to feel like you have to use a certain kind or buy anything special to make one single recipe. For most recipes, any medium-heat oil will do fine (see Chapter 4 for a detailed breakdown of oils and their uses) meaning any refined oil such as canola, sunflower, safflower or light olive oil. All of the salad dressing recipes will work with any liquid oil you have, but you might enjoy the flavor of an extra-virgin olive oil or another unrefined oil.

CHAPTER 7

Breakfast

Breakfast is the most important meal of the day. But that doesn't mean you need to slave over it or eat it in a breakfast nook. Of course, cereal is always a great option, but if you are like me and eat breakfast at work or on the way to work, cereal is not very portable. And cereal gets old. Try something new!

Here are some easy ideas for work-day breakfasts plus a few fun things to try out on a lazy weekend morning when you have more time.

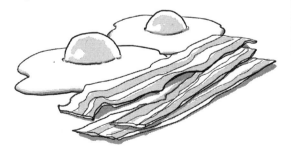

WORK-DAY BREAKFASTS

Yogurt Parfait

So easy, it's barely a recipe.

In a bowl or plastic container, put a cup of yogurt (I like plain, fat free yogurt but you can use whatever you want). Top that with a small handful of almonds, walnuts, or pecans. Add some berries (fresh or frozen) or a sliced banana. Top that with some dry cereal or homemade granola.

Eat it now or put a lid on it and take it to work like I do. Pardon, I mean, "like the cool kids do." (I'm cool. I swear.)

Toast

The only reason I included toast is so I can tell you this story. One time when I was six or so, I got confused at my grandma's house and I couldn't remember if the butter went on the bread before or after it went into the toaster. My six year-old brain logic told me that it was probably before it went in, because how else would the butter get all melted? Smart, right? So the toaster caught fire, and I started yelling, and my grandma ran in wearing this big silky kimono number and dumped a box of baking soda all over it and saved our lives. The toast and toaster were ruined, but we were saved. So let that be a lesson to you.

However, if you are so lucky to have a toaster oven or broiler, you can, in fact, butter the bread before you put it in the toaster oven. Your toast will be all the toastier for having done so.

Cinnamon Toast

Spread bread with a teaspoon of butter, sprinkle with 1 teaspoon of sugar and a few dashes of cinnamon. Put it in the toaster oven or under the broiler for a couple of minutes until the sugar is all melty and crunchy and awesome. As with all broiling, watch it carefully and don't forget about it or you could start a fire. Think about my grandma while you eat it.

Oatmeal

The directions are on the package. Follow them. Then add some nuts and dried fruit, butter and maple syrup, or peanut butter and honey and mix it all up and put it in your talk-hole. A pinch of salt makes oatmeal taste a lot better, too.

Oatmeal Buyer's Guide

If you've never checked out the oatmeal section at the grocery store, boy, are you in for a stupid surprise. Real quick, here's the four major forms that oatmeal takes on the shelf:

Steel Cut Oats — Whole oat grains that have been chopped up. These are almost exclusively eaten as a hot cereal and require 30 minutes or more to cook. You can cook a pot on the weekend and microwave servings during the week. Probably not ever what a recipe means when it calls for "oatmeal."

Rolled Oats — Whole oat grains that have been rolled out flat. They can be cooked into a nice cereal in five to ten minutes. I prefer these for baking because they hold up well, provide a nice texture, and have more fiber than the quick and instant types. AKA "old-fashioned oats."

Quick Oats — Oat grains with the outer husk removed, then rolled out flat. They cook up in into cereal in one to three minutes and are also fine for baking, but have a softer, less chewy texture than rolled oats.

Instant Oats — These are quick oats that have been even further rolled and chopped up to make them edible the minute they hit hot water. It's like eating predigested oatmeal (that may be an exaggeration). I don't recommend these for anything really, unless you are really in a bind. Or you are an infant.

Cinnamon Apples

My mama made these to go with French toast. Mmm. They would also be bad-ass on some ice cream. Just sayin'.

- » 1 apple
- » 1 tablespoon butter
- » 1 tablespoon sugar
- » ¼ teaspoon cinnamon

1. Cut the apple into eight wedges.

2. With a paring knife, remove the center bit of each wedge to cut out the seeds.

3. Heat the butter in a skillet over medium heat until it melts.

4. Add the apples and stir to coat them in butter.

5. Sprinkle with sugar and cinnamon. Stir occasionally until the apples are tender, about five minutes.

6. Eat them hot now or cool them and eat them with yogurt later. You can hog it all up or share with a friend. Yumsies.

Serves 1-2

Scrambled Eggs

These are easy. Here's how to make them in a skillet. Two eggs is probably good for you; if you have a date over then you might want to double this recipe.

- » 2 eggs
- » ¼ teaspoon salt
- » ¼ teaspoon pepper
- » 1 tablespoon butter

1. Crack the eggs into a bowl and add the salt and pepper.

2. Use a fork or whisk to beat the hell out of those eggs. Poke the yolks to get them started. Beat them very fast, kind of moving your wrist in a circular motion so that the utensil sweeps the bottom of the bowl. (I hope I am not coming off like an asshole here; I'm sure you know how to beat eggs, but just in case...) Keep beating them until the white and yellow parts have become one—everything is consistently light yellow. Perfect.

3. Heat up your skillet over medium heat and add the butter. After the butter melts, it will foam up. That's the time to put the eggs in.

4. Just pour them in and let them sit for a minute, then stir gently, scraping the bottom.

5. Keep moving them around, scraping the bottom, until they are almost totally cooked: still shiny-wet looking, but firm. The whole process should be done within a couple of minutes.

6. Remove from the heat and serve on a plate or on toast with mayonnaise and tomato for my favorite breakfast sandwich ever!

Eggs in the Microwave!

A great trick to know when you're cooking a big breakfast for your anarchist group and the stovetop is covered in homefries, bacon, pancakes, and manifestos.

1. Beat the eggs like usual, in a microwave safe bowl. Add the butter, salt and pepper to the eggs and microwave one minute on high.

2. Stir. Microwave another 30 seconds and check them; maybe they're done. If not, stir again and go for another 30 seconds. Surely they are done now.

Bacon

Here's how to cook bacon the old-fashioned way.

1. Lay your bacon strips in a cold skillet and turn the heat to medium. Starting the bacon in a cold pan will keep it from curling up as much.

2. Cook the bacon about four minutes on each side or longer depending on how crispy you like it.

3. Serve. You can drain it on some paper towels or newspaper after it's done to remove some of the grease but I don't usually, so my arteries are clogged all to hell.

Bacon in the Microwave!

The neatest, tidiest way to cook a small amount of bacon quickly. Also the most paper-towel-wasting, but sometimes . . . oh, what the hell, right?

1. Lay a few strips in a single layer on a couple of paper towels (on a microwave safe plate) and cover with another paper towel. Microwave about 3 minutes.

2. Check crispiness. Swap out the paper towels for new ones if they are terribly saturated. Zap for another minute and check again.

3. Keep going in 30 second increments until bacon reaches desired crispiness.

Homemade Granola

This is how my great-grandma made it, except I cut way down on the sugar and oil because I don't live on the prairie. This is really easy, but you need to be able to pay attention to something for two whole hours so you might want to skip this if you skipped your Adderal.

- » 4 cups oatmeal (rolled oats)
- » 1½ cups wheat germ (this will be near the oatmeal in the cereal aisle)
- » 1 cup sesame seeds
- » 2 cups chopped raw pecans, walnuts, almonds, or any raw nuts
- » 1 cup sunflower seeds
- » 1 cup frozen apple juice concentrate, thawed but not mixed with water
- » ¼ cup oil (canola, corn, light olive, or coconut)
- » 1 teaspoon vanilla
- » Optional: 2 cups dried fruit (raisins, cranberries, cherries, chopped apples, pineapple, or apricots)

1. In a huge bowl, toss together the oatmeal, wheat germ, seeds, and nuts.
2. Combine apple juice concentrate, oil, and vanilla, and pour over dry ingredients.
3. Mix well; your hands are the best tool.
4. Spread out on a cookie sheet (or a pizza pan if that's what you have) and bake at 300º for 90 minutes, stirring every 15 minutes.
5. When it is looking and smelling toasted and pretty well dried out, turn the oven off and leave it in there to cool with the oven door cracked a bit.
6. Once completely cool, mix in optional fruit and store in an airtight container.

Makes a shitload of granola. (That's prairie terminology for about 10 cups of granola, 20 servings)

Learn to Cook

Berry Muffins

The best muffins ever. You can use any kind of berry you desire. If you use frozen fruit, thaw it first then separate the juice and use that in combination with the apple or orange juice to make up ½ cup total. Makes 12 muffins. Store muffins in an air-tight container or plastic baggie for up to a week in the refrigerator or two weeks frozen. Thaw over night in the fridge or for a few seconds in the microwave. I like making these with whole wheat flour to make me feel healthier.

- » 1½ cups flour (white or whole wheat or a combination)
- » ½ cup sugar
- » 2 teaspoons baking powder
- » 1 egg
- » ½ cup apple or orange juice
- » ¼ cup canola oil, olive oil, or other vegetable oil
- » 1 tablespoon yogurt or sour cream or milk
- » 1 cup sliced strawberries (or other berries)

1. Preheat the oven to 400°. Get out a muffin pan and grease each hole or put cupcake liners in each.

2. Whisk the dry ingredients together in a bowl.

3. Beat the wet ingredients together in another bowl.

4. Add the wet mix to the dry mix and stir together. Don't worry about getting all the lumps out; lumps are a fact of life when you're making muffins. Just get all the flour moist.

5. Gently stir in the berries.

6. Scoop the batter into the muffin tins, about ¼ cup of batter for each.

7. Bake about 25 minutes or until the center muffin passes the toothpick test. Alternatively you can bake in a greased 8" round cake pan for 30 minutes and make berry bread.

WEEKEND BREAKFASTS

Sometimes you have some extra time and you want something fancy, or it's the weekend or maybe it's your mom's birthday and you want to break into her house and scare the shit out of her with some breakfast in bed like you used to do back when life didn't suck. The least you could do is learn to make some decent French Toast so she doesn't have to choke it down like she had to back then.

Breakfast Tacos

Tacos for breakfast are the best if you are not a fan of a sweet breakfast. This is how I make two bacon, egg and cheese tacos (which are my fave), but you can make as many as you need. Figure it out!

- » 2 eggs
- » 2 strips of bacon
- » 2–3 tablespoons grated cheese (cheddar or monterey jack or American or whatever you got)
- » 2 flour tortillas
- » For serving: salsa, pico de gallo, guacamole

1. Cook your bacon in a skillet. Set aside on a plate when it's crisp but leave that grease in the pan!

2. Beat the eggs in a bowl. Beat them good.

3. Add the eggs to the bacon grease skillet. Cook like you do scrambled eggs. (I don't salt since the bacon is salty, but you can add a little.)

4. When they are almost finished, sprinkle with cheese and turn the heat off.

5. Warm your tortillas (see *Chapter 9, Tacos*, for instructions.)

6. Put half your cheesy eggs in each tortilla, top with a piece of bacon and salsa if you like. EAT.

7. Or wrap tightly in foil and take it to work with you and make your coworkers jealous.

Pancakes

Make some pancakes on Sunday morning and be like Alice on
"The Brady Bunch."

- » 1 cup buttermilk
- » 1 cup flour
- » 1 teaspoon baking powder
- » ½ teaspoon baking soda
- » 2 tablespoons butter, melted, or oil
- » 1 egg
- » For Cooking: 2 teaspoons butter or oil
- » For Serving: butter, maple syrup, powdered sugar, jam

Fake Buttermilk!

If you don't have buttermilk you can "fake it" with one of the following combinations:

- 1 cup milk (or 1 cup fake milk, e.g., soy milk) + 1 teaspoon vinegar or lemon juice
- ½ cup milk + ½ cup plain yogurt

1. Whisk the dry ingredients together. In a separate bowl, mix the wet ingredients well. Add the wet to the dry and stir to combine well. The whisk works well for this.

2. Preheat a griddle or large skillet over medium heat.

3. Grease it with a teaspoon of oil. Smear the oil around with a spatula. (Or just use some spray oil; I don't care.) Let the oil heat up until it pops when you throw a drop of water on it.

4. Using a ¼ cup measuring cup or a ladle or a big-ass spoon, dip into your pancake batter and put about a quarter cup of batter on the skillet. (Smaller pancakes are easier to flip.) You will probably be able to fit three pancakes on there. Leave it alone for a minute.

5. Watch them and as they cook—you will see bubbles form and pop around the edges. When the pancakes look cratered like the moon and the outer edges are dry, it's time to flip them. If you try to flip them too soon, you will end up with a sad mess.

6. Wiggle a spatula under one and then with a sharp, confident hand, thrust (thrust!) the spatula under the pancake, lift, and flip. The first few times you do this, you might misfire and end up with one pancake on top of another. But that's not the end of the world; you'll have extra batter unless you're eating with several friends, and if they don't know how to flip the pancakes they should shut up and just let you start over.

7. Flip them all and cook for another 2–3 minutes. You can check by lifting the edge and peeking to see if it is nice and brown. When it is, you're done.

8. Serve with butter and maple syrup and reap the praise. Makes about eight 4" pancakes.

Serves 2-4

French Toast

hilahcooking.com/
how-to-make-french-toast

Easier than pancakes and a great use for some stale bread. Plus, as I recall, your mom loves it.

» 4 slices of bread (stale bread actually works better for this, but fresh is fine)

» 1 egg

» ¼ cup milk

» 1 tablespoon sugar

» For Cooking: 2 teaspoons oil or butter (or spray oil)

» Optional: ½ teaspoon vanilla extract and/or orange zest

» For Serving: butter, maple syrup, powdered sugar, jam, cinnamon apples

1. In a wide bowl, beat the egg, milk, sugar, and optional flavorings together. Whisk it good—you don't want any egg white or yolk visible. It should all be an even, light yellow color.

2. Preheat a skillet over medium heat.

3. Put the oil or butter on it and smear that around (or do the spray oil thing like you do).

4. Dip a slice of bread into the egg mix, then flip it and get the other side into it. Let any excess egg drip off, then lay it in the pan.

5. Do that with the other bread slices.

6. Cook two minutes, then check by lifting the edges of the bread and seeing if they're nice and brown. If they're brown, flip 'em and brown the other side for two more minutes.

7. Serve with butter and syrup, or powdered sugar, or jam, or cinnamon apples.

8. Makes 4 slices, but you can easily double the recipe.

Serves 2

Frittata

A frittata is an Italian omelet. It's also very similar to the Spanish tortilla. It's super easy to throw together and super hard to mess up. Plus, it's a great way to use up any leftover bits of cheese, cooked vegetables, grains or meat you have around. Serves 3–4 people.

- » 4 eggs
- » 2 tablespoons fresh parsley or herb of your choice
- » 2 tablespoons grated parmesan
- » ¼ teaspoon salt
- » ¼ teaspoon pepper
- » 2 cups sliced raw or cooked vegetables or meat or cooked grain or pasta
- » 1 ½ tablespoons butter

1. Beat the eggs with the parmesan, parsley, salt, and pepper and set aside

2. Melt the butter in a cast iron or other oven-safe skillet over medium-high heat.

3. Saute the raw ingredients until cooked, about 5 minutes. Add any cooked filling ingredients now.

4. Arrange the filling evenly in the skillet and pour the eggs on top. Make sure the eggs are even, too.

5. Lift the edges of the frittata as the eggs begin to set to allow the runny eggs to flow underneath.

6. When the top is nearly set, pop the skillet under a broiler on low heat for about 2 minutes or until just cooked.

7. Cool briefly then slice into wedges and serve warm or at room temperature

Serves 4

Filling Combination Ideas

. . . .

ham/potatoes

bell pepper/onion

spinach/cheese

sausage/broccoli

tomato/herb/cheese

shrimp/pasta/artichoke

red bell pepper/goat cheese/bacon

a Note on Presentation

If you are into presentation, try this trick with any fruit or mayonnaisey salads (tuna, chicken, etc.):

Get a head of Boston, Bibb, or red or green leaf lettuce and pull off as many entire leaves as the number of people you are serving. Wash the leaves carefully, shake gently to dry, break off any unsightly stems and put them in the fridge for 20 minutes to get really crisp and cold. Chill your plates in the freezer while this is going on. Put one leaf on each plate, top with a scoop of salad, and serve. Just like they do at fancy tearooms in London.

You can also use fresh lettuce to line platters and plates to present smoked salmon and its accoutrements, small sandwiches cut into triangles, or wedges of a frittata.

Brunch

Sometimes you want to have your friends over and get them drunk at noon on a Sunday but the only way you can validate that is by calling it a "brunch" and then you have to serve food. Here's some good recipes for when that happens to you. (Some good drink recipes are in Chapter 16!)

Salmon Platter

This is the absolute easiest mother-effing thing you could make for brunch, and yet it gets people so excited. Probably because smoked salmon is expensive. But your friends are worth it ... right? This platter will give 6 people a taste of the high life. If you are hosting, just throw a fruit salad together and make some Screwdrivers or Mimosas. You're done.

» 1 pound thinly sliced smoked salmon (aka lox)
» 1 8-ounce package cream cheese (Leave it out on the counter for 30 minutes to an hour before you put your platter together so it gets soft.)
» ¼ cup minced red onion or shallots
» 1 jar capers (usually around 3 ounces)
» 1 lemon, cut into 6 or 8 wedges
» Optional Garnish: fresh dill or parsley sprigs
» For Serving: a baguette, thinly sliced; 12 mini bagels, halved (and toasted if you care enough), or a box of fancy crackers

1. Get out your biggest plate, platter, pizza pan, or trash can lid. If it's ugly, cover it with aluminum foil, a doily, or some butcher paper or something.

2. Put the cream cheese in the center. Sprinkle it with chopped onion or put the onion in a bowl on the side.)

3. Arrange the salmon slices around the cheese chunk in a pretty way; presentation is gonna make or break it.

4. Drain the capers and sprinkle them over the salmon. (Or serve them separately in a cutesy bowl.) Arrange the lemon slices and herbs whimsically and evenly around the platter.

5. Provide a couple of forks for serving the salmon and butter knives for the cheese. Put out a pepper grinder, too, if possible, with black pepper in it. Serve the bread or crackers in a basket.

Capers

Capers are the unopened flower buds of a Mediterranean plant, which have been salted or pickled then jarred and mailed to your store.

They have a sharp, spicy, mustardy flavor but also taste like salt due to the preservation methods. Some people like them; if you like strong flavors like olives and pickles and mustard, you probably will like them. If not, you probably won't.

They are used a lot in Italian cooking (salads, sauces) and also in tartar sauce. I like to keep them around to mix in to various things when I am feeling sassy. You will find them in the store near the olives most likely.

Fruit Salad

Again, super duper easy. You can put whatever fruits you want in a fruit salad, but a good rule of thumb is no more than five different fruits. More than that and it starts to look and taste cluttered.

Cut everything up to approximately the same size, no bigger than your thumb I'd say. Strawberries can just be cut in half and other berries left whole (washed of course). You can also jazz it up by adding fresh herbs, citrus juices, or other seasonings.

If you want to use bananas, apples, or pears, sprinkle the cut pieces with lemon juice before mixing in to prevent them from getting brown and unsightly. Fruit salads are best made the day you plan to eat them, but will keep okay in the refrigerator for a couple of days.

Here are some of my favorite combinations, but keep in mind that the best fruit salads are made with fruit that is in season and perfectly ripe, so make your decisions based on the time of year and what looks good.

Combo 1: Serves 8
1 cantaloupe, peeled and cubed; 1 quart box strawberries; 4 kiwis, peeled and cubed; 1 tablespoon poppy seeds

Combo 2: Serves 8
8 cups watermelon, honeydew and/or cantaloupe melon cubes; 2 tablespoons lime juice; 1 teaspoon fresh chopped ginger; ½ teaspoon chili powder

Combo 3: Serves 8
1 pineapple, peeled, cored and chunked; 1 pint blueberries; ½ cup shredded coconut, 2 mangoes, peeled and chunked, 2 tablespoons chopped fresh mint

Waldorf Salad

This is a famous fruit salad from the Waldorf Hotel in New York City. The original recipe calls for mayonnaise, but I prefer to use plain yogurt instead since I find mayonnaise a little heavy, but do what you think you will like best. This is good for four people and can be doubled if you are serving more. Don't peel the apples—the peels add nutrition and beautiful color to an otherwise plain-looking salad. You can also add cooked chicken to the salad for more of a luncheon dish.

- » 1 cup diced apple (Gala or Fuji are great but Red Delicious apples look prettier)
- » 1 teaspoon lemon juice
- » 1 cup diced celery
- » ½ cup coarsely chopped walnuts
- » ¼ cup plain yogurt or mayonnaise (or do half of each for the best of both worlds)

1. Toss the apple in the lemon juice and then mix everything else in. (The lemon juice isn't really necessary to prevent browning, since the yogurt or mayonnaise will prevent it, but I like how it tastes, and it's a little extra insurance.)

2. Refrigerate until serving time

Makes enough for 2 people.

Vegetable Pie

This is kind of like a cross between a frittata and a quiche. In many ways, it is easier than either of those things even though there looks to be many ingredients.

- » 2 teaspoons butter or oil (or spray oil) for greasing the pans
- » ¾ cup diced onion
- » 1 zucchini or summer squash, grated, about 1 ½ cups
- » 2 carrots, grated, about 1 cup
- » 1 cup flour (white or whole wheat)
- » 1 teaspoon baking powder
- » 1 tablespoon dried dill weed or basil or another herb
- » ½ teaspoon salt
- » ½ teaspoon black pepper
- » ¼ cup oil
- » 4 eggs
- » 1 cup grated cheddar cheese (or whatever kind you have)

1. Preheat oven to 350° and grease two pie pans well.
2. Combine the vegetables in a bowl and sprinkle over the flour, baking powder, and seasoning. Toss to combine.
3. Beat the eggs with the oil separately and then add that and the cheese to the vegetable mixture. Stir to combine well.
4. Split between the greased pie pans and bake 25 minutes or until it passes the toothpick test.
5. Cool 10 minutes before slicing. Serve warm or at room temperature.

Serves 4-8, depending on appetites.

Brown Sugar Coffee Cake

This is sweet and yummy, and it travels well so if you get invited to a brunch, bring this. You should also bring a bottle of cheap champagne.

> » 2 cups brown sugar
>
> » 1 cup sifted flour
>
> » 1 teaspoon cinnamon
>
> » 1 teaspoon salt
>
> » ½ cup butter (= 1 stick = ¼ pound), cold
>
> » 1 teaspoon baking soda
>
> » 1 teaspoon baking powder
>
> » ¼ teaspoon ground cloves or allspice
>
> » ¼ teaspoon ground nutmeg
>
> » 1 egg
>
> » 1 cup buttermilk

1. Grease a 9" x 9" inch pan. Preheat the oven to 350º.

2. Mix together brown sugar, flour, cinnamon, and salt.

3. Cut the stick of butter into small cubes. Toss the butter cubes into the sugar/flour mixture and use a fork or your fingertips to cut the butter into the dry mix until it resembles coarse meal with some bigger chunks.

4. Set aside one cup of this mixture to use for topping the cake.

5. To the remainder, add baking soda, baking powder, spices.

6. In another bowl, beat egg and buttermilk; add this to the dry mixture.

7. Stir minimally, just until the flour disappears. Lumps are okay, as long as there are no big streaks of flour. Sweep the bottom of the bowl a few times to make sure there's no flour hiding out down there.

8. Pour the batter into the greased pan and sprinkle with the reserved one cup of sugar/butter crumbs from the beginning.

9. Bake at 350º F for 35 minutes. Cut into 9 or 12 pieces.

CHAPTER 11

Lunch

I'm going to assume you are all brown-bagging it for school, work, road trips, or conjugal visits. Some of these recipes require a microwave to reheat, which you probably have at work, but if a microwave is not at your disposal, there are lots of other recipe choices here.

If you're fortunate enough to work at home, you can use these suggestions or check out the supper recipes for some quickies. Also, many of the recipes under "Snackies" could totally qualify as lunch.

Anything left over from dinner can make a great lunch. Chop up leftover meats or vegetables and add them to a salad or inside a bean burrito. Leftover rice pilaf becomes fried rice in a jiff; leftover pasta makes pasta salad.

You will soon be a master of this game.

SALADS

It's something to be able to put together a beautiful, delicious salad. These are healthy and portable, perfect for lunch and picnics, too! Or just for suppertime side dishes. Salads are so versatile!

The Big Salad

I love a big salad for lunch. But I hate paying ten bucks for it at a restaurant. This is what I like to put in my big salad, but obviously you do not have to do the same. It's best if you have a refrigerator at your avail to keep this in until lunch time, but an insulated lunch bag will suffice, especially if you use some frozen vegetables like I do. Layer all the ingredients in a 4-6 cup plastic container, in the order given. If you're at home and you want to make this salad, arrange it in the almost-opposite order: lettuce on the bottom, then hard vegetables, then soft vegetables and cheese or eggs, then drizzle the dressing all over and mix gently with two forks.

- » 2–3 tablespoons salad dressing of your choice (my choice is given to you below)
- » ¼ cup frozen peas and/or corn (they will thaw out by lunch time)
- » 1 carrot, grated
- » ½ cup cherry tomatoes or diced tomato
- » ¼ cup nuts and/or raisins
- » Some cheese chunks or a peeled, boiled egg, cut into wedges (or leftover diced meat from dinner)
- » 3 cups washed, torn lettuce leaves (or you can buy a baby lettuce blend, but that gets pricey)
- » ¼ cup fresh parsley or cilantro leaves

1. Put everything into a traveling container, starting with the dressing on the bottom, then your harder vegetables, nuts, protein, then lettuce. Keeping the lettuce away from the dressing will prevent it becoming soggy.

2. When it's time to eat, shake it up to mix everything. It's just like those stupid shake `em up salads they used to have at McDonald's. But way better.

Orange Juice Dressing

This is one of my favorite homemade dressings. You can buy salad dressing of course, but homemade dressing is lighter and more flavorful, and people get excited about you when you feed it to them. There are a couple more salad dressing recipes in Chapter 11 if you'd like to try those, too.

» 1 clove garlic, put through garlic press or finely minced

» ¼ cup orange juice

» 1 teaspoon mustard

» 2 teaspoons safflower, sunflower, or canola oil

» 2 teaspoons cider vinegar

» ¼ teaspoon salt

» ¼ teaspoon black pepper

1. Combine all in a jar with a tight lid and shake the shit out of it. Refrigerate up to three weeks.

2. Makes about 1/3 cup dressing, enough for three salads I bet. Double this recipe if you eat a lot of salad.

Lettuce

Iceberg might be the most familiar lettuce, but it's essentially worthless in terms of nutrition content. For the most vitamins/minerals/fiber/bang for your buck, go with Romaine. It also, wonderfully, lasts longer in the fridge than softer lettuce like Boston or red and green leaf.

When you get home from the store, shake the whole head over the sink to get excessive water off of it, because sitting in water is bad for vegetables and makes them rot. Store it in a plastic grocery bag in the crisper drawer.

To make salad, pull off some leaves (for a side-salad, figure 3 leaves per person) and rinse in cold water. If you're making a lotta salad, fill up a large bowl in the sink, put all the leaves in and swish around. Pull them out and lay them in a single layer on a clean tea towel with another towel on top. Press down gently to absorb the water. Get them mostly dry, then tear into pieces—one or two inches across is good for eating. Put in your salad bowl and refrigerate until ready to add your other ingredients and serve.

Pasta Salad

This is great because you can make up a big batch on the weekend and then have it for a few lunches during the week. For variety, add some beans one day or some tuna another day. Here's a very basic recipe to start, with lots of options and substitutions to pick from and customize it. It's extremely flexible so don't be a feared of experimenting. If you like a vegetable or an herb, it will probably be just great in here, so put some in.

- » 2 cups (half-pound) any bite-sized pasta
- » 3 cups broccoli florets (or cauliflower, halved green beans, 1" zucchini chunks, or a mixture)
- » 1 cup mozzarella cheese, cubed (or some other kind of cheese, or 1 cup of cooked beans)
- » ½ cup chopped parsley or spinach, torn up
- » 2 tablespoons fresh herbs, chopped (or 1 tablespoon dry herbs)
- » 1 pint cherry tomatoes, cut in halves (or 2 cups cucumber chunks or bell pepper chunks)

Dressing:
- » 2 tablespoons red wine vinegar
- » 4 tablespoons olive oil (or whatever you have)
- » 2 teaspoons dijon mustard
- » ½ teaspoon salt and pepper, each
- » ½ teaspoon dried basil
- » ¼ teaspoon dried oregano and crushed red pepper, each

1. Cook pasta according to directions on package, except add broccoli florets (or whatever vegetables you are using) to the pasta water for the last 3 minutes of cooking time. Drain in a colander.

2. Combine dressing ingredients in a small jar and shake well to combine.

3. When the pasta has cooled slightly, mix everything together in a big bowl, pour the dressing over, and chill at least an hour.

This will make about 10 cups of salad, about 5 lunches

Tabouli

hilahcooking.com/
how-to-make-tabouli

This is kind of like pasta salad, but with cracked wheat instead of pasta. It has all the same benefits (keeps well, easy as shit to make) and is nice for a change of pace. Mix it up by putting some tabouli, lettuce, and some hummus in a pita bread and wrapping it up like a burrito. **Bonus Tip:** *you can use cooked rice or barley or quinoa or couscous instead of bulgur—no need to adjust anything else.*

- » 2 cups cracked wheat
- » 2 cups very hot water
- » 1 cucumber, diced (~1½ cups)
- » 1 bunch green onions, sliced thinly (~1 cup)
- » ½ cup fresh mint, dill, or cilantro, chopped
- » 2 cups fresh parsley, chopped
- » 1 clove garlic, minced
- » ½ cup fresh lemon juice
- » ¾ cup olive oil
- » 1 tablespoon pepper
- » 2 teaspoons salt

1. Soak the bulgur in hot water about 30 minutes, until water is absorbed and bulgur is softened. Drain off any extra water.

2. Mix everything together and let stand at least 30 minutes. Serve at room temperature.

This makes about 8 cups of tabouli, about 6 lunches

SANDWICHES

You might be thinking, "What kind of A-hole needs to read about how to make a sandwich?" but ... well, okay, that is a valid point. I still think I might have some ideas here to enlighten even the most advanced sandwich maker, as I have held not just one, but two, positions in my time on Earth as a Professional Sandwich Artist.

Number One: *Mix it up!* If you're saving money by eating out of a fucking bag at your desk, at least get yourself some nice bread. Some of that rye or pumpernickel or seven grain or whole wheat with the little nuts on top for Christ's sake. Some pita bread. Walk on by the yellow mustard and cheese slices and check out the fancy cheese or mustard or pickles once in a while. Live a little. Please. Sandwiches don't have to be all ham-and-cheese all-the-time. Exhibit A:

Sandwich Guts

If you're stuck in a stupid sandwich rut, here are some new filling combinations you can try out.

Cream Cheese, Avocado, Tomato: Spread a thin layer of cream cheese on your bread slices (a tablespoon each or so), top with avocado slices and black pepper, and close it up. Pack your tomato slices separately and put them on when you're ready to eat. Try it on rye bread.

Ham, Spinach, Pickled Beets: I love pickled beets on a sandwich, and you might too, if you like pickled beets. Put a little mayo on some bread with a couple of ham slices and some mustard in between if you like. Pack some pickled beet slices and and washed spinach leaves separately to add at lunch time.

Brie, Fruit Jam, Spinach Or Watercress Leaves: Cut the rind off the brie if you want. Put a few slices of brie on one piece of bread and spread the jam on the other and close it up. Pack the greens separately. Try with dark bread like pumpernickel.

Peanut Butter, Banana: Spread a tablespoon of peanut butter on each slice of bread. Slice half a banana and put that down, then add a tablespoon of raisins sprinkled around or a teaspoon of honey or maple syrup drizzled over. Close that bad boy up, and it should be fine until lunch.

Sauteed Vegetables: Thinly slice half a red bell pepper and a small zucchini lengthwise (¼" slices). Heat a teaspoon of olive oil in a skillet over high heat and put the vegetables in. Brown quickly, about 2 minutes each side, then salt and pepper them and remove. You can use them now for a hot sandwich or let it cool and refrigerate for a sandwich the next day or the day after that. Great with hummus or mozzarella cheese with some lettuce, tomato and fresh basil if you have it. Roll that up in a pita bread and wrap it in foil for neat and tidy transport and eating.

Number Two: *Do it right!* Learn how to properly pack a sandwich so it doesn't get soggy.

1. Make the bread-and-protein part of your sandwich and put it in a baggie or container (I reuse my sandwich baggies until I can't anymore). If you're using mayonnaise or cream cheese or a spread containing one of those, it's okay to spread a little right on the bread. Mustard might make the bread soggy so try to sandwich that in between the cheese'n'meat if possible. I mean, like this: bread, mayo, cheese, mustard, meat, bread again. Something like that.

2. Pack your sandwich vegetables separately. Slice up tomatoes and wash some lettuce and pack those together in another container. Whatever other vegetables you're putting on your sandwich go in here, too: onion, cucumber, pickles. Just put the lettuce on top so it doesn't get crushed.

3. Pack those things plus a piece of fruit and some nuts or chips or carrot sticks into a bag or a lunchbox or whatever.

4. Time to eat: add your vegetables to the sandwich. Eat your balanced lunch.

MAYONNAISE SALADS

These must be kept refrigerated, so don't bother if you don't have a chiller at work.

Boiling Eggs

The best way to hard boil an egg (hard boiled means the yolk is completely cooked and set) is to put a couple of eggs in a pot and add water until they are barely covered. Put a lid on the pot and put it over a high heat. As soon as the water boils, turn the heat off, leaving the lid on. Let the eggs sit in the hot water for 10 minutes. Then rinse them in cold water and you are all set to peel them. To do that, pick up the boiled egg and tap it gently and repeatedly on a hard surface, rotating it as you go so as to make cracks all over the egg. Once it's good and cracked all over, pick the shell off like a scab. Rinse it under cold water occasionally to help the shell move along. Keep picking and rinsing until it's clean.

Egg Salad

Here's a recipe to make enough egg salad for one sandwich. It doesn't keep super well, so I recommend just making what you want for the day. If you're making sandwiches for your boss or something, too, then just double or triple the recipe and don't forget to put poison in the one for your boss. *

» 1 egg, hard boiled
» 1 tablespoon mayonnaise
» 1 teaspoon mustard
» ¼ teaspoon salt or celery salt
» ¼ teaspoon pepper
» Optional: ½ teaspoon dried dill and/or 1 tablespoon minced celery or onion

1. Peel the egg and mash it up in a bowl with a fork.

2. Add everything else and mix it around. Mash it until it's as smooth or chunky as you like.

3. Eat it with crackers or take some bread and sliced tomato and cucumber with you and make a sandwich. If you're in a rush in the morning, you can just put everything but the egg in a container, then peel and mash the egg into it when you're ready to eat.

Never put poison in food or drinks.

Tuna Salad

Tuna, like eggs, can be kind of stinky, so if you work with a bunch of uptight dickwad complainers, bring a tuna sandwich for lunch and give them something to complain about.

» 1 5-ounce can tuna

» 2 tablespoons mayonnaise or olive oil

» 2 teaspoons mustard

» ¼ cup diced celery

» 1 tablespoon pickle relish or minced pickles, sweet or dill

» 1 teaspoon black pepper

» Any combination of these seasonings: 1 tablespoon chopped fresh parsley, 2 teaspoons capers, a few dashes Tabasco sauce, 1 teaspoon lemon juice, or ½ teaspoon lemon pepper

1. Open the tuna can but hang onto the lid to help you squeeze the liquid out. Hold the can over the sink and push the lid into the tuna, letting the liquid run into the drain and back into the Earth from whence it came. Or give it to your cat.

2. Now use a fork to get the tuna out of there and into a bowl and break it up a bit.

3. Add everything else, including whatever seasoning you want, and mash it around.

4. Make a sandwich or put it atop a Big Salad.

Canned Tuna

I may get accused of libel for writing this, but canned albacore ("white") tuna has been shown by FDA testing to have as much as three times the amount of mercury as canned "light" tuna (which encompasses just about all the other species of tuna: skipjack, bluefin, yellowfin, tongol). For that reason I avoid albacore, and even then I limit my canned tuna consumption to about once a month. Also, I recommend buying water-packed tuna as opposed to oil-packed. The healthy omega-3 fatty acids in tuna are soluble in oil and you will lose some of the nutrition along with the packing oil when you drain it. Since oil and water don't mix, the omega-3 fatty acid stays in the water-packed tuna where it belongs!

Chicken Salad

I hardly ever have leftover chicken around, and you probably don't either, so here's how to start from scratch. If you do have leftover chicken, you're awesome! You just go chop up about 2 cups of it and skip ahead to the mixing stage of the recipe.

» 2 boneless chicken breast halves
» Optional seasonings for chicken: a bay leaf, ½ teaspoon salt, ½ teaspoon thyme, ½ teaspoon pepper, 1 clove garlic
» 1 cup diced celery
» ½ cup mayonnaise
» Optional mix-ins (any or all of these): ½ cup slivered almonds, ½ cup diced apple, ½ cup halved grapes, ¼ cup chopped fresh cilantro or parsley, ½ teaspoon chili powder or curry powder

1. Put your chicken in the smallest pot it will fit into and cover it with about an inch of water. Add any of the optional seasonings you want. Cover the pot and turn on the heat, medium. Bring the chicken to a simmer then turn the heat down to low to keep it at a simmer. Now you are *poaching*!

2. Poach (simmer) the chicken for 5 minutes, then turn the heat off and let it sit in the hot water for another 10 minutes.

3. Take it out, cool on a cutting board until you can handle it, then dice.

4. Let it cool some more then put it in a bowl with all the other ingredients.

5. Taste it and add a sprinkle of salt and pepper if it needs it.

Chicken Breasts

So, there's kind of a confusing thing about whole breasts versus half breasts; boneless/skinless or not. Chickens, like humans, have two boobies (not literally!), so a "whole breast" means both of those, still attached to each other.

It's fairly uncommon anymore to find whole chicken breasts and usually what you see are halves, but they are just labeled "chicken breasts." You may see "split chicken breasts" which have not been deboned or skinned; they are a much better value than boneless/skinless breasts because there is less processing involved.

If you want to save a little money but don't want to bother with boning the chicken, you can at least buy boneless, skin-on chicken pieces (breasts and thighs are sold that way) and pull the skin off yourself before or after cooking. So, now you know.

OTHER MOISTIES FOR SANDWICHES

Sandwiches don't have to be just mayo and mustard, either. Oh no. Try making one of these easy-ass spreads to jazz things up. **Bonus Tip:** These recipes can all also be used as party dips with crudités or chips! Yay!

Red Pepper Spread

This is good for vegans and vegetarians and anyone who likes red bell peppers. If you want to get some of those roasted red peppers in a jar, you can skip the saute step and head right into the blending in the blender step, using about a cup of chopped roasted peppers. This keeps refrigerated up to one week.

- » 2 tablespoons olive oil
- » 1 red bell pepper, cut into ½" squares (about one cup)
- » ¼ teaspoon salt
- » 1½ cups raw cashews or walnuts
- » ¼ cup raw sesame seeds
- » ¼ cup water
- » 1 teaspoon nutritional yeast (or parmesan cheese)
- » ¼ cup lemon juice (about one lemon)
- » 1 tablespoon liquid amino acids or soy sauce

1. Saute pepper with salt in 2 tablespoons of oil over medium-low heat for about 10 minutes, until soft.

2. Transfer pepper and oil to a blender or food processor and add all remaining ingredients. Blend until smooth.

Makes about 1½ cups

Cucumber Spread

This is my friend Natalie's mama's recipe. Myra makes sandwiches with this on very thinly sliced whole wheat bread and wraps them up for us when we take long car trips. Myra is nice.

» 1 smallish-medium cucumber

» 3 ounce package cream cheese (the tiny square package)

» 2 teaspoons minced red or white onion

» 2 teaspoons lemon juice

» salt to taste (not more than ¼ teaspoon)

» ⅛ teaspoon pepper (white if you have it)

» ⅛ teaspoon hot red pepper sauce, like Tabasco

1. Cut the cucumber lengthwise and use a spoon to scrape out the seeds and toss them. Grate the cucumber on a cheese grater (the biggest holes)—it should be about a cup. Squeeze the cucumber shreds between paper towels or in a clean tea towel to get some of the liquid out.

2. In a bowl, beat cream cheese until fluffy with an electric mixer or a strong arm and a wooden spoon.

3. Mix in onion, seasonings and cucumber.

Makes about 1 ½ cups

Hummus

You need tahini to make this. Tahini is like peanut butter but made from sesame seeds. You'll find it near the peanut butter if you have a decent grocery store in your city. If you have a dinky store, they might keep it with the "Natural Foods" or the "Ethnic Foods." It might also be called "sesame paste." If you really can't find it, throw in a couple tablespoons of sesame seeds instead. Anyway, hummus is darn good in a pita bread wrap with a bunch of crunchy vegetables and some olives or feta cheese.

- » 1 can chick peas, rinsed and drained, or 1 ½ cups cooked drained chick peas
- » 2 cloves garlic
- » 2 tablespoons tahini
- » Juice of one lemon (about 3 tablespoons)
- » 2 tablespoons olive oil
- » ¼ cup water (maybe a little more)

1. Put everything in the blender and make it smooth. Or leave it lumpy, it's up to you.

2. Keeps in the 'frigerator a week or so.

Makes about 2 cups

Pimiento Cheese

Am I the only one who LOVES pimiento cheese? I fear it's gotten a bad rap because the crap they sell in the little tubs at the grocery store ain't nothing like the real thing, baby. Real pimiento cheese is a time-honored tradition in Texas; it is a thing of beauty, wonderment, cheese … and happiness.

» 2 cups grated sharp cheddar

» 8 ounces cream cheese, softened

» 2 tablespoons mustard (Dijon, brown, or yellow)

» 1 tablespoon mayonnaise

» 4 ounce jar pimientos, drained and minced

» Optional: 1 tablespoon capers, drained and chopped; chopped pickled jalapenos to taste

1. Mash all that together. It helps if the cream cheese is softened.

2. Eat that with healthy stuff like celery sticks or just make a sandwich. This'll keep in the fridge for a week or more.

Makes about 2 cups of heaven.

Pimientos

Pimientos seem kind of old-fashioned, I guess, but all they are is very mild peppers in a jar. Not unlike the fancy, imported, fire-roasted, red bell peppers that were all the rage in 2008. Lots of casserole recipes from the 1950s call for pimientos. Then they fell out of fashion for some reason. You'll find them near the olives, probably, in tiny jars, like little red gems hidden amongst the modular shelving units. I'm bringing pimientos back.

HOT LUNCH!

If you've ever sent the movie Born Yesterday, the phrase "Hot lunch" might mean something to you. If you haven't seen it, I recommend it. Most of these are things you would make at home if you are at home because you work at home or it's the weekend. Or Columbus Day.

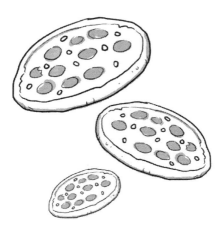

Microwave Burritos

*I love **Taco Bell** bean burritos, but I know they are not very healthy. Plus, I know that I can make my own for half the price or less, and that is DIRT CHEAP. I like to make a dozen of these at a time and store them in the freezer. At lunchtime I can just wrap one in a damp cloth or napkin and microwave for a minute until it gets all gooey and stuff, and then if I'm lucky I find a sticky packet of Taco Bell hot sauce wedged under my chair seat and I go to town on that shizz! Or I just use some other hot sauce.*

» 1 dozen flour tortillas (I like whole wheat for this)

» 1 can (or 2 cups) refried beans; either pinto or black beans are fine

» ½ cup diced onion

» 1 cup grated cheese—cheddar, monterrey jack, pepper jack, muenster, what you please

» Optional: leftover diced meat or vegetables

1. Set yourself up an assembly line: tortillas at one end and a plastic container that you can stick your burritos in at the other end.

2. Pull out a tortilla and spread 3–4 tablespoons of refried beans down the middle of it. Top with a tablespoon of chopped onion and 2 tablespoons of cheese (and a little of your optional leftovers).

3. Fold up the ends and then fold over the sides so all your fillings are wrapped up good. Keep doing that and then pack them all into a container or containers. Freeze.

4. When you take one or two to work, just let them hang out until lunch; you don't really have to refrigerate them. Then wrap 'em in a damp towel or napkin and microwave about a minute for each one. Add an orange or something to round that meal out. Blammo. Lunch. At home or the office.

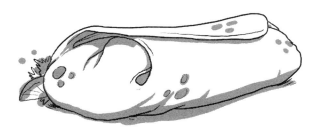

Tiny Fake Pizzas

Pretty intriguing name, right? I know. I'm kind of a master of naming things.

Basically, this is:

> » some kind of small bread thing (English muffin, bagel, pita bread)
>
> » spread with some kind of sauce (leftover chili, leftover spaghetti sauce, sweet chili sauce, pesto, mustard)
>
> » topped with vegetables and/or meat (diced peppers, onions, leftover cooked meat, lunchmeat, capers, olives, etc.)
>
> » sprinkled with some cheese
>
> » and baked in the oven for 5–10 minutes at 350º or put under the broiler for 2–3 minutes until melty and toasty. Easy-peasy.

Here are my favorite tiny fake pizzas:

1. English muffin with sweet chili sauce, sliced green olives, bell pepper, onion, mozzarella or provolone

2. Pita bread with pesto, diced broccoli or fresh spinach, parmesan cheese

3. Bagel with mustard, tuna, lots of black pepper, pickled jalapenos, cheddar cheese or swiss

4. Chapati with butter, garlic, parmesan cheese

5. Pita bread with a sprinkle of parmesan or mozarella, topped with a shitload of arugula or spinach, then some roasted red bell peppers.

Learn to Cook

Ramen Noodle Casserole

Ummm, this is delicious and I don't care what anyone says about ramen noodles: I still love them, even though I know I should make more healthful and desirable meals. I had a boyfriend in college who would make this, and he taught me about adding ketchup to ramen noodles! He also gave me a venereal disease then broke my heart. On to the noodles.

» 1 package ramen noodles (the square kind with the seasoning packet—YOU KNOW—any flavor you like)

» 1 cup various cut-up vegetables (peas, carrots, corn, broccoli, green beans, whatever)

» 2 tablespoons grated cheese (whatever you have on hand)

» Optional jazzifiers: 1 tablespoon ketchup; 2 tablespoons diced onion; hot sauce; 1 boiled egg, sliced; 1 hot dog, sliced

1. Boil some water in a pot. Break the noodle block in half and drop it in the boiling water. Add the vegetables. Cook 3–4 minutes or however long the package says, then drain.

2. Mix in half the seasoning packet (or even less—that shit is SALTY), the cheese and whatever else you want to jazz it up.

3. Now you have two options. You can just eat it out of the pot like that.

4. OR, if you really want to impress, you can put it into an oven-safe bowl or a small baking pan, top it with a couple of crumbled crackers or more cheese, and pop that sucker under the broiler for a minute. Blammo. It's like a real casserole that your mom might make, if your mom was a nineteen year-old college douchebag with shaved nipples.

Fried Rice

If you have leftover rice or rice pilaf from earlier in the week, you can make this in ten minutes flat. No joke. Adjust the amounts depending on how much rice you have and how many people you are feeding. The beauty of fried rice is that it absolutely requires cold, leftover, dried out rice. If you try to make a pot of fresh rice to use here, you'll end up with a gummy mess.

» 1 clove garlic, minced

» 1 egg

» 1 tablespoon oil (sesame oil is perfect if you have it)

» 1 cup cooked rice

» 1 cup chopped vegetables (onion, celery, carrots, green beans, broccoli, peas, corn, you name it)

» 1 teaspoon soy sauce

1. Beat the egg with the minced garlic.

2. Heat the oil in a skillet over medium heat and cook the egg, then put it in the bowl you will be serving from (save a washin').

3. Add a little (`bout a teaspoon) more oil if the skillet is dry and saute the vegetables over medium-high heat for 2 minutes.

4. Make some room in the center by pushing the vegetables to the outer edges and put in the rice. Break it up if it is clumpy.

5. Stir it all around to get the rice heated up, add the egg and stir again to break that up.

6. Sprinkle with soy sauce and serve. (If you want to leave the egg out, just put the garlic in with the vegetables.)

Grilled Cheese and Tomato Soup

This is a hardcore classic combo that I know y'all's triflin' third grade asses went crazy for. The grilled cheese is easy no secret—but the homemade tomato soup will have your clubhouse flippin' out.

Grilled Cheese

- » 2 slices of bread
- » 2 teaspoon butter
- » 2 slices of cheese that are approximately the same size as the bread (or 1/4 cup grated cheese)—cheddar, monterey jack, swiss, whatevah
- » Optional: 2 slices tomato, 4 dill pickle slices, mustard or sweet chili sauce

1. Make a sandwich with the bread and cheese.
2. Spread each slice of bread with one teaspoon of butter.
3. Turn a skillet or griddle to medium heat and lay the sandwich down.
4. Cook it about two minutes or until the underside is good and toasty.
5. Flip it and cook on the other side another 2 minutes or so.
6. Take it out and cut it diagonally into triangles.
7. Dip it into **Tomato Soup**.

Tomato Soup

You will find that this is nothing like the canned stuff, but that's probably a good thing since the canned stuff tastes like extra salty ketchup anyway. This soup is good without the carrots, too, if you are in a hurry; if you have the inclination and the carrots, though, they add a mellow sweetness to round out the tomatoes' fruitiness. How's that for some poetic license with the food descriptions.

- » 1 cup minced carrots
- » 1 tablespoon olive oil
- » 1 pound tomatoes, diced (about 3 cups)
- » 1 teaspoon basil
- » ¼ teaspoon black pepper
- » ¼ teaspoon salt
- » ½ cup water
- » 1 cup cream or milk

1. Soften carrots in oil over medium heat 5 minutes.
2. Add tomatoes and cover. Simmer 5 minutes until tomatoes begin to break down.
3. Add basil, pepper, salt, and water. Simmer, covered, 10 minutes.
4. Add cream and reheat over low heat for 5 minutes.

Makes about 4 cups, enough for two big bowls.

Tuna Patties

You can just eat these with a salad or put on bread for a tuna patty sandwich. Try canned salmon or crab in place of the tuna, too!

» 5 ounce can tuna

» 1 egg

» ¼ cup minced green onion, red onion, or other onion

» ¼ cup minced celery (half a stalk)

» ½ cup breadcrumbs or cracker crumbs

» 1 teaspoon dill, basil, or lemon juice

» ½ teaspoon pepper

» ¼ cup more breadcrumbs, cracker crumbs, or cornmeal

» 1 tablespoon oil

1. Drain the tuna and mix with everything else, except the extra ¼ cup of crumbs and the oil. Your hands work well for this.

2. Divide into two portions and make each portion into a patty shape.

3. Put the ¼ cup crumbs on a plate and dredge each patty in the crumbs on both sides.

4. Heat the oil in a skillet and pan-fry the patties three minutes on each side until browned. Serve with **Secret Tartar Sauce**. (You can also bake these in the oven: coat with crumbs, lay on a lightly greased cookie sheet and bake at 350° for 12–15 minutes.)

Makes 2 patties

Breadcrumbs

When a recipe calls for breadcrumbs and you have none, take heart. Toast a piece of bread until it's really crispy and then stick it in the blender. Viola! Crumbs. Works for crackers, too, but you don't toast them first. A money-saving tip (granted, it's not much money) is to save stale bread and heels in the freezer until you have a bunch then toast and grind them all up at once to make your own breadcrumbs. Store in an airtight container.

Corn Fritters

hilahcooking.com/
corn-fritters

You can make this with grated zucchini as well, or part corn and part zucchini. Eat these for lunch with some sour cream or sweet chili sauce for dippin' or you could even serve these as a hot party snack—fry them ahead of time and then reheat on a cookie sheet in the oven at 350º for 10 minutes.

- » 15 ounce can corn (or 1½ cups frozen or fresh kernels—requires about 3 fresh cobs)
- » ½ cup diced onion
- » 1 egg
- » 2 tablespoons whole wheat flour or white flour
- » 1 teaspoon pepper
- » Optional Jazzifiers: ¼ teaspoon cayenne pepper, 1 teaspoon dill, 1 tablespoon fresh cilantro or parsley, 1 minced jalapeno
- » 3 tablespoons oil (for frying)

1. Drain the corn if it is canned; thaw it if it is frozen and see the corn chowder recipe on page 150 for instructions on cutting kernels from cobs. Mix with everything else and let it stand 10 minutes for the flour to absorb the liquid and thicken the mixture.

2. You will need to cook the fritters in two batches unless you have a giant flat-top griddle like at Waffle House.

3. Heat a skillet over medium heat with about half of the frying oil for a couple of minutes.

4. Use a soup spoon or your tablespoon measure to drop the corn mixture into blobs on the griddle and fry about a minute or two on each side.

5. Remove to a plate and tent (cover loosely) with foil to keep warm.

6. Add the rest of the oil to the pan and let heat again; fry the rest of the fritters.

7. Serve hot with sweet chili sauce or **Secret Sour Cream Sauce**.

Makes about 14 fritters.

SECRET SAUCES!

Secret Tartar Sauce

The secret is that even if you only have mayo and pickles, you can still call it tartar sauce. Mix all this together:

- » ¼ cup mayonnaise
- » 2 tablespoons lemon juice (if you have none, use a tablespoon of pickle or caper juice!)
- » 1 tablespoon minced dill pickle
- » 1 teaspoon minced capers
- » 2 tablespoons minced parsley
- » ¼ teaspoon cayenne pepper (optional)

Secret Sour Cream Sauce

The secret in this case is that this would be used over lots of things besides corn fritters: sautéed fish or chicken, steamed cruciferous vegetables, carrots or asparagus. Mix together:

- » 2 tablespoons sour cream (or plain yogurt or mayonnaise)
- » 2 teaspoons lime juice
- » ½ teaspoon dill
- » ½ teaspoon honey

CHAPTER 9

Dinner

Probably the last thing you want to do when you get home from work is head to the kitchen for two hours of cooking. I hear you; I do. So let's keep it simple, yeah? Good idea.

In the first section, I present to you a collection of easy, mostly one-pot, meals using moist-heat methods (simmering, stewing, braising) and dry-heat methods (baking, roasting, sautéing and pan frying). Then we'll move on to the main-and-two-veg style of cooking, where things get a little more complicated because you have timing to think about, but I will share some ways to get around that and other neat tricks.

MOIST HEAT METHOD

SIMMERING STEWS, BUBBLING BRAISES

Truthfully, many of these begin with sautéing, which you now know is a dry-heat method. But in the end, soups and stews and braises are all wet so there you have it. Serve any of these with one of the salads in this book and a piece of toast, garlic bread, or homemade bread or biscuits for a well-balanced meal.

Creamy Zucchini Soup

This is a light soup that would be nice in the summertime when the living's easy. There's actually no cream in it, but the texture is rich and silky from the soluble fiber in the zucchini. And that might be the least appetizing sentence I've over written, but please don't let that deter you. This is surprisingly delicious, requires only a few basic ingredients, and it's healthy. It's also just as easy and good made with a pound of spinach (washed well) instead of zucchini.

- » 4 large zucchini, sliced 1/2" thick (about 6 cups)
- » ¼ cup diced onion
- » 1 clove garlic
- » 1 teaspoon salt
- » 1 teaspoon pepper
- » 2 tablespoons butter (olive oil to make it vegan)
- » 4 cups water or chicken or vegetable stock, not to be used all at once

1. Put everything except 2 cups of the water or stock in a pot and bring to a boil. Simmer 5-10 minutes until zucchini is soft.

2. Turn off the heat and add the remaining 2 cups of liquid. Adding it now instead of earlier cools the soup off for safer blending. Have I told you yet to use caution when blending hot liquids? Very important! The pressure can build up and blow the top off the blender. Hold the lid down firmly while blending hot things.

3. Puree in a blender in batches or with an immersion blender. This is wonderful served hot, but may also be served cold. I'm not much on cold soups, personally, but don't let that stop you if it sounds good to you.

Makes about 6 cups, enough for 4 people.

Learn to Cook

Potato Soup

hilahcooking.com/
potato-soup

My mama made this a lot when I was a wee babe. I loved it, and I still do. It's super easy and tastes awesome, and it's great on a chilly evening with some crackers and the cucumber spread from the last section. Using leeks instead of onions makes this a little fancier and Frenchy-er.

- » ¼ cup chopped onion
- » 2 tablespoons bacon fat or butter
- » 3 cups water
- » 1 teaspoon salt
- » 2 cups diced potatoes (peeled or not)
- » 1 15-ounce can evaporated milk (or 2 cups of milk or heavy cream)
- » Garnish: chopped parsley, dill, celery leaves, or paprika

1. Heat your fat of choice over medium heat in a saucepan. Saute onion about 5 minutes or until translucent.

2. Add water, salt, and potatoes. Bring to boil then simmer uncovered until tender, about 20 minutes. By this time most of the water should have cooked off, but if not, let it go a little longer; there should just be enough water left to come about half-way up the potatoes.

3. Use a large spoon or immersion blender to mash up about half the potatoes, leaving the remainder in chunks. Mashing the potatoes is crucial to acquire the right thick'n'creamy texture! Don't skip this step.

4. Add milk and reheat over medium heat until steaming hot.

5. Serve with garnish of choice (it's okay if your choice is no garnish, too).

Makes about 6 cups of soup, which will serve 3-4 people.

Peanut Soup

It might sound weird, but peanut soup has been around a long time, originating in West Africa in like the 1550s after peanuts were brought over from South America. So it's a worldly dish, you see. I like it with the carrot/arugula salad in this book, but you can also serve it over cooked rice, couscous, or millet if you want a heartier meal. Cooked chicken also makes a fine addition.

- » 2 tablespoons butter or olive oil
- » 2 stalks celery, finely chopped
- » 1 cup onion, finely chopped
- » 1 serrano or jalapeno pepper, seeded and minced
- » 1 clove garlic, minced (1 teaspoon)
- » 2 tablespoons flour
- » 3½ cups chicken or vegetable stock
- » 4 ounce can tomato sauce
- » 1 cup diced sweet potato (¼" cubes)
- » ½ cup peanut butter
- » 2 teaspoons lemon juice
- » ¼ cup chopped cilantro (or parsley)

1. Heat butter or oil in a large pot over medium heat. Add celery, onion, peppers, and garlic, then saute five minutes.

2. Reduce the heat to low and sprinkle with the flour. Stir that around.

3. Add a cup of the stock, slowly pouring it in while stirring. (Just like making gravy!) It will spatter but keep stirring to make sure there are no flour lumps.

4. Add the remaining stock and tomato sauce. Also fill the empty tomato sauce can with water, swirl it around, and add that in.

5. Bring to boil, then reduce heat and simmer uncovered 10 minutes.

6. Add sweet potato and cook another 5 minutes.

7. Stir in peanut butter and lemon juice. Serve garnished with cilantro or parsley.

Makes about 5 cups, serving 2–3 people (more if you are serving over grains or as a first course.)

Learn to Cook

Corn Chowder

This is best made with fresh corn in the middle of the summer when corn is cheap and good, but it's also hard to want to eat hot chowder in the middle of the summer, so you can totally do it with frozen corn in the winter. Or whenever. Scout's honor; frozen corn never ruined anything.

Corn Cobs

The easiest way I have found to cut kernels from corn cobs is to shuck them and remove the silks, then lay them down and cut off a few rows along the side. Then roll it so it's stable and sitting on that flat side. Keep cutting off rows until it's all clean. To get all the corny goodness now, stand the cob upright and scrape downward, using the back (blunt) edge of your knife. White stuff will ooze out. This is called the "milk," and it imparts a great sweet corn taste and smooth texture when you add it to your stuff.

- » 1 cup chopped onion
- » 1 cup chopped celery
- » 1 cup diced red potatoes (½" cubes)
- » 2 tablespoons butter + 1 tablespoon oil
- » 3 tablespoons flour
- » 3½ cups chicken or vegetable stock
- » 2 cups corn (cut from 4 fresh cobs or frozen)
- » ½ teaspoon thyme or tarragon
- » ½ teaspoon salt
- » ½ teaspoon pepper
- » 1 cup milk or half and half
- » Optional: grated cheese

1. Heat butter and oil over medium heat. Saute onion, celery, and potatoes for 5 minutes.
2. Sprinkle in flour and stir.
3. Add stock, a cup at a time, until all is incorporated.
4. Add corn. If using fresh corn, scrape the milk from the cobs as well (see sidebar).
5. Add spices and simmer until potatoes are soft.
6. Add milk and heat until steaming.
7. Garnish bowls with grated cheese if you like.

Makes about 8 cups of soup, about 4 servings.

Lentil Coconut Soup

OMG this soup is so good I dream about it. Hearty, healthy, warming, spicy, and even vegan. You can serve over some cooked rice or with chapati bread if you want to round it out. Mmm, an orange and red onion salad would be great with this.

- » 1 teaspoon oil
- » ½ cup chopped onion
- » 1 clove garlic, minced (1 teaspoon)
- » ½" piece fresh ginger root, peeled and minced (about a tablespoon)
- » 1 tablespoon curry powder
- » 1½ cups red lentils (you can use brown if that is all you can find; it just won't be as pretty, but whatever)
- » 3½ cups water
- » 15 ounce can coconut milk
- » ½ teaspoon salt
- » 1 tablespoon lime juice (lemon will work, too!)
- » Optional: cilantro, fresh jalapeno slices, cooked rice, chapati

1. Heat the oil in a large sauce pan over medium heat. Sweat the onion, garlic, and ginger (cook over low heat with the lid on) for 5 minutes.

2. Add the curry powder and stir until you can smell it real good, 30–60 seconds.

3. Add the lentils and water. Bring to a boil and then simmer, covered, 30 minutes, until the lentils are cooked. If you need to add more water and let it cook a little longer to get the lentils very soft, that's okay.

4. Add the coconut milk and salt and reheat gently.

5. Add lime juice just before serving. Sprinkle each serving with cilantro and jalapeno slices.

Makes 4 big bowls.

Chili

Everyone needs a good chili recipe. I asked my dad to email me his chili recipe and this is what I got, verbatim:

chili is easy. keep it simple, and don't do any yankee stuff like add cinnamon or funky spices, all they do is make it sweet. throw everything in a pot and cook until the meat is tender. you may want to use two kinds of meat, like ground and stew, add ground meat after the stew meat is tender for a thicker meatier stew. don't cook at the same time or the ground will dissolve. give people the option of adding beans, but texans generally eschew beans in their chili. salt to taste. serve with chopped fresh jalapeños and onions on top. love dad

My favorite part is when he tells me not to do any "yankee stuff." He's right about the "no beans in Texas chili" of course, but adding beans is a great way to stretch this recipe to feed more. Make a batch of cornbread to go with it, and you may achieve World Fame. Anyway, here we go:

- » 1 pound coarsely ground beef (in Texas you can find "chili grind," or use 1 pound stew meat chunks)
- » 28 ounce can tomatoes (diced or whole tomatoes or 1½ pounds fresh tomatoes)
- » 16 ounce can tomato sauce (or an additional ½ pound fresh tomatoes)
- » 1 big onion (softball-sized)
- » 6 cloves garlic, minced (2 tablespoons)
- » 2-5 jalapeños, chopped (depending on your taste)
- » 1 tablespoon ground cumin
- » 3 tablespoons chili powder
- » 1 tablespoon corn masa (this is the flour used for making tortillas. You can use a corn tortilla, diced, in its place)
- » 1 teaspoon salt
- » Optional: 15 ounce can kidney or pinto beans; for more heat, add a couple of chili pequins (similar to bird-eye peppers)

1. Break up the meat into small chunks in the bottom of a big pot. Turn to medium-high heat and brown part way.

2. Add everything else (except the beans if you want to use them) and bring to a boil over medium heat. Reduce heat, cover, and simmer 1 hour if using ground meat, 2 hours if using stew meat.

3. Add the beans if you want them. Taste the broth and add more salt if you want, or more chili powder. Simmer another 30 minutes or so until the meat is tender.

This batch feed 4–6 people but can easily be doubled if you have a large enough pot. Leftover chili is never bad and always good.

Learn to Cook

Vegetable Curry

This is a total bastardization of real Indian curry, I am aware, but who cares? It's quick, easy, and you probably have everything you need to make it right now. I listed the spices as I make this, but if all you have is curry powder, do not be discouraged. Just double the curry powder and move on with your life.

» 1 tablespoon oil

» 1 teaspoon ground cumin

» 1 teaspoon ground coriander

» 1 teaspoon mustard seeds

» 1 teaspoon turmeric

» 2 tablespoons curry powder

» 1 onion, minced, about a cup

» 3 cloves garlic, minced

» 1 teaspoon grated or dried ginger

» 1 15 ounce can tomatoes (or 1 pound fresh, chopped tomatoes)

» 1 jalapeno or serrano, minced, or 1 whole dried red chili (if you like it spicy!)

» 4 cups assorted vegetables, cut into bite-size pieces (Cut the dense ones into smaller pieces than the soft ones.)

» 15 ounce can of beans (chick peas, kidney beans, lentils, whatevs), drained and rinsed

» ½ teaspoon salt

» For Serving: 1 cup rice, cooked, or 1 batch chapatis *(Page 132)*, Cucumber Raita *(next page)*

1. Heat the oil in your big pot over medium heat 'til it is hot. Throw in your spices of choice (or availability) and stir them around to toast them, about 30 seconds.

2. Add the onion, garlic, ginger, tomatoes, and pepper and stir that around. It will bubble and pop at you but just tell it to behave and keep stirring. Cook for a couple of minutes.

3. Add the vegetables and a cup or two of water so that the vegetables are almost covered. Add the salt and stir it up. Simmer about 15 minutes until the vegetables are soft.

4. Add drained beans and heat through. Stir in cilantro before serving.

Serves 2-4, depending on if you're serving it alone or with rice or chapati

Cucumber Raita and Tsatsiki

Raita is a cooling kind of relish that is used to temper the spicy effects of curries. It is similar to the Greek tsatsiki, and I might as well just tell you how to make that here, too. (Tsatsiki goes well atop grilled meats.)

- » 1 cucumber, peeled and grated (about 1 cup)
- » 1 cup plain yogurt (fat free works, but full fat is traditional)
- » ½ teaspoon salt
- » For Raita: ¼ teaspoon ground cumin
- » For Tsatsiki: 1 clove garlic, minced and 1 teaspoon dried mint

To make the raita, just combine cucumber, yogurt, and salt in a bowl and mix quickly with a fork. Top with cumin and refrigerate until serving time.

To make tsatsiki: Put the cucumber in a colander and sprinkle with the salt. Set aside for 10 minutes, then press down on it to squeeze the liquid out. Put into a bowl with the yogurt, mint, and garlic and combine well. Refrigerate until serving time.

Mushrooms

People say that you shouldn't wash mushrooms because they get soggy or don't brown in oil properly with all that extra water. That might be true, but with something like this curry, you needn't worry about that since they are going to be cooked in water for a long time anyway. Be smart. Go ahead and wash those mushrooms since they grow in dirt and poop. Then just dry them off on a towel if you want to get them browned in some oil or something for some new dish you create.

155

Beans and Greens

This colorful, healthful, Italian-y stew makes a good replacement for chili when you're entertaining some vegetarians or your heart just can't take another gram of cholesterol. Plus, the name rhymes and who can argue with that. Be sure to use sodium-free broth or water or risk the beans not softeneing properly. If you want, you can substitute two cans of beans for the dried beans. Reduce the broth to 2 cups and drain, rinse, and add the beans in with the greens.

- » 1 cup dry cannellini or Great Northern beans (or any large-ish bean of your choosing)
- » 2 tablespoons olive oil
- » 1 medium onion, diced (about a cup)
- » 2 cloves garlic, minced
- » 1 teaspoon oregano
- » 1 bay leaf
- » 4 cups water or sodium-free broth
- » 4 cups chopped greens (kale, escarole, collards, or arugula)
- » 1 lemon
- » 1/2 teaspoon salt
- » 1/2 teaspoon black pepper
- » For Serving: grated parmesan cheese, fresh chopped basil

1. Soak the beans over night. Drain.

2. Heat the oil in a large pot and add the onion. Saute 5 minutes or until beginning to brown.

3. Add the garlic, oregano, bay leaf, broth, and drained beans. Cover. Bring to boil over high heat.

4. Reduce heat and simmer 1 hour, or until beans are soft.

5. Add the greens and cook 5-10 minutes more.

6. Add the juice of the lemon, salt and pepper. Serve hot with cheese or fresh basil if desired and garlic bread.

Serves 4

Beef Vegetable Stew

This is how my mommy makes it. The tarragon is delish if you have some; if you don't, use basil or dill. You can also substitute ground beef and reduce the initial simmering time to 30 minutes.

- » ½ pound sirloin steak, cut into 1" cubes
- » 16 ounce can whole tomatoes or 1 pound diced fresh tomatoes
- » 1 tablespoon fresh tarragon or 1 teaspoon dried
- » 2 cloves garlic, minced (2 teaspoons)
- » 1 tablespoon oregano
- » 1 tablespoon Worcestershire sauce
- » 1 teaspoon salt
- » 1 teaspoon black pepper
- » 2 cups water
- » 2 carrots, sliced
- » 1 large potato, diced
- » ½ cup chopped onion
- » 2 stalks celery, sliced
- » 1 cup peas
- » 1 cup corn
- » Optional: 1 turnip, diced; 1 cup chopped cabbage

1. Combine beef, tomatoes, seasonings and water in a large pot.
2. Bring to simmer, cover, reduce heat, and simmer 1 hour.
3. Add vegetables (including any optional ingredients) and simmer 30 minutes until potatoes are tender.

Serves 4

Learn to Cook

Green Beans Giachini

This is simple, but really bad ass. You could use it as a side dish with some roasted chicken or fish, but I almost always just serve it for dinner with bread. So simple and so perfect. And you can also use all zucchini in place of the green beans if they are on sale at the store. Or you can leave the potato out and use the green beans as a sauce for spaghetti. Yumzos.

- » ¼ cup olive oil
- » 1 large onion (as big as a softball)
- » 2 cloves garlic, minced (about 2 teaspoons)
- » ½ cup chopped parsley
- » 2 pounds fresh green beans, stems trimmed off
- » 2 fat zucchinis
- » 2 big white or red potatoes
- » 1 pound tomatoes (about 4) or 1 15 ounce can whole tomatoes)
- » 1 teaspoon salt
- » 1 teaspoon pepper
- » Optional: red pepper flakes and/or lemon wedges

1. Heat the olive oil in a large pot over medium-low heat.

2. While it heats up, grate the onion on the large holes of a cheese grater or mince it fine.

3. Add it and the garlic to the oil.

4. Let that cook five minutes while you cut the zucchini into 1" slices and the potatoes into ½" cubes.

5. Add them and the green beans to the pot.

6. Coarsely chop the tomatoes and add them.

7. Give it a stir, add salt and pepper, and cover.

8. Simmer 30 minutes, covered. Remove the lid and simmer another 10 minutes to thicken the sauce.

Serves 4-6 depending on what else you got going on the table.

Braised Pot Roast

As you know, braising is great for less tender cuts of meat because the long slow cooking time tenderizes the meat. Pot roasts are even better the next day as leftovers. If you have a crock pot, just put all the ingredients in there (vegetables on the bottom, roast on top) for 8 hours on low, or 4 hours on high.

» 3–5 pound beef roast

» 2 teaspoons salt

» 2 teaspoons black pepper

» 2–3 tablespoons vegetable oil

» 2 large onions, cut into quarters (3 cups)

» 2 large carrots, cut into 1" lengths (2 cups)

» 4 red, yellow, or russet potatoes, cut into 2" pieces

» 1 cup sliced celery

» 4 garlic cloves, minced (4 teaspoons)

» 1 cup beer, red wine, or beef or chicken stock, or water

» 1 bay leaf

1. Preheat the oven to 325º. Get out a roasting pan or Dutch oven.

2. Heat a large cast iron (or steel) skillet or your Dutch oven, if you have one, over high heat on the stove and add the oil. Let it get hot.

3. Coat the roast with the salt and pepper. Brown it on all sides in the oil. This may take 15 minutes. Seriously. It takes longer than you might think to brown a huge hunk like that. Transfer the roast in your roasting pan or, if you're using a Dutch oven, just leave it in there. (P.S. This is traditional, but optional; your pot roast will be different but still delicious if you skip the browning step.)

5. Put the vegetables and garlic around the roast, pour in the liquid, and stick the bay leaf in there. Cover with the lid or foil and roast 2 hours.

6. Check to see if it is tender: when you put a fork in it and twist, meat should shred off. It may need up to 4 hours, depending on the size and shape of the roast. When the roast is tender, remove from oven and let rest 20 minutes before slicing and serving. (Make a salad while it's resting!)

7. Alternatively, you could do this on the stovetop, on very low heat, as long as you have a Dutch oven or a deep enough pot with a tight lid.

Servings vary; figure 3-4 servings per pound of roast.

Learn to Cook

Red Beans and Rice

hilahcooking.com/
red-beans-and-rice

A Cajun classic, made popular with the masses by Popeyes fried chicken. This recipe tastes a lot like Popeyes, which is a terrific thing, IMHO. Plus it's vegetarian and feeds a ton of people. You could also serve these beans with cornbread or carrot muffins instead of rice. Also, a citrus/avocado salad might be nice with this.

» 1 pound dry red beans or kidney beans

» 1 cup diced onion

» 1 cup diced celery

» 1 cup diced green bell pepper (green pepper actually works better here than red; another victory for the little and poor guy!)

» 4 cloves garlic, minced (4 teaspoons)

» 3 bay leaves

» 1 teaspoon thyme

» ¼ teaspoon rosemary

» ½ to 1 jalapeño, diced

» 1 tablespoon honey (or molasses or brown sugar)

» 1 teaspoon balsamic vinegar

» 1 teaspoon salt

» ½ teaspoon celery salt

» ½ teaspoon soy sauce

» 2 cups rice (I like brown rice but you can use white)

» 4 cups water

» 2 tablespoons butter

1. Soak beans overnight in enough water to cover them by 3 inches.

2. The next day, drain that water and put them in a big ol' pot with the onion, celery, pepper, garlic, spices, and jalapeño (everything up to the honey) and cover it with new water by 1 inch.

3. Cover it. Bring it to a boil, then turn to a simmer and simmer 2 hours.

4. Check to see if they are done by scooping a bean out, letting it cool a bit, then trying to mash it with your fingers. It should mash easily. If not done, let them cook another 30 minutes to an hour until they are. Add the honey, vinegar, salt, celery salt, and soy sauce now and turn the heat off. Let that sit while you cook your rice.

5. Mix rice and water in a saucepan. Cover and bring to a boil. Simmer 15 minutes for white rice or 45 minutes for brown. Add butter and fluff.

6. Reheat beans if necessary; they are probably still warm enough.

7. Serve beans over rice and pass the Tabasco sauce!

Serves 8-10

160

Cooking Dried Beans

To cook beans from scratch, the first step is to sort the beans. If you usually skip that step, take heed, children, for I too was once of the mind that a quick look-over would suffice until the woeful day when I chomped into my chalupa and found a rock.

Put two cups (one pound) of dry beans in a colander and look through them … really look at them. Pull out any funky looking beans or anything that is not, in fact, a bean. Then rinse them and put them in a big ass pot.

Now you have two options: To soak or not to soak. Soaking may remove some of the gaseous qualities of legumes, but it also requires forethought. With some beans, such as black or kidney, it also drains away their color. I usually do not soak, but here are the two methods.

Soaking Method 1: Cover the beans in the big ass pot with 3" of water. Cover and leave to soak at room temperature 8 hours or overnight. Drain and cover with 2" of fresh water. Bring to boil over high heat, then reduce heat to a simmer and cook partially covered 1-2 hours depending on the bean, until they are softened enough that one can be easily mashed between your thumb and finger.

Soaking Method 2: After sorting and rinsing, put beans in a large pot and cover with 1" water. Bring to boil on high heat, then turn off heat and let beans soak in hot water for 1 hour. Drain and cook as above.

No-Soaking Method: Cover the beans in the big ass pot with 4" of water and bring to boil over high heat. Reduce to medium and cook at a strong simmer for 2–3 hours, adding hot water as necessary to keep the beans covered, until they are softened enough that one can be easily mashed between your thumb and finger.

Now Season: Always salt beans AFTER they are softened. For a pound of beans, start with 2 teaspoons of salt and add from there until they are seasoned to your liking. Remember the most reliable way to taste the beans is to taste the bean cooking liquid, rather than a bean itself. Once the liquid is salty enough, so are your beans. Seasonings like whole peeled garlic cloves and halved onion or jalapeño may be added at the beginning of cooking time. Avoid adding tomatoes or other acidic seasonings at the beginning because they could make the bean skins tough. Add those when you salt the beans.

Perfectly Good Fish

I came up with this recipe one day when I was in a bind and all there was to eat were some shriveled vegetables and frozen tilapia. This could be called shallow poaching, or even steaming, but whatever it is, it's easy, fast, cheap, and good. The fish must be completely thawed before cooking. I'd serve this with some buttery rice, Cajun-style.

- » 1 tablespoon butter
- » 1/2 cup thinly sliced onion
- » 1 stalk celery
- » 2 tablespoons dry vermouth, white wine, or water
- » 1 pound boneless tilapia, cod, or catfish fillets (four 4 ounce portions all about the same size)
- » 1 tomato, diced (about 1/2 cup)
- » 1 jalapeño, sliced (seeded if you like)
- » 1 large clove garlic, minced (about 1 teaspoon)
- » 1/2 teaspoon dried thyme
- » 1/4 tespon salt
- » For Serving: lemon wedges, fresh parsley, cooked rice, hot sauce

1. Melt the butter over medium heat in a skillet that has a lid. Begin to saute the onions.
2. Slice the celery lengthwise in half, then crosswise 3 times to make 8 thin sticks. Add them to the onions and saute another minute until softened.
3. Add the vermouth or wine.
4. Lay the fish fillets over the vegetables in a single layer and scatter the tomato, jalapeño, garlic, thyme, and salt over that.
5. Put a lid on the skillet and simmer for 10 minutes, or until the fish is cooked through. You'll know it's cooked when it can easily be pierced with a fork and it looks opaque rather than slightly translucent.

Serves 4.

Salsa Chicken

Another "desperation meal," you can actually make this with still-frozen boneless chicken breasts if you must. It won't get any kind of pretty brown color, but it'll be just as edible as anything. In this recipe, chicken is shallow-poached in salsa, making it super-duper easy and fast. You could serve it with beans and rice or make it into tacos. Oh, and you could do the same thing with boneless chicken thighs which are usually cheaper than breasts.

- » 1 tablespoon oil
- » ¼ teaspoon salt
- » ¼ teaspoon pepper
- » ½ teaspoon dried oregano
- » 2 boneless chicken breasts, frozen or not
- » 1 cup salsa of your choice

1. Heat the oil in a skillet over high heat.
2. Sprinkle the salt, pepper, and oregano on the chicken.
3. Sear the chicken on both sides (skip this if using frozen chicken).
4. Add the salsa and cover tightly.
5. Poach the chicken in the salsa over low heat for 10 minutes for thawed chicken breasts, 20 minutes for frozen chicken breasts. Chicken is done when a fork can easily pierce it, the juices run clear, and the internal temperature reaches 165° F.

Serves 2-4

DRY HEAT METHOD
BAKING & ROASTING

Okay, now we'll get into the oven. Most of these recipes would fall into the category of casseroles, and many of them qualify as one-pot meals, although you may end up dirtying more than one pot in preparing the components of each. Those recipes, I guess would really be classified as "combination" cooking method recipes, since they start out with something wet like a sauce and then go into the oven to bake. Whatever. To round out any of these meals, make a green salad while the main dish bake or steam some vegetables real quick (see Side Dishes in Chapter 11).

Rice, Corn, and Cheese Casserole

Another recipe from the good old days, this is a good thing to do with leftover rice. You can use white rice if you prefer. Chopped broccoli can also be added for a truly one-dish meal; just add in about 2 cups of finely chopped fresh or frozen broccoli before baking. This also goes really well with Spinach and Orange Salad (Page 225). Instructions for microwaving are included if you don't want to heat up the whole dang house. Leftovers make a hearty, healthy breakfast, too.

- » 3 cups cooked brown rice
- » 2 cups corn (can substitute 3 cups chopped broccoli)
- » 1 small onion, chopped (you can saute it first if you like, but I just throw it in raw)
- » 2 cups grated sharp cheddar (6 ounces by weight)
- » 1½ cup milk
- » ½ teaspoon each salt, chili powder, black pepper
- » Paprika for toppin'

1. Set oven to 350º F
2. Combine all ingredients except paprika.
3. Pour into a greased 2 quart casserole (a 9x13" dish will work, too) and smooth out evenly.
4. Sprinkle with paprika and bake for 40–45 minutes. Top will be browned and casserole will be firm.
5. You could also microwave this for 10 minutes on full power, turning half way through if your microwave has no turntable dealie.

Serves 6.

Chicken Divan

This is a classic dish, invented in the 1950s at a swanky hotel restaurant in New York City. The original recipe used gruyere and parmesan cheeses instead of cheddar, but this is how my mom made it, and so this is how I give it to you.

» 3–4 stalks broccoli (one "bunch" as they are sold in the store)
» 2 cups sliced cooked chicken breast (poach it as directed in the chicken salad recipe, or use leftover roasted chicken, cut up)
» 1½ cups milk, half-and-half, or cream (I prefer milk)
» 4 tablespoons butter
» 3 tablespoons flour (white or whole wheat)
» ½ teaspoon salt
» 1 tablespoon lemon juice
» 1 tablespoon curry powder
» 1 cup grated cheddar
» 2 slices whole wheat bread, buttered on one side and then cubed

1. Preheat oven to 350º F.
2. Cut each stalk of broccoli lengthwise into 4–6 pieces. Put it in a steamer basket in a large pot with a ½ inch of water in the bottom. Heat on high, covered, until boiling. Reduce heat slightly and steam broccoli 3–4 minutes. Remove from heat.
3. Arrange in an 8x8" or 9x9" dish, with florets facing outwards and stems in the center. Place chicken on top of the stalks. Set aside.
4. Melt butter in a sauce pot over medium heat and add flour. Stir with a whisk until bubbling. Add milk, a few glugs at a time, whisking after each addition until it's all in there. Heat until thickened, about 4 minutes, stirring constantly.
5. Remove from heat. Mix in salt, lemon juice, and curry powder.
6. Pour over chicken. Sprinkle with cheese. Top with bread cubes.
7. Bake for 20–30 minutes to heat through and toast bread cubes.

Serves 4

Pineapple Lemon Chicken

I imagine my mom got this recipe from the back of a can of pineapple slices. She used to make it when I was a kid. I bet she served it with rice and green beans; that sounds good, anyway. I've changed it here to use fresh pineapple, but if you want to use canned, just get a 20 ounce can of pineapple slices, use the juice in the sauce, and lay the slices over the chicken at the end.

- » 2 cups fresh pineapple cubes (1" cubes)
- » 1 clove garlic, minced (1 teaspoon)
- » 2 teaspoons Worcestershire sauce
- » 4 teaspoons mustard
- » 1 teaspoon dried rosemary or thyme
- » 4 boneless, skinless chicken breast halves (about 2 pounds)
- » ½ teaspoon salt
- » 1 lemon, sliced thinly

1. Turn the oven to 400° F.

2. Put 1 cup of the pineapple chunks in a blender with the garlic, cornstarch, Worcestershire sauce, mustard, and rosemary. Puree.

3. Arrange chicken in an 8x8" or 9x9" pan or 2 quart baking dish (use one with a lid if you have it; otherwise use foil). Sprinkle with the salt. Give the sauce another stir and pour it over the chicken. Cover with a glass lid or a piece of foil. Bake 30 minutes.

4. Remove the lid or foil. Top with pineapple and lemon slices, baste with sauce from the bottom of the pan. Bake 5–10 minutes longer.

Serves 4

Learn to Cook

Tuna Noodle Casserole

If you want to shortcut this, use a can of cream of mushroom or celery soup in place of making your own white sauce, although making your own white sauce is kind of a rite of passage around here: The White Sauce Rite. If you choose not to go for it this time, mix soup, tuna, spices, and cooked noodles together and bake.

- » 8 ounces egg noodles
- » ¼ cup chopped celery
- » ¼ cup chopped onion
- » 2 tablespoons butter
- » 2 tablespoons flour
- » 1½ cups milk
- » 1 teaspoon dill weed (teehee)
- » 1 teaspoon pepper

- » ½ teaspoon salt (omit if using canned soup)
- » 2-5 ounce cans tuna
- » Optional: ½ cup grated cheese (cheddar, Swiss, whatever you like); ½ cup bread or cracker crumbs mixed with 1 teaspoon oil; 1 teaspoon paprika

1. Put a large pot of water on to boil. Once it boils, drop the noodles in. Set a timer for the lowest number of minutes the package says. Set the oven to heat to 400° F.

2. In a saucepan over medium heat, melt the butter and saute the vegetables about 5 minutes, until the onion is getting translucent and soft. Sprinkle the flour over the vegetables in a fairly even layer. Stir it around so that all the vegetables are coated in sticky butter-flour goo.

3. Now add the milk, a half-cup at a time, stirring after each addition to get any lumps out. Add the spices and seasoning and turn off the heat.

4. By now it is probably time to drain your noodles. So, do that, then dump them in your saucepan if there's room; if not, mix everything in the noodles pot.

5. Open and drain the tuna and gently mix that in.

6. Pour the whole kit and caboodle into a greased casserole (8" or 9" square or a 2 quart). Top with cheese, oily breadcrumbs, and/or paprika if you like cheesies, crunchies, or pretties on top of things. Bake uncovered 20 minutes. Make a salad or something.

Serves about 4 people.

Baked Macaroni and Cheese

Now that you've mastered the white sauce, making some homemade mac'n'cheese will be a snap. Omigod, am I the only one who LOVES mac'n'cheese with a side of peas? It's the best thing in the world. The little trick here is not cooking your noodles all the way before combining with the cheese sauce so that in the oven they can absorb cheese sauce flavor without getting overcooked and mushy. Mushy noodles are gross.

- » 2 cups small elbow macaroni
- » ¼ cup (4 tablespoons) butter
- » 3 tablespoons flour
- » ⅛ teaspoon dry mustard (or ½ teaspoon prepared mustard)
- » ½ teaspoon salt
- » ½ teaspoon pepper
- » 2 cups milk, warmed up
- » 2 cups grated sharp cheddar
- » 1 cup croutons or bread cubes, optional

1. Bring a large pot of water to boil and add the macaroni. When it begins to boil again, set a timer for 3 minutes. After three minutes, drain. The pasta will still be very firm. That's okay. Set aside.

2. Preheat the oven to 375º F.

3. Melt butter in 2 quart saucepan over medium heat. Sprinkle flour and spices over the butter and stir with a whisk until a smooth paste forms. Cook, stirring, for another minute or two, until it begins to smell toasty.

4. Add ½ cup milk at a time, whisking after each addition to incorporate fully and get rid of any lumps. Once all milk is added, continue to cook, stirring (take special care to get the corners of the pan) until mixture comes to boil.

5. Remove from heat and add cheese. Stir to melt. Add macaroni.

6. Pour all of it into a greased, 2 quart casserole dish. Top with croutons or bread cubes. Bake for 25 minutes. Serve with buttered peas and carrots if I am coming over.

Enough for 4 people.

Learn to Cook

Vegetable Shepherd's Pie

hilahcooking.com/
shepherds-pie

You could make this with meat, of course. This is one of those "recipes" that changes every time I make it and is utterly dependent on what's hanging out in the fridge. The method stays the same and it does require some mashed potatoes, which I hope you have leftover from some time ago. If you want to make a meaty pie, brown one pound of ground beef or lamb in the oil until cooked through before adding the vegetables. Also, check my website for a more traditional lamb and beer shepherd's pie.

» 1 tablespoon oil or butter

» ½ cup chopped onion

» ½ cup chopped celery

» ½ cup chopped carrots

» 1 clove garlic, minced (1 teaspoon)

» 2–3 cups assorted vegetables, roughly chopped (frozen, fresh, or leftover)

» 8 ounces tomato sauce

» ½ teaspoon thyme and/or rosemary

» Leftover (or canned) beans or leftover cooked meat

» About 2 cups of mashed potatoes

» Optional: ½ cup grated cheese; 1 teaspoon paprika

1. Preheat the oven to 425º F.

2. Heat the oil in an oven-safe (cast iron) skillet. Saute the onion, celery, carrot and garlic in the oil for about 5 minutes.

3. Add the other vegetables and stir around.

4. Add the tomato sauce and herbs, and any meat or beans you want, and simmer it all together until thickened. Add a little water if it seems like it's going to stick.

5. Plop the mashed potatoes on top and spread around as best you can. Sprinkle with cheese or paprika if you like and bake for 20 minutes until the potatoes are heated through and the cheese is melty.

Serves 4

DRY HEAT METHOD

SAUTEEING, PAN-FRYING, & STIR-FRYING

This is where you'll find the quickest dishes. Because these all use direct heat, they cook fast!

A blessing indeed, when you're tired and cranky and really need to eat something STAT before you keel over headlong into a vat of ice cream.

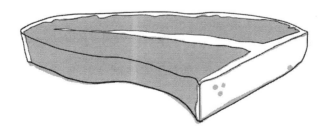

Sauteed Steaks

Drop a little dough on some tender steak like sirloin, filet, or strip. You'll want fairly thin steaks, ¾" to 1¼" thick. For even cooking throughout, have the meat at room temperature before you begin—just set them out on the counter for an hour, covered. You will also want to pat them dry before seasoning to minimize splattering when they hit the hot oil. Bake some potatoes (p. 216) and keep them warm in the oven while you cook the steaks. Have a salad at the ready and present your loved one with a classic meal you made yourself. This way will produce medium-rare doneness; if you want them more done, cook another minute or two.

> » 2 boneless beef steaks, about 6 ounces each
>
> » ½ teaspoon salt
>
> » 1 teaspoon black pepper
>
> » 1 tablespoon olive oil
>
> » ½ cup red wine, beef stock, or chicken stock
>
> » 2 tablespoons butter
>
> » 1 tablespoon fresh parsley

1. Pat the steaks dry. Sprinkle both sides of each with salt and pepper.

2. Heat a heavy skillet over high heat and add the oil. When it is good and hot, put the steaks in. Don't move them for 5 minutes.

3. Flip and cook another 5 minutes.

4. Take them out and put on a plate to rest for 5 minutes while you make a light sauce, like so:

5. Pour the wine or broth into the hot pan to deglaze it; stir to pick up all the browned bits and simmer to reduce by about half (meaning you have about ¼ cup of liquid left).

6. Add the butter and parsley and pour the sauce over your steaks.

Serves 2

Pan Fried Chicken Breasts

Ha ha, I said "breasts." Here's how to do them so they don't get all shriveled up and dried out. Make some mashed potatoes, rice pilaf, or garlic bread to go with these. Round it out with a green vegetable.

» 4 chicken breast halves

» ½ cup flour

» ½ teaspoon salt

» 1 teaspoon pepper

» 2 tablespoon oil

» 2 tablespoon butter

» ¼ cup white wine (or more broth)

» ½ cup chicken or vegetable broth

» *Optional:* 1 tablespoon capers, 1 tablespoon lemon juice, 2 tablespoons fresh parsley or dill, 1 tablespoon dijon mustard

1. Before salmonella gets everywhere, get out your biggest skillet. Get out a plate, too, and mix the flour, salt, and pepper together on it. Get out another plate for after the chicken is cooked.

2. Butterfly the chicken breasts *(see p. 86)*. You will now have 4 heart-shaped pieces if you did it right, and the world is your Valentine.

3. Lightly dredge each side of your chicken hearts in the seasoned flour. Just a dusting of flour is all you need. Then wash your hands. Duh.

4. Turn the skillet on to high heat. Heat for one minute and add the butter and oil. Heat another minute.

5. Put the chicken in and cook for 3 minutes on one side. Flip and do two more minutes.

6. Remove and set on the clean plate you have nearby to rest while you make a sauce, like so: Pour the wine into the hot skillet and stir it around until it evaporates. Add the broth and whatever other optional things you like (they are all good, and any combination is good). Stir that around for a minute.

7. Add the chicken back to the skillet and serve.

Serves 4

Learn to Cook

Pan Fried Bean Burgers

hilahcooking.com/
veggie-bean-burgers

Mix and match your beans, grains, nuts and seasonings to customizethese. They are super flexible. Like yogis. You don't have to pan fry these vegan burgers, either, but it makes them crunchier. You could bake them on a greased sheet at 350° for 30 minutes instead. Either way, these will hold together better if you can let the patties sit for a bit before cooking. How about this: make the patties and leave them while you slice tomatoes and onion and wash your lettuce for the burgers? Chill your lettuce while you cook the burgers. Win!

» 1 ½ cups cooked beans or 1 15-ounce can

» ½ cup oatmeal, breadcrumbs, or wheat germ

» ½ cup cooked grain (rice, quinoa, etc.) or more oatmeal

» ½ cup grated carrot, sweet potato, or squash

» ½ cup sunflower seeds (or any other seed or nut you like, chopped small)

»

» ½ cup chopped onion

» 2 tablespoons soy sauce or liquid aminos

» 1 tablespoon vinegar

» Seasonings, pick some: 1 teaspoon thyme, rosemary, or oregano; Tabasco sauce, cayenne pepper, or chili powder; 1 teaspoon fresh garlic and/or ginger

» 3 tablespoons oil

» Optional: an additional ¼ cup breadcrumbs for dredging

1. Rinse and drain the beans.

2. Put the beans into a food processor with the onion and oatmeal to finely chop. Lacking a food processor, mince the onion by hand and mash the beans with a spoon.

3. Mix all ingredients well with your hands, except oil. If it seems too dry to hold together, add a teaspoon of water at a time until it sticks; if too moist, add a spoonful more oatmeal or crumbs.

5. Form into 4 equal-sized patties about an inch thick. Dredge in crumbs if you like an extra crispy crust. Let sit as long as you can.

7. Heat the oil over medium heat in a heavy skillet and fry for 5 minutes on each side. Eat them hot and crispy! **Bonus Tip:** These can also be cooled and frozen after cooking. Reheat in the oven or microwave.

Serves 4

Learn to Cook

Chicken Lo Mein

A very good approximation of the noodles you might get at a Chinese buffet. Some may complain that it's not an authentic Chinese dish and to them I say: bah, go suck on a fortune cookie. Just because something isn't authentic doesn't mean it's bad. You could also substitute a pound of whole, peeled, raw shrimp and make shrimp lo mein just like that (*snaps fingers)!

- » 8 ounces linguine or fettuccine
- » 2 skinless, boneless chicken breasts or 4 skinless, boneless thighs
- » 3 tablespoons soy sauce
- » 2 teaspoons cornstarch
- » ¼ cup vegetable oil
- » 2 cups sliced napa or savoy cabbage, bok choy, or mushrooms
- » 1 cup snow peas (leave whole) or thinly sliced celery
- » 2 green onions, cut into 1" lengths (or ¼ cup thinly sliced onion)
- » 1 red bell pepper, sliced thinly
- » ½ cup water (or chicken broth if you've got it)

1. Put on a large pot of water for the noodles; put a lid on it so it will boil faster.

2. Slice your vegetables thinly and set them aside.

3. Slice chicken thinly (¼") and put it in a bowl with the soy sauce and cornstarch—toss around.

4. Your water's probably boiling by now; cook the noodles according to package directions. Drain, rinse, and leave them in the colander for now.

5. Put a large skillet over high heat.

6. Add the oil and heat for about a minute.

7. Add chicken and stir fry 2–3 minutes, until partially cooked.

8. Add all the vegetables. Stir fry another minute.

9. Add water or chicken broth and noodles. Toss to combine. Bring to a simmer, stir again, and serve.

Serves 4

Learn to Cook

Tofu Stir Fry

I've been making this since high school. Are you smarter than a stoned teenager? If you remember to put on a pot of rice before you start the stir fry you are! Use any vegetables you like and cut them all up to bite-size pieces. Refer to Chapter 6 if you need to refresh yourself on the relative density: size rule of cutting vegetables for stir fries and medleys. Serve in a tortilla if you forgot the rice. Or over those fried chow mein noodles you buy in a can if you want to take a fairly healthy meal and make it fairly unhealthy. If you want to. It is good.

- » 8–16 ounces firm tofu (not silken)
- » 2 tablespoons oil
- » 3 cups or more chopped vegetables:
    - » **Dense:** carrots, potatoes, beets, sweet potatoes, winter squash
    - » **Medium:** onion, summer squash, broccoli, celery, green beans
    - » **Soft:** greens, spinach, asparagus
- » 2 cloves garlic, minced
- » 2 teaspoons or more soy sauce

1. Slice the tofu into ⅓"–½" thick slices and press between clean tea towels for five minutes or longer to pull some moisture out so it won't splatter so much when you fry it. Set a heavy skillet on top of the tofu-towel-sandwich to put some pressure on it. The longer it is pressed, the better.

2. Heat your oil over high in a big skillet for a minute until it shimmers.

3. Put in your tofu and step the hell off. It will get you. If you have a splatter screen, now is the time to use it.

4. Fry on high for 3–4 minutes until you can see the crispy brownness start to creep up the sides of your tofu slices. Flip carefully and cook another 3 minutes until the other side is golden. Remove from skillet.

6. Throw in your hard vegetables and stir for 2 minutes. Add medium vegetables and stir another 2–3 minutes until they are almost done. Add the softies. Stir it around. Add your tofu, garlic, and soy sauce. Toss quickly for another 2 minutes until everything is done. The End!

Serves 2–4

Learn to Cook

SUMMER TIME SUPPERS

Here are some ideas for suppers to make when it is too damn hot outside to do much of anything, especially slave over a hot stove all day, and all you really want is something cool and refreshing, and you can't have popsicles for dinner again.

Sushi Bowl

Faster than rolling up a buncha shit, but with all the great taste of sushi rolls? Sign me up! You could serve this on its own or with sauteed fish. It would also make a good bag lunch.

» 1 cup sushi rice (white or brown)

» 2¼ cups water

» 2 tablespoons rice vinegar

» 1 tablespoon sugar *(Optional, see sidebar)*

» ½ teaspoon salt *(Optional, see sidebar)*

» 1 avocado, pitted and sliced or diced

» 1 cucumber, diced

» 1 red bell pepper or carrot, cut into strips

» 1 bunch green onions, thinly sliced

» 4–8 sheets nori (toasted seaweed wraps)

» Extras: 4 tablespoons sesame seeds; wasabi powder (mixed with an equal volume of water) or paste; pickled ginger; soy sauce

1. Cook the rice with the water (15 minutes for white, 45 for brown). When it's done, spread it out on a plate or cutting board. Combine the vinegar, sugar and salt; stir to dissolve. Sprinkle over the rice a little at a time, stirring it around after each sprinkling, until the rice is cool and all the vinegar mixture has been absorbed. Divide the rice into 4 bowls.

2. Cut up the vegetables. Sprinkle over each bowl evenly.

3. Tear up one or two sheets of nori and sprinkle over each bowl. There is a lot of sprinkling in this recipe.

4. Then sprinkle each with a tablespoon of sesame seeds.

5. Serve with a small dish on the side of wasabi, ginger, and soy sauce for … sprinkling.

Serves 4

Rice Vinegar

You can purchase "Seasoned Rice Vinegar" as well as plain old rice vinegar (that may be labeled "Sodium-free Sugar-free" or it may not). Seasoned vinegar has had some sugar and salt added, the idea being that if you use that to season your sushi rice, you need only use that because it's already got everything in it. Basically, it's up to you which you buy, just make sure you don't add more sugar and salt if you're using seasoned vinegar.

Learn to Cook

Peanut Noodles

Soba noodles are made from buckwheat and are from Japan. They are kind of a gray-brown color with a nutty flavor, and they cook really fast. I think they look like worms, but they taste good and it's a nice change from regular old wheat noodles. If you can't/don't want to find soba noodles, just use some angel hair (capellini) pasta. This is also good as a cold salad if you omit the eggs and refrigerate it for an hour before serving.

- » 10 ounces soba noodles
- » 2 tablespoons peanut butter
- » 1 tablespoon soy sauce
- » 1 tablespoon rice wine vinegar or cider vinegar or white wine vinegar
- » ½ teaspoon red pepper flakes
- » 2 cloves garlic, minced (2 teaspoons)
- » ½ pound green beans
- » 2 eggs, beaten (you can leave these out and make it vegan)
- » 1 tablespoon sesame oil or vegetable oil
- » ½ cup sliced green onions

1. Bring a pot of water to boil for the noodles.
2. In a bowl, combine peanut butter, soy sauce, vinegar, red pepper, and garlic and set aside for later.
3. Trim the stems off the green beans and then cut them in half.
4. Heat the oil in a skillet and add the eggs. Cook over medium-high heat, stirring quickly until they are cooked, then remove to a bowl.
5. Add the green beans to the skillet and stir fry a couple of minutes.
6. By now your water is probably boiling, so put in the noodles and set a timer.
7. Keep stir frying those green beans; turn the heat down if you are getting nervous.
8. Drain the noodles and add them to the skillet along with the peanut sauce, eggs, and onions. Toss everything around to coat all the noodles in the sauce.

Serves 4

Learn to Cook

Taco Salad

This is my friend Emily's go-to summertime supper. She said some people like ranch dressing on theirs, but we both agreed that is not as friendly to bikini bodies as salsa.

Taco Part:

- » 1 pound ground beef (sometimes I add cooked beans or use only cooked beans)
- » ½ cup diced onion
- » 2 cloves garlic, minced (2 teaspoons)
- » 1 tablespoon chili powder
- » 1 teaspoon cumin
- » ½ teaspoon salt

Salad Part:

- » ½ head romaine lettuce, washed and torn into bite-sized chunks
- » 2 tomatoes, diced
- » 1 avocado, diced
- » 1 bunch green onions, sliced
- » 4 handfuls tortilla chips (or make tostadas and crumble them, *see Tostadas p. 260*)
- » 1 cup salsa (store bought *or use the recipe on p. 248*)

1. Over medium-high heat, saute the beef and onion together, stirring to break up the meat into small chunks.
2. When the onions are tender and the meat is brown, add the spices and turn the heat to simmer while you prepare the salad stuffs.
3. Put the lettuce on bottom with tomatoes, avocado, and green onions on top. Crumble the tortilla chips over the top. Distribute the taco filling over that and serve with salsa (or ranch).

Serves 4

TACOS

Here are three taco options, from fast, cheap and on-the-fly to exotic, impressive, and takes-planning. You can make some *Spanish Rice* (p. 214) to go with them or some *Refried Beans* (p. 216). If you want to. Or you could try the *Fried Plantains* in garlic (p. 220). But part of the beauty of tacos is that you don't need a fork to eat them so don't feel pressured to make a side dish. You can also make your own *Flour Tortillas* really easily (p. 233). And there's some badass recipes for guacamole and salsa in Chapter 14.

Tortillas

Reheating tortillas is easy. A couple ways to do it: on the stove, in the oven, or in the microwave. These work for flour or corn tortillas.

Stovetop (my favorite because they get a little browned and taste like they just came off the comal): toss them right onto the gas flame or an electric stove on high. Watch them the entire time and flip after just a few seconds. Do NOT start a tortilla fire. Use tongs to flip them. Put on a plate and cover with another plate until you are ready to eat.

Oven: wrap your tortillas in foil; sprinkle a little water on them first from your fingertips if they are stale; put into a 300º oven for 10–20 minutes while you cook everything else.

Microwave: put them on a plate, sprinkle with water and microwave 30 seconds; flip the stack over and move the inside ones to the top and microwave another 30 seconds.

Veggie Tacos

This is a go-to meal for me, perfect for the end of the week when we don't have much in the way of food around and want to use up all the leftovers. All you need is some tortillas, some basic seasonings, and whatever vegetables you can scrounge up from the fridge, freezer, or pantry. This is just a basic guideline—you are expected to exchange any or all of these vegetables for what you have on hand.

- » 1 tablespoon oil
- » ½ cup chopped onion
- » 1 clove garlic, minced (1 teaspoon)
- » 1 cup frozen corn (or more or different vegetable)
- » 1 shriveled zucchini, chopped (J/K! It's just that mine is usually shriveled by now; you can use something else that is green if you have it)
- » 1 cup diced starchy vegetable like carrots, potatoes, or sweet potatoes
- » 1 can beans, drained (if you don't have these use some more vegetables or any leftover cooked grain)
- » 1 teaspoon chili powder
- » 1 teaspoon cumin
- » ½ teaspoon oregano
- » 4–6 tortillas
- » Optional: salsa, cheese, avocado, diced tomato, shredded lettuce, cilantro, sour cream

1. Saute all the vegetables in the oil until they are softened and slightly browned.
2. Add the beans and spices and turn heat to low. Add a coupla tablespoons of water if it's sticking.
3. Stir around and mash the beans up a little with your spoon.
4. Heat the tortillas and make tacos. Serve with any of the optional things you have on hand.

Makes enough for 2–3 people

Fish Tacos

hilahcooking.com/
fish-tacos

You can make these in about 10 minutes if you have some fish in the freezer. And you thought ahead to thaw it. Otherwise, it will take a bit longer, but it's still pretty fast. If you don't have the anise seed, leave it out. But if you can spring for it, it gives a really nice background flavor.

» 1 pound any white fish (tilapia, cod, halibut, whatever is your pleasure)

» 1 teaspoon ground cumin

» ¼ teaspoon anise seed, crushed

» ½ teaspoon black pepper, crushed

» ½ teaspoon chili powder

» ½ teaspoon salt

» ¼ cup cornmeal

» 2 tablespoons vegetable oil

Toppin':

» 2 cups thinly sliced cabbage

» ⅓ cup diced onion

» ¼ cup chopped cilantro

» ½ jalapeno, minced (remove seeds if you want it less hot)

» 1 lime (2 tablespoons juice)

» 1 teaspoon salt

» 1–2 tablespoons mayonnaise

» 8 corn or flour tortillas

1. For fish: Combine spices and cornmeal. Cut fish into 8 even-sized pieces and roll in cornmeal mixture. Set it aside while you make the toppin'—the cornmeal will adhere better when you cook it.

2. For toppin': Combine vegetables with lime juice and salt. Mix it up good. Add mayonnaise right before serving.

3. When you're ready to cook: heat your skillet up real good on high heat and add the oil. Let that heat up a minute.

4. Put in the fish and let it set still for about 3 minutes. When you can lift it easily and it doesn't stick, flip it and turn your heat down to medium-high.

5. Cook another 3 minutes until you cut one open, and it's not raw; it should be opaque white, not translucent. Remove from heat.

6. Add mayonnaise to the cabbage and mix it up.

7. Heat your tortillas and make tacos with the fish topped with the slaw.

Makes 8 tacos, serves 4.

Learn to Cook

Tacos al Pastor

hilahcooking.com/
tacos-al-pastor

My favorite kind of tacos. It's totally worth whatever trouble you have to go to to find the dried chilies. I promise. The End. But wait there's more. You can use a can of pineapple chunks for this, drain the juice to use for the 1 cup of pineapple juice and save the chunks to cook with the meat. Or use fresh pineapple chunks.

» 3 guajillo chilies

» 1 ancho chili

» 1 cup pineapple juice

» 1 tablespoon white or cider vinegar

» 1 teaspoon cinnamon

» 1 teaspoon salt

» 1 teaspoon pepper

» 1 teaspoon oregano

» 5 cloves garlic

» ½ cup chopped onion

» ½ teaspoon achiote powder (aka, annatto; you can leave this out if you want or buy it and add it to some Spanish rice)

» 1½–3 pounds pork tenderloin (depending on how many people you are serving and what they have at the store. 1½ lbs will serve 6 people)

» 1 cup pineapple cubes

» 12–24 corn tortillas

» **For Serving:** diced onion and minced cilantro

1. Combine everything but the pork, pineapple and tortillas in the blender. Make it smoove. Pour it over the pork and marinate it in the fridge up to 24 hours.

2. Remove from the fridge and bring to room temperature (let it sit out for an hour). Preheat the oven to 350º F.

3. Pull it out of the marinade and put into a roasting pan or a big casserole with the pineapple chunks.

4. Roast it for an 30 minutes to 1 hour (depending on weight) or until a meat thermometer stuck in the middle reads 165º.

5. Alternatively, you can slice the tenderloin and grill the slices outdoors or in a cast iron skillet on high for 4 minutes on each side.

6. Alternative to that, skip the marinating and put the whole thing with the sauce in a crock pot for 8 hours on low.

7. Serve with onion and cilantro on corn tortillas.

Serves 6–12, depending on how much pork you got

Learn to Cook

PASTA & FRIENDS

Besides pasta, here you will find the old stand-bys like marinara and meat sauce and also some new-and-easy things to do with pasta once you've reached your saturation point with tomato sauce.

When cooking pasta, remember: have the sauce ready and waiting on the pasta (not the other way around). Use at least 12 cups (3 quarts) of water per pound of pasta and add a tablespoon of salt to flavor the pasta. Put a lid on the pot to bring it to boil faster. Make sure the water is at a full boil before you drop the pasta in (otherwise it will clump up nasty). Stir briefly after dropping it in, partially cover the pot, and return to boil. Remove the lid once the pot boils again and set a timer for the minimum time listed on the package; stir frequently and taste frequently until the pasta is cooked al dente. Drain in a colander and return to the pot. Add a tablespoon or so of oil or butter to help keep the pasta from sticking together. Do not rinse pasta unless you are using it for a cold salad.

Al Dente

Sometimes people say to me, they say: "Hilah, how do I know when the pasta is done?" Seems like a silly question, but I will admit that even my own dear dad is one of those people. The answer to this question lies in your heart. No, I'm kidding, but it does lie in your mouth.

"Al dente" is a description that's bandied about quite often since they started importing real Italian pasta, and it's great to cook your pasta "al dente," except that it's a concept that non-Italians are not familiar with. Sure, we know it translates to: "to the tooth," but really? Are you fucking kidding me? That really has no meaning to me as an English speaker; there's no action verb in that phrase. I NEED AN ACTION VERB FOR SENTENCES TO MAKE SENSE TO ME.

Now, imagine putting in this action verb: resist. Now we have "resist the tooth," and we are getting somewhere. So what you are looking for, when you pull out a piece o' pasta and taste it is a piece o'pasta that is tender enough to bite through, yet offers a tiny bit of resistance in the center. Not so much that you end up with hard pasta jamming up your molars, but a pleasant chewiness remains. To figure out what this means to you, do some trials. When you cook pasta, set the timer for the minimum time specified. Usually it will say something like "boil 5–8 min" or whatever, so start with 5 minutes. Try a piece. If it sticks in your teeth, let it go another minute and try again. Keep doing that.

Marinara Sauce

Okay, I know this may look overly simple. I was shocked when I learned the ingredients, thinking "Is this all there is?!" But let me assure you, I learned this from a very sexy Italian man when I was traveling through Ireland, and we cooked it together in a hostel kitchen and received a very nasty note the next day for using someone else's salt. But it was totally worth it to have a very sexy Italian man make me marinara sauce the way his mama used to. I spoke no Italian and he spoke no English, and yet we communicated through the language of love. (I don't mean French, either.)

» ¼ cup olive oil

» 6 cloves garlic, minced (2 tablespoons)

» 28 ounce can whole tomatoes (or 2 pounds diced fresh tomatoes)

» 2 tablespoons dried basil (or 4 tablespoons chopped fresh basil)

» Salt, if necessary

1. Heat the oil over a medium-low heat and add the garlic. Cook just a few minutes until the garlic smells up your kitchen.

2. Add the tomatoes and stir. Put a lid on the pot and simmer 15 minutes.

3. Use a spoon to kind of break up the tomatoes, mashing them against the sides of the pot.

4. Add the basil and simmer another 5 minutes with the lid off. Taste. You might want to add a little salt, depending on the tomatoes.

5. Serve over spaghetti ... or something else.

Makes about 4 cups of sauce

Meaty Sauce

I originally did this in my pressure cooker, but here's how to do it the old-fashioned way. If you have a pressure cooker, get everything together and then seal it, bring to pressure and cook 15 minutes, followed by a natural release. You can use this sauce over spaghetti or to make lasagne.

- » 1 pound ground beef
- » 1 large onion, minced
- » 1 carrot, minced
- » 1 stalk celery, minced
- » 4 cloves garlic, minced (4 teaspoons)
- » 1 teaspoon rosemary
- » 1 tablespoon oregano
- » 1 tablespoon basil
- » 1 teaspoon fennel seeds
- » ½ teaspoon thyme
- » ½ teaspoon sage
- » 1 28 ounce can tomatoes (or 2 pounds chopped fresh tomatoes)
- » 8 ounces tomato sauce
- » 4 ounces tomato paste
- » 1 cup water
- » 1 tablespoon balsamic vinegar
- » ¼ cup chopped parsley

1. Brown the meat in a large pot over medium heat until cooked.
2. Add the onion, carrot, and celery. Saute in the meat grease for 5 minutes.
3. Add garlic and herbs, tomatoes, and water. Bring to a boil, then reduce heat and simmer uncovered for one hour.
4. Add the vinegar and parsley and taste for salt.

Makes about 8 cups of sauce

Pasta with Tomato Cream Sauce

It is no lie that the closest I've ever come to working in a professional kitchen was dating boys who did. (Also a brief stint at the Alligator Grill, but I don't really like thinking about that time of my life.) Anyway, this is something I learned from one of those boys. This is like fettuccine alfredo but better. Really easy and really delicious. Win-win.

- » ½ cup minced onion
- » 2 cloves garlic, minced (2 teaspoons)
- » 2 tablespoons olive oil
- » 2 cups cream
- » 1 tablespoon tomato paste
- » 1 teaspoon salt
- » 1 tablespoon fresh tarragon or 1 teaspoon dried
- » 1 pound of spaghetti, linguine, or fettuccine
- » Optional: ½ cup or more grated parmesan

1. Put on a large pot of water for your noodles.
2. Heat oil over medium heat in a saucepan. Add onions and garlic and saute until translucent, about 5 minutes.
3. Add cream. Simmer 5 minutes.
4. Add tomato paste and salt. Simmer 5 more minutes until slightly reduced in volume. Turn off heat.
5. Add tarragon. Let steep a few minutes, until your noodles are cooked and drained.
6. Mix the sauce and noodles together; stir a few minutes until the sauce is absorbed.
7. Sprankle wit' cheez.

Serves 6–8.

Pasta Primavera

hilahcooking.com/
pasta-primavera

I invented this one night when I had a bunch of cool rocker-types over for dinner and made lasagna for them. Only after my cool rocker guests arrived did I find out that one rocker shunned dairy. A lactose-intolerant rocker?! I thought rockers were tolerant of everything! So, ever the Good Hostess, I whipped this up out of what I had around and it turned out awesome, and the rockers were impressed, and I became cool forever and ever. Amen.

- » 1 pound pasta (originally I used gemelli but you can really use any shape you want to)
- » 3 tomatoes, diced (about 2 cups)
- » 2 cloves garlic, minced (2 teaspoons)
- » 2 tablespoons minced onion
- » 1 teaspoon oregano (or 2 teaspoons fresh minced)
- » 2 tablespoons olive oil
- » 2 tablespoons lemon juice
- » 1 tablespoon balsamic vinegar
- » 1 teaspoon salt
- » 2 cups chopped vegetables (carrots, zucchini, broccoli, green beans, whatever you want or have)

1. Bring a big pot of water to a boil and put your noodles in it. Set a timer for 2 minutes less than the cooking time specified on the package.

2. Mix the tomatoes with all the spices, juice, vinegar and oil and let that sit while you cut up your vegetables.

3. When the timer goes off, add the vegetables to the pasta pot and bring back to a boil.

4. Boil 2 more minutes.

5. Drain and mix with the tomato mess.

6. Serve with parmesan cheese if you aren't serving to a lactose-intolerant rocker or a person of the vegan persuasion.

Serves 8.

Spaghetti and Meatballs

Everybody's favorite! Remember that part in Lady and the Tramp? *That was so romantic. Maybe you'll get a smooch out of somebody if you make this for them. If you want a salad, put it together before you begin the spaghetti and put it in the refrigerator to crisp. As alternative to spaghetti, you could toast some hoagie rolls and make meatball subs for everyone! Melt mozzarella over the top under the broiler or in the oven. Less smooching potential, but delicious nonetheless.*

» 1 pound spaghetti

For Meatballs:

» 1 pound ground meat

» 1 egg

» ½ cup dryish, starchy particles (breadcrumbs, oatmeal, cornflakes, you get the picture)

» ½ cup finely chopped onion

» 1 clove garlic, minced

» a handful of parsley (¼–½ cup), chopped

» ½ teaspoon salt

» 1 teaspoon pepper

» 1 tablespoon olive or vegetable oil

For Sauce:

» ½ cup red wine

» 15 ounce can tomatoes or 2 cups diced fresh tomatoes

» 4 ounce can tomato sauce

» 2 cloves garlic, minced

» 1 teaspoon oregano

» 2 teaspoons basil

» ½ teaspoon crushed red pepper

1. Put on a large pot of water to boil for the spaghetti.

2. Make the meatballs: combine the beef, egg, starchy bits, onion, garlic, parsley, salt and pepper in a bowl. Mix with your hands until the onion pieces are evenly distributed. Form into 1½" balls, about the size of golf balls. You'll probably get around 12 balls.

3. Heat the oil in a skillet over high heat and brown the meatballs, turning once or twice. When they are well browned, add ½ cup red wine and cook until it is nearly evaporated.

4. Add the other sauce ingredients. Cover and turn heat to low. Simmer 20 minutes.

5. Cook your spaghetti while this is simmering. When it is al dente, drain and return to the pot. Serve with meatballs and sauce.

Serves 4–6, depending on appetites and whether there's salad first.

Eggplant Parmesan

I like to make this in individual servings by baking it in small ceramic dishes. You very likely do not have any small ceramic dishes, so just make it in whatever size casserole or cake pan you have. If you want to get fancy, cook up some spaghetti to serve this with. Put on your pasta water to boil when you put it in the oven; it will time out just right to have the noodles and eggplant done at the same time. Or make garlic bread. Or make hot hoagies out of it. Yum!

- » 1 eggplant (about 1 pound)
- » 2 eggs
- » 2 tablespoons flour, white or whole wheat
- » ¼ cup olive oil
- » 1½ to 2 cups tomato sauce (see recipe for *Marinara Sauce, p. 186* or buy a jar)
- » ½ cup grated parmesan cheese (4 ounces by weight, grated)

1. Wash and dry eggplant. Cut crosswise into ¼" thick slices, discarding stem and bottom ends. You will have 12–15 slices. Pat dry on a clean towel.

2. Beat eggs and flour together until smooth.

3. Heat half the olive oil over medium heat in a large skillet.

4. Dip eggplant slices in egg mixture and carefully lay in oil in a single layer. Fry gently (not too much bubbling or popping) about 5 minutes on each side until browned.

5. Arrange half the browned slices in a 9" x 13" dish.

6. Top with half the tomato sauce and half the cheese.

7. Brown the remaining eggplant slices, then layer on top of the cheese. Top with remaining sauce and cheese. Bake at 350° until bubbly, 20 minutes.

Makes 3 large servings, 4 if you serve with bread or spaghetti.

Vegetable Lasagna

This is the recipe I came up with when I was a High School Vegetarian. It's still good, and you don't even have to eff with boiling the noodles first. If you want garlic bread with this, get it ready while the lasagna is baking, then put it in the oven next to the lasagna for the last 15 minutes of uncovered cooking time.

Bonus Tip: *If you want to make a meaty lasagna, just follow these same directions but replace the tomato sauce with Meaty Sauce and replace the vegetables with a 10 ounce package of frozen spinach, thawed and drained or 1 pound of fresh spinach, washed and cut up.*

» 8 ounces lasagna noodles

» 28 ounce jar spaghetti sauce (or make the recipe for *Marinara Sauce, p. 186*)

» 1⅓ cup water

» 12 ounces ricotta cheese or cottage cheese

» ½ cup grated mozzarella

» ⅓ cup grated parmesan

» 1 egg

» 1 tablespoon fresh oregano and basil, each; or 1 teaspoon dried, each

» ½ teaspoon black pepper

» 1½ cups diced summer squash (yellow, pattypan, or zucchini)

» 1 small tomato, diced

» ½ cup diced red bell pepper

1. Combine sauce and water in a large pitcher or bowl.

2. In another bowl, mix ricotta, mozzarella, half the parmesan, the egg, oregano, and basil; combine well.

3. Lightly oil a 9" x 13" baking dish. Pour in about a cup of the tomato sauce/water. Lay 3 lasagna noodles (uncooked) over that. Spread half of the cheese mixture over them, then half the mixed vegetables. Pour another cup of sauce over that.

6. Make one more layer of noodles, cheese, vegetables, sauce. Pour last of sauce over top layer and sprinkle with remaining parmesan.

7. Cover with foil and bake at 350° for 45 minutes. Remove foil (carefully!) and cook 15 minutes longer.

8. Let stand at least 10 minutes before serving.

Makes 6–8 servings.

CHAPTER 10

June Cleaver Cooking

Okay, maybe now you are ready to try some multi-course meals. Like, a meat and two sides that all have to be ready at the same time!

Exciting!

Here are four pre-planned meals, complete with sides, detailing what you should be doing at any given moment. Make sure you have a functioning kitchen timer or something you can use as such. This symbol ✳ will alert you when it's time to multi-task or pause one recipe to attend to another.

All of these are meant to serve four people of average appetites. If you need to stretch it a little to feed five or six, add some cheese and crackers before the meal or an extra salad or even make a dessert ahead of time!

That would really be something!

Practice on these menus a couple of times until you feel like you've got the hang of timing courses. Mostly what "getting the hang of it" means in this frame is practicing multi-tasking in your brain-space. Take the pressure off yourself and just try making one of these for yourself and a close friend the first time. Once you've done it once, try it again with a couple more guests. Soon, it will seem easy.

When you're ready to come up with your own menus, here are a few things to keep in mind:

Simplify. You don't need to make every single thing fancy and complicated. Indeed, you will be more relaxed (therefore, a better host) if you keep your focus on the entree and make the other dishes fairly simple.

Make it pretty. Think about colors when planning what you will make. A plate full of beige food is unappealing. A plate full of brown, green, and yellow however is a thing of beauty. Learn to appreciate the beauty of color. (Not to mention the antioxidants!) Easy things you can add at the last minute to brighten a bland-colored plate are roasted red bell peppers sprinkled with a little olive oil and minced garlic; a bright sauce like pico de gallo or cranberry sauce; even a couple store-bought pickles, olives, or marinated artichoke hearts can perk up a plate and add visual interest.

Avoid redundancy. Complimentary flavors are wonderful; similar flavors can work well; the same ingredients or textures over and over again throughout a meal get old. Don't serve a tomato salad with a tomato pasta dish; Don't serve a fondue appetizer when the main dish is macaroni and cheese. You get the idea.

MEATLOAF DINNER

MEATLOAF, POTATO BAKE, GREEN BEANS AMANDINE

Meat and potatoes is a classic for a reason. Here we have a basic meatloaf recipe and a potato casserole which I think is a bit better for beginners since mashed potatoes don't "hold" as well in the case that your timing gets off a little. And if your guests run late, don't stress too much. Meatloaf and potato bake will both stay hot enough if you cover them with foil and the green beans can be cooked at the last minute once everyone has arrived.

Gameplan: You should be able to get this together from start to finish in an hour and a half, so plan to start cooking about 90 minutes before you want to serve dinner.

1. The first thing to do is get started on the meatloaf and put that in the oven. Then you have 40 minutes to get the potatoes together and ready to go into the oven.

2. Add the potatoes to the oven for the last 20 minutes of the meatloaf cooking, then wash and prepare the green beans.

3. When it's time, pull the meatloaf out to rest and turn the oven off, but leave the potatoes in there to keep warm.

4. Cook the beans while the other things hang out.

Learn to Cook

Meatloaf

This is essentially a giant meatball. If you need to stretch it to feed 6, add another egg and another cup of "filler" or more finely chopped vegetables. Some recipes use a mixture of ground beef and ground pork or ground beef, pork, and veal. You can try either of those if you like. Everything else remains the same. If you want to serve more people with this plan, double all the ingredients and form into two loaves. The cooking time will still be about an hour.

» 1 pound ground beef

» 1 egg

» 1 cup oatmeal, bread crumbs, cracker crumbs, Rice Crispies, or cornflakes (this is what's known as "filler")

» ½ cup minced onion

» 2 cloves garlic, minced (2 teaspoons)

» 1 teaspoon salt

» 1 teaspoon pepper

» ½ cup chopped fresh parsley (or fresh spinach, no problem)

» Optional thingies: ½ cup grated carrot or zucchini, ½ cup minced bell peppers, ¼ cup ketchup for slathering atop

1. Turn the oven to preheat for 350°. Get out a loaf pan or a cookie sheet and have it at the ready.

2. Put the meat in a big bowl. Add the egg, "filler," onion, garlic, salt, pepper, and parsley. Also add any other chopped vegetables you want to add. Wash your paws well and then use those to mash everything around well. Make "squoosh" sounds with your mouth while you do it for added enjoyment.

3. Once everything is well combined, plop it into the loaf pan or onto the cookie sheet. If you use a loaf pan, smooth the top out nice-like; if you use a cookie sheet, shape the blob into a shape reminiscent of a loaf. Wash your hands and put it in the oven.

4. It needs to bake for one hour total, but for meal-timing purposes, set your timer for 40 minutes, which is the point at which you'll spread the top with ketchup if you like and put the potatoes in to bake.

Learn to Cook

② Potato Bake

This is very similar to scalloped potatoes, but without having to make a white sauce first. It's faster, and you save washing a pot. Pretty badass combo. This serves 4 people, but can easily be doubled to serve 8 (just use a 9" x 13" cake pan instead).

> » 1 pound potatoes (about 4 small russet potatoes)
> » 1 tablespoon butter (for the pan)
> » 1 cup grated cheddar or jack cheese
> » 1 cup cottage cheese
> » ½ teaspoon black pepper
> » 1 tablespoon chopped parsley
> » paprika

1. Wash the potatoes well and poke them a few times with a fork; four stabs per potato is sufficient. Microwave the potatoes on a plate for 8–10 minutes until soft. Let them cool a few minutes or you will burn yourself. Peel them now if you want to; I don't, but I never have company over. Slice potatoes about ¼" thick.

2. Butter a 1.5–2 quart casserole or a square cake pan. In another bowl, combine cheeses with pepper and parsley. Layer potatoes and cheese in dish, beginning with potatoes and ending with cheese. Sprinkle with paprika.

3. This needs to bake for 20 minutes.

✳ ***Put the potato bake in the oven when the 40-minute timer for the meatloaf dings. Set the oven for another 20 minutes.** (This is when you should spread ketchup on the meatloaf, too, if you like that.)*

While that cooks,
start on the green beans:

197

Learn to Cook

Green Beans Amandine

- » ½ pound fresh green beans
- » 2 tablespoons olive oil or butter
- » ¼ teaspoon salt
- » ⅓ cup sliced or slivered almonds
- » 1 tablespoon lemon juice

"Resting"

You'll come across this a lot in recipes about meat. "Let it rest". The reason for doing this, as opposed to slicing right into whatever meat thing you just cooked (steak, roast, meatloaf, et al), is to let the juices calm down a little bit so they don't spray all over the place in a hot fury like so much magma when you break the surface. Just let it cool for 10 minutes. Then slice it and serve.

1. Rinse the beans in a colander. Snap the ends off the green beans and discard them.

✳ ***Stop now until you take the meatloaf out of the oven.***

2. Once the meatloaf is out and resting (see sidebar) and the potatoes are staying warm in the oven (which is now turned off), continue.

3. Heat the oil or butter in a large skillet over medium-high heat for 30 seconds or so.

4. Saute the beans for about 5 minutes, then add salt and almonds and saute another 5 minutes until the green beans are tender and the almonds are toasted.

5. Stir in lemon juice.

4 Serve your meal at once and please pass the ketchup!

Learn to Cook

ROASTED CHICKEN DINNER

CHICKEN, RICE PILAF, ROASTED ASPARAGUS

{ *A nice thing to serve if your grandma is coming for dinner one spring evening.* }

Gameplan: *Depending on the size of the chicken, a novice can expect to have this meal done in an hour and a half to two hours from start time.*

1. Get your chicken in the oven. That's gonna give you at least an hour of time to wash up, get the rice going, and prep the asparagus. No problem.

2. Start the rice about 20 minutes before the chicken is done.

3. The asparagus roasts quickly while the chicken rests; the rice stays hot enough in its pot as long as you leave the lid on.

   Voila. Everything is done at the same time.

Roasted Chicken

Roasted chicken is super easy and very economical if you can manage to not eat the whole thing at once. Use leftovers for chicken salad or chicken fried rice or chicken divan. One thing: don't stick a cold-ass chicken right from the fridge into the oven. Let it sit out at room temperature for at least 1 hour before cooking. Putting a cold chicken in the oven is a sure way to end up with a brown-on-the-outside-raw-on-the-inside chicken. Yuck.

» 1 whole chicken (3–4 pounds, take note of the weight because it determines the cooking time)

» 4 sprigs rosemary, oregano, thyme, or sage (a "sprig" is about 3" long, FYI) or 1 lemon

» 2 tablespoons butter or olive oil

» 1 teaspoon salt

» 1 teaspoon pepper and/or paprika

» 1 large onion, cut into ½" slices

1. Have your chicken out at room temperature. Preheat the oven to 425°. Put the onion slices in the bottom of a shallow roasting pan or a 9 x 13 cake pan.

2. Check inside the chicken and make sure there's not a bag of giblets in there; if there is, toss that out. Pat the outside dry with a paper towel.

3. Put the sprigs of herbs inside the cavity. If you use a lemon, cut it in half and squeeze it in there, then toss in the rind, too.

4. Rub the skin with butter or oil and sprinkle with salt and pepper.

5. Tie the legs together with cotton twine or just tuck them under the bird.

6. Place the bird breast side up in a roasting pan, on top of the onion slices.

7. Roast 20 minutes per pound, 1 to 1 ½ hours total depending on the size of your bird. (It's done when a thermometer reads 180° F in the thigh or when the juices that run when you poke between the leg and the breast with a fork are clear, not pink. Let the chicken rest 15 minutes before carving. You'll cook the asparagus while it's resting.)

Take 20-30 minutes now to clean up a little, then start on the rice pilaf.

② Rice Pilaf

Rice pilaf is easy to make and goes with pretty much everything. Feel free to add a few pinches of any herb or spice you like. Just make sure that the herbs and spices you use will compliment the ones you used in the chicken (check the chart!).

- » ¼ cup chopped onion
- » ¼ cup chopped celery
- » 2 teaspoons butter or oil
- » 1 cup white rice
- » ½ cup peas
- » 1 clove garlic, chopped
- » 1 bay leaf

- » ½ teaspoon salt
- » 1½ cups chicken broth, vegetable broth, or water
- » Garnish with: ¼ cup chopped toasted almonds or other nuts; ¼ cup chopped parsley

1. Saute the onions and celery in the butter or oil over medium-high heat for 10 minutes, stirring frequently, until lightly browned.

2. Add the rice and saute 5 more minutes to lightly toast the rice and get it all covered in butter.

3. Add the peas, garlic, bay leaf and any other seasonings and the broth.

4. Bring to a boil, stir, cover, and turn down heat simmer for 15 minutes. When it's finished, turn off the heat but leave it covered so it'll keep warm.

While that simmers, prepare the asparagus... or, to use the latin, preparagus:

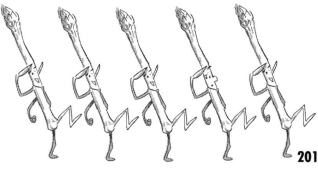

201

③ Roasted Asparagus

Or green beans or okra. They all look the same in the oven. Best thing: if your timing gets off, roasted vegetables are also good at room temperature.

- » 1 pound asparagus
- » 1 tablespoon olive oil
- » 1 tablespoon parmesan cheese or 1 teaspoon lemon zest or both!

1. Give the asparagus a rinse. Break or cut off the butts of the asparagus stalks (the whitish or brownish end).

2. Lay the asparagus on a baking sheet in a single later and drizzle with olive oil. Toss around delicately with your hands to get them coated in the oil. Set aside until the chicken is done.

* When the chicken is cooked, remove it from the oven to rest and turn the heat on the oven up to 450°. Roast asparagus for 10-15 minutes.

Sprinkle the asparagus with cheese and/or lemon, carve the chicken, and serve it all UP!

Carving

Start by sharpening your knife, oh, and roasting a chicken. Grab a leg and jiggle it; you should be able to see where the joint lies under the skin. Holding the leg with one hand and pulling it away from the rest of the chicken, cut through the skin to reach the thigh joint. (This is not for the faint of heart or queasy of stomach.) Separate the drumstick from the thigh by cutting through the joint; if your knife is in the right place it should be fairly easy.

Now cut through the skin along the line where the breast and thigh join. It should be easy to cut in the joint, separating the bones.
Now the breasts: Locate the center breast bone that runs along the chicken and using that as a guide, cut along with the tip of your knife, making short strokes from butt to wing end. Then follow the curve of the wishbone down towards the wing. Use your hands to pull the breast meat away and continue making small cuts to separate it from the body. Now you have a big, boneless breast that you can slice crosswise. Cut the wings off now, too. (For turkey, you will want to slice the meat off the drumsticks, too. Just hold it upright and slice parallel to the bone.)

FISH DINNER

PAN FRIED FISH, OVEN FRIES, COLESLAW

{ *This is kind of like fish 'n chips from Ye Olde England, but healthier because it's not all deep fried, and I threw in some coleslaw for good measure.* }

Gameplan: You should be able to get this meal together in under 45 minutes.

1. Make the coleslaw and put it in the fridge (this is one reason why salads are so great as sides because you can make them in advance). Make some Secret Tartar Sauce, too (see Chapter 8) and refrigerate that.

2. Cut up the potatoes and put them in to bake. Set a timer for 10 minutes.

3. During those 10 minutes, bread your fish and set aside.

4. Flip the potatoes and set the timer for another 20 minutes. Start cooking the fish 10 minutes before the potato timer goes off.

5. Everything will be ready within 5 minutes of everything else, and you will be so proud.

Learn to Cook

① Coleslaw

No mayonnaise bullshit, this slaw will actually keep quite well overnight if you wanted to make it that far ahead of time.

- » 3 cups finely chopped or shredded cabbage (half a small head)
- » 1 stalk celery, thinly sliced
- » 1 carrot, grated
- » 2 tablespoons cider vinegar, red wine vinegar, or white vinegar
- » 2 tablespoons canola oil, olive oil, or vegetable oil
- » 1 teaspoon mustard
- » 1 clove garlic, minced (1 teaspoon)
- » 1 teaspoon black pepper
- » ¼ teaspoon salt
- » Optional: 1 canned chipotle pepper ("chipotle en adobo"), minced (makes it hot and smoky)

1. Mix everything together and set aside in the refrigerator to mingle.

Make Secret Tartar Sauce and put it in the refrigerator.

Start on the potatoes:

Oven Fries

Not as greasily-delicious as French fries, but heartier and neater. Also less temperamental. It's pretty hard to overcook these. Serve with steaks or fried fish.

- » 1 pound Russet potatoes (about 4 small ones), red potatoes, or sweet potatoes for a change
- » 2 tablespoons oil
- » 1 teaspoon salt
- » 1 teaspoon pepper
- » Optional Jazzifiers: ½ teaspoon oregano, coriander, chili powder, or dill; ¼ teaspoon cayenne pepper

1. Turn the oven to 450º.

2. Wash the potatoes well and dry. I leave the skin on, but you can peel them if you don't like potato skin. Cut each potato into about slices about ½" wide by ½" thick; the length is not important.

3. Put them on a cookie sheet and drizzle with oil and add salt and pepper. Use your paws to jumble them around so every wedge is coated. Put them in the oven.

4. Set a timer for 10 minutes

✳ ***Get the fish ready and breaded in that time.***

5. When the potato timer goes off, pull them out, flip them all over with a spatula and put them back in the oven for 20 more minutes or until the fattest wedge can be easily punctured with a small knife and the potatoes are browned.

✳ ***Cook the fish during this second half of potato cooking!*** *(If you need to hold them while you finish cooking the fish, just leave them in the oven (turned off now) for up to 10 minutes, and they will stay hot and crisp.)*

While those bake, work on the fish:

Learn to Cook

Pan Fried Fish

You can use any fairly firm white fish (not flounder and its ilk). I always use skinless fillets because fish skin weirds me out, but that's a personal decision between you and your fishmonger.

- » 4 fish fillets, around 6 ounce each, all roughly the same size and no more than 1" thick (tilapia, catfish, cod, mahi-mahi, etc.)
- » 1 egg
- » 2 tablespoons water
- » 1 cup bread crumbs, cracker crumbs, or cornmeal
- » ½ teaspoon salt
- » 1 teaspoon paprika
- » 3 tablespoons oil for frying
- » Lemon wedges

1. In a bowl large enough to fit one piece of fish, beat the egg and water together well. Combine the crumbs, salt and paprika on a plate. Dip each piece of fish in the egg to coat both sides; let any excess drip off. Dredge each side in the crumbs, patting the crumbs on to help them stick.

✳ Set the coated fillets on a plate to rest until after you have flipped the potatoes.

2. Once the potatoes have been flipped, turn a large skillet or griddle on high heat and add the oil.

3. Once hot, put the fish in gently and fry for 3 minutes. Flip carefully.

4. If the fillets are less than one inch thick, cook another 2–3 minutes until a fork slides in easily. If they are closer to an inch thick, turn the heat down to medium and cook another 5 minutes or so. (If you need to hold them while you wait for something, just leave them in the pan, uncovered, heat turned off, for up to 5 minutes.)

(5) Serve hot crisp fish and potatoes with cool coleslaw and tartar sauce and cold beers.

Learn to Cook

VEGETARIAN DINNER

STUFFED PEPPERS, BAKED GRITS, CARROT ARUGULA SALAD

{ *This is a gorgeous meal that everyone will like, vegetarian or not.* }

Gameplan: This might be the most advanced meal plan in the section because roasting and peeling peppers might be something you've never tried. It's easier than you think, and I'll bet you can get this meal together in an hour, even faster once you've got the hang of the peppers.

1. Make the salad and refrigerate it.

2. Start the grits and bake them while you roast and peel the peppers.

3. Get the filling made, peppers stuffed, and into the oven.

4. Have some wine and relax for a while.

5. Serve dinner. You're done.

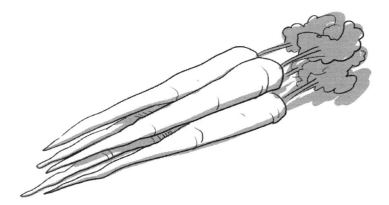

(1) # Carrot and Arugula Salad

Much better than the old mayonnaise thing that shows up at Luby's.

- » ½ pound carrots, grated or minced
- » ¼ cup sunflower or pumpkin seeds
- » 3 tablespoons lemon juice
- » 2 tablespoons olive oil
- » ½ teaspoon whole cumin seeds or ¼ teaspoon ground cumin
- » ½ cup minced parsley
- » ½ teaspoon salt
- » ½ teaspoon pepper
- » 1 bunch arugula, washed well and stems removed, torn into bite-sized pieces

1. Mix everything except the arugula and refrigerate for up to an hour. (You'll toss in the arugula at serving time.)

Next up: get ye to the Grits!

② Baked Grits

Get yellow grits if you can find them. Or you can use coarse-ground yellow corn-meal. Have patience when adding the grits to the water to prevent lumps.

- » 1 cup cornmeal or grits
- » 4 ½ cups water
- » ½ teaspoon salt
- » 4 tablespoons olive oil
- » ½ cup cooked beans (pinto, black, kidney)
- » 1 teaspoon oregano
- » Optional: ¼ - ½ cup grated Monterey Jack cheese

1. Preheat oven to 350º F. Grease an 8 x 8" pan.

2. Bring water to boil in a saucepan. Add the salt. Add the cornmeal, a handful at a time, sprinkling it over the water and stirring with a long-handled spoon after each addition.

3. When you are getting close to the end, it will start popping and bubbling like a cauldron (this is why you're using a long-handled spoon).

4. When it is all in, add 2 tablespoons of the oil, reduce the heat to low, and simmer 5 minutes, stirring frequently.

5. Turn off the heat and stir the beans and oregano.

6. Pour the grits into the pan. Drizzle with remaining 2 tablespoons of oil. Top with cheese if you want.

7. Bake 30 minutes (but they can happily bake for up to 45 minutes if you're running behind getting the peppers in the oven) .

Now get to work on the peppers:

Learn to Cook

Stuffed Peppers

If serving the very young or very old, you may want to use red bell peppers in place of the spicier poblanos.

» 4 large poblano peppers

» 1 sweet potato, about a pound

» ¼ cup raisins

» 1 tablespoon coconut oil or butter

» 1 tablespoon brown sugar

» ½ teaspoon salt

» Dash cinnamon (⅛ teaspoon)

» **Sauce:**

» 1 tablespoon oil

» ½ cup sliced onion

» 2 cloves garlic (2 teaspoons)

» 1 bay leaf

» 1 cup tomato sauce

» 1 cup water

1. Roast and peel the peppers (See next page).

✳ Prepare the sweet potato filling while they sit and cool off.

2. Peel and cube the potato and put into a pot with just enough water to cover. Bring to boil and cook 5–10 minutes until they are tender. Drain, mash, and mix with the raisins, coconut oil, sugar, salt, and cinnamon.

3. In a large skillet, sauté the onion in the oil until translucent.

4. Add the garlic and sauté until golden. Add the bay leaf, tomato sauce, and water. Simmer while you stuff the peppers:

5. Cut the peppers in halves lengthwise and remove the seeds and ribs. Fill each half with about ¼ cup potato filling.

6. Place the peppers in a 9 x 13" pan and pour the sauce over.

7. Bake for 10 minutes alongside the grits, just long enough to get them heated through.

Toss the arugula into the salad and serve everything at once!

Roasting Peppers

Roasting peppers softens them and deepens their flavor and allows you to remove the skin.

Hot peppers like poblanos and jalapeños can irritate your skin, though, so you may want to wear gloves when handling them. I hate wearing gloves myself, so I just end up with burny hands afterwards. My friend calls them "Hunan Hands." You needn't worry when peeling mild bell peppers, though.

To make your life better and more worth living, pick out the smoothest, least creviced peppers you can find; that will make peeling them much easier.

Method 1: Gas stove
Hold the peppers over a high flame for about a minute or two on each side until the skin is black and blistering. Use tongs to turn them.

Method 2: Broiler
Put the peppers on a baking sheet and put under the broiler for a minute or two. Turn them and broil the other side until they are black and blistering.

After roasting in one of those two ways, put the hot peppers in a paper bag, rolled closed, or a bowl with a plate over top. Let them sit and steam until they have cooled off, 10–15 minutes.

Now the skins will be loose enough that you can rub them off with your hands or a paper towel. Don't rinse the peppers or you'll be rinsing off all the toasty flavor!

Learn to Cook

CHAPTER 11

Side Dishes

Here you will find potatoes, salads, and things like that. Things that you could make to go with other things. Or things that you could just eat on their own and be the world's laziest vegetarian.

Plain Old Rice

The directions are on the package, but in case you think they might be lying ...

- » 1 cup rice
- » 2 cups water
- » Optional: ½ teaspoon salt and/or 1 tablespoon butter

1. Combine in a pot with a lid. Put over high heat. Bring to a boil.
2. Turn the heat down to the lowest setting.
3. Cook 15 minutes for white rice; 45 minutes for brown rice. Don't stir or take the lid off. Just leave it.
4. Turn the heat off when the timer dings and leave it alone until its time to eat. That is all.

Makes 2 cups cooked rice, which is 4 servings

Spanish Rice

Just another rice pilaf, really. But it goes well with Mexican food and it looks pretty and pink.

- » 1 cup white rice
- » 1 tablespoon butter
- » ½ cup thinly sliced onion
- » 1 bay leaf
- » ½ cup tomato sauce (or 1 small diced tomato)
- » 1 ½ cups chicken broth or water

1. Saute the onion and rice in the butter until the rice is slightly toasted.
2. Add the bay, tomato, and stock. Bring to a boil, reduce heat, cover and simmer 15 minutes.

Makes 3 cups cooked rice, or 4 servings.

Other Grains

Grains are easy. Pretty much just cook 'em like rice. Pretty much just put them in a pot with some water and a lid, bring to a boil over high heat, then turn the heat down to simmer until they are softened and the water has been absorbed. Start your timer as soon as the pot has come to a boil and you have turned it down to simmer. See Chapter Four for descriptions of some grains you may not be familiar with. It'll be fun to familiarize yourself with them and change up your usual side o' rice for a side o' something else.

For bulgur and couscous, you need put the grain into a pot of boiling water, turn the heat OFF, and let soak with the lid on for about fifteen minutes. Here's a handy chart for measurements and times.

GRAIN COOKING GUIDE

White rice	1 cup rice	2 cups water	Simmer 15 min	Makes 3 cups
Brown rice	1 cup rice	2 ¼ cups water	Simmer 45 min	Makes 3 cups
Wild rice	1 cup rice	2 cups water	Simmer 45 min	Makes 3 cups
Quinoa	1 cup quinoa	2 cups water	Simmer 10 min	Makes 2 cups
Bulgur	1 cup bulgur	2 cups boiling water	Soak 15–20 min	Makes 2 cups
Couscous	1 cup couscous	2 cups boiling water	Soak 10–15 min	Makes 2 cups

Learn to Cook

hilahcooking.com/
refried-beans

Refried Beans

Use black beans or pinto beans. You can make any quantity you like, just use about a tablespoon of oil per cup of beans and salt to taste. Nothin' like some smooth refried beans.

» Cooked beans, with liquid

» Oil

» Salt

1. Heat the oil in a skillet and add the beans.

2. Mash with a big spoon or potato masher. Taste for salt.

3. Mash some more until smooth.

Baked Potatoes

Begin with medium to large Russet potatoes and scrub them well to get any dirt off. Dry them with a cloth. Stab them a few times with a paring knife or a fork. Now you are ready to cook either:

In the microwave: Put them on a plate and microwave 7–10 minutes for one potato (15–20 minutes for 4), stopping half-way through to flip them over. If your microwave didn't come from a pawn shop, it probably has a button marked "potato" which is handy to use. Just hit that button and then enter the number of potatoes. They are done when a knife goes in easily.

In the oven: Preheat the oven to 350°. Rub the potatoes very lightly with oil and sprinkle with salt. Put on a cookie sheet and bake about 1 hour, until a knife inserted goes in easily.

Now they are baked. Pull them out and use a fork to poke a line of holes down the middle (this keeps them fluffier than cutting with a knife). Using a towel to protect your hands, give the top a little mash with your fist, then squeeze the potato on either end of the slit you made to open it up and fluff up the guts. Top with butter, sour cream, cheese, bacon, onions, broccoli, salsa, chili, or French fries (I kid!).

Mashed Potatoes

hilahcooking.com/
mashed-potatoes

Russet potatoes make the best mashed potatoes, but red or yellow potatoes will do fine. Mashed potatoes don't wait very well so if you are trying to time them out with another course, you may hold the boiled potatoes in their hot cooking water until ready to serve, then drain and mash with the cream and butter when you're ready.

- » 2 pounds Russet Potatoes
- » ¼ cup cream or half-and-half
- » 3–4 tablespoon butter
- » 1 teaspoon salt
- » 1–2 teaspoons pepper

1. Peel the potatoes if you desire peel-free mashed potatoes. I like peels.

2. Cover with water in a large pot and bring to a boil over high heat, covered. They are done when a knife easily pierces through. (Stop here if necessary for up to 15 minutes)

3. Drain the water and return the potatoes to the pot.

4. Heat the butter and cream and seasoning in the microwave or a small pot so that the butter melts.

5. Pour over potatoes and mash with a potato masher or with an electric mixer. Don't try to use a food processor because the potatoes turn sticky and gluey with too much speed.

Serve 4–6 people ASAP!

Learn to Cook

Steamed Broccoli

You can steam cauliflower this way, too. Both are delicious just with a little butter and salt, some lemon juice, a sprinkle of Parmesan cheese, or some garlic butter. For an extra special side, steam the broccoli until just bright green, then saute quickly with a couple tablespoons of butter and a clove of minced garlic. Yum!

- » 1 head of broccoli
- » Salt
- » Lemon juice and/or butter

1. Rinse the broccoli. You can cut off the big stem and toss it or slice it into ½" x ½" sticks and steam them, too, which is what I usually do. Cut the top part into florets. You want them all to be about the same size.

2. Put about a half inch of water in the bottom of a large pot (one with a lid) and put a steamer basket on top. Put the broccoli in the basket, stems on the bottom if you're using them.

3. Put the pot over high heat and cover it; listen and watch for it to boil. Steam will come out around the lid. Reduce the heat a little bit and let it steam for 5 minutes.

4. Check it. If it's bright emerald green, it's ready.

Serves 4-6

Frozen Vegetables

I'm gonna be real with you. Frozen vegetables actually have instructions on how to cook them, right there on the package! But the general rule is to bring the water to a boil, then add the vegetables, put a lid on the pot and boil or simmer for about 5 minutes (more like 15 for lima beans and black-eyed peas). All I will tell you to do is to drain most of the water off before adding salt and pepper and butter or oil. Yum yum. And figure a serving is about a half-cup vegetables per person.

Sauteed Collard Greens

Or any greens: kale, chard, mustard, turnip. This is my favorite way to cook them. Still firm, not overcooked, not oversalted. Just perfect.

- » 1 bunch of greens
- » 1 clove garlic, minced (1 teaspoon)
- » 1 tablespoon olive oil
- » ¼ teaspoon salt (maybe more)
- » 1 tablespoon balsamic, red wine, or cider vinegar
- » ½ teaspoon crushed red pepper flakes

1. Wash the greens and cut or tear them into 1" pieces.

2. Heat the oil in a large skillet over medium-high heat. Add the garlic and cook it for 30 seconds or so.

3. Add the greens and salt and toss around. They won't fit at first, but as they cook, they will wilt. Just keep moving them around so the top layer gets down to the bottom.

4. When they have turned a fairly uniform shade of bright green, add the vinegar and red pepper.

5. Toss it around again and serve.

Serves 4

Fried Plantains

Plantains look like big, badass bananas, and in a way, they are. Their peel is thicker and tougher than a banana's, they can't be eaten raw, and they are harvested by Hell's Angels. They are an interesting fruit in that they go through several stages of ripening, changing from starchy and bland (green) to soft and sweet (black). They can be used in any stage with wonderful results. My favorite time to cook them is in their yellow stage, when they are just slightly sweet. You might need to use a knife to peel them. Cut off the ends first and use a paring knife or vegetable peeler to get all the fibers and skin off.

» 4 plantains, green to yellow

» 2 tablespoons butter or oil

» ½ teaspoon salt

» **Optional:** 2 tablespoons honey (for sweet yellow plantains);2 cloves minced garlic and/or chopped parsley or cilantro (for savory green plantains)

1. Peel the plantains and slice them on the diagonal, ¼" to ½" thick.

2. Heat the oil over medium heat. Add the plantain slices and saute about five minutes.

3. Stir and flip and add salt and either honey or garlic. Turn heat to medium-low.

4. Saute another 5 minutes, until they are browned around the edges and softened.

5. Sprinkle with parsley if you're using it.

6. Good with grilled meat, tacos, or as a dessert with ice cream (if you make them with honey).

Serves 4

Succotash

This is a great thing to do with frozen vegetables. Serve with glazed sweet potatoes and salad for a healthy and pretty vegetarian meal. It's also good with roasted chicken or for a barbecue.

- » 1 cup chopped onion
- » ½ to 1 cup chopped tomato
- » 1 tablespoon oil
- » 2 cloves garlic (2 teaspoons)
- » ½ teaspoon thyme
- » ½ teaspoon salt
- » 2 cups corn kernels (frozen or fresh)
- » 2 cups baby lima beans or blackeyed peas (frozen)
- » ¼ cup water

1. Saute the onion and tomato in the oil for about 5 minutes over high heat.

2. Add everything else, including the water. Put a lid on it and simmer 15 minutes.

Serves 4–6

Learn to Cook

Stuffed Tomatoes

These look fancier than they are. They are best with big, summertime tomatoes. If you wanted, you could probably serve these as a main dish, even, accompanied by a pasta salad or soup.

- » 4 large tomatoes (beefsteak or "slicing" tomatoes)
- » 1 clove garlic, minced (1 teaspoon)
- » 1 cup bread crumbs
- » 1 teaspoon lemon pepper
- » 1 teaspoon basil
- » 4 tablespoons olive oil
- » Optional: ¼ cup grated Parmesan cheese

1. Preheat oven to 400° F.

2. Cut the tops out of the tomatoes, cutting a cone-shaped wedge out to remove the stem and part of the center core. Scoop the seeds out.

3. Mix the rest of the ingredients together (including the cheese if you are using it) and stuff about a quarter of it into each tomato.

4. Set them on a baking sheet and bake for 15–20 minutes until they are soft and the breadcrumbs are toasted.

Serves 4

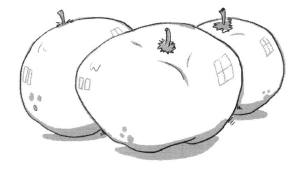

Maple Glazed Sweet Potatoes

A quick, braised sweet potato thing that goes well with chicken and pork dishes.

- » 1½ pound sweet potatoes
- » ½ cup water
- » 2 tablespoons maple syrup
- » ¼ teaspoon salt

1. Peel potatoes and cut into 1½" chunks.
2. Put them in a saucepan with the water and cover. Heat over medium heat until simmering. Cook over low heat about 15 minutes until soft.
3. Add maple syrup and salt. Stir to coat.

Serves 4

Orange and Red Onion Salad

This is totally a classic combo in Spain. Fancify your life.

- » 2 oranges
- » 1 grapefruit (or another orange if you're not keen on grapefruit)
- » ½ red onion, thinly sliced
- » 1 avocado, sliced or cubed
- » 1 tablespoon lime juice (about ½ lime)
- » ¼ teaspoon salt
- » ½ teaspoon pepper
- » Optional: handful of kalamata olives

1. Peel the oranges and grapefruit and cut into circles about ⅓" thick. Pick the seeds out with the tip of a knife.
2. Arrange among 4 plates, top with onion and avocado slices.
3. Sprinkle with lime juice, salt, and pepper. Top with olives if you like.

Serves 4

Green Salad, Wicked-Good

Just because it's green doesn't mean it's not delicious. This is a great salad dressing recipe that you can use on any kind of salad you throw together, or you can copy this salad exactly and claim all the credit for being a Salad Genius.

» ½ head Romaine lettuce, washed and torn

» 1 avocado, diced

» ½ red bell pepper, diced

» 1 small apple (Gala or Fuji work well), cored and diced

» Optional: sunflower seeds, pumpkin seeds, chopped walnuts

Worcestershire Dressing:

» ¼ cup Worcestershire sauce

» Juice of 1 lime (3–4 tablespoons)

» 2 tablespoons olive oil

» 1 tablespoon balsamic vinegar

» ¼ teaspoon dried oregano

» 1 teaspoon honey

» 1 teaspoon mustard

» 1 clove garlic, minced (1 teaspoon)

1. Combine dressing ingredients in a jar and shake well or whisk together in a small bowl.

2. Just before serving, drizzle 3–4 tablespoons of dressing over lettuce and sprinkle other salad ingredients over top.

Salad serves 4 people, but the leftover dressing will keep for at least 3 weeks in the refrigerator.

Learn to Cook

Spinach and Orange Salad

A classic and so pretty! The sweet poppy seed dressing would also be nice over apples. If you like, substitute 2 cans of mandarin orange segments, peeled, for the fresh oranges. If you also like, use any other salad dressing in this book.

» 1 bunch spinach, washed well (or a 1 pound bag of baby spinach)

» 4 oranges

» ½ red onion, sliced into thin rings

Poppy Seed Dressing:

» ¼ cup honey or maple syrup

» 3 tablespoons cider vinegar

» 2 teaspoons Dijon mustard

» 1 teaspoon poppy seeds

» 2 tablespoons olive or vegetable oil

1. Shake all dressing ingredients together or whisk in a small bowl.

2. For the oranges, peel them, and then cut crosswise into 4–6 slices so that each slice resembles a sunburst. Pick the seeds out with a knife or fork.

3. Arrange the orange slices and onion slices over the spinach and drizzle about half the dressing over it. Serve and pass the remaining dressing at the table.

Serves 4

Macaroni Salad

This is a classic, mayonnaise-y macaroni salad that goes with fried chicken in the park or a weenie roast on the beach. Watch for sand.

- » 12 ounces elbow macaroni
- » 1 bunch green onions, sliced thinly
- » 2 cups chopped celery
- » 1 cup cubed cheddar cheese (¼" cubes)
- » 1 pound ham, cubed
- » ½ pound frozen peas
- » ½ teaspoon pepper
- » ½ teaspoon celery salt
- » ¼ cup pickle relish
- » 3 cups mayonnaise
- » ¾ cup sour cream
- » 1 cup light cream
- » 3 tablespoons Dijon or brown mustard

1. Cook and drain macaroni.
2. Combine with other ingredients.
3. Refrigerate 6–8 hours.

Makes a ton. That's not very helpful. Serves 12 or more.

Potato Salad

Finally a use for those five-dollar-a-pound organic fingerling potatoes you've been coveting at the Whole Foods! What? You don't care for potatoes that cost more than gasoline? Oh, well, then by all means, use any waxy potato such as red or yellow new potatoes. Just don't come crying to me when that hippie girl with the pink dreads doesn't call you back.

» 2 pounds potatoes, all roughly the same size

» 2 cups sliced celery

» ½ cup sliced green onions

» 1 cup sliced or grated carrots

» 2–4 tablespoons vinegar

» 2–4 tablespoons olive oil

» 1 teaspoon salt

» 1 teaspoon pepper

» Optional: ½ cup mayonnaise

1. Boil whole potatoes until tender. Depending on the size, this may take 8–20 minutes.

2. Drain, cool slightly, and cut into 1" cubes.

3. Mix with vegetables and sprinkle with vinegar.

4. Add oil, salt and pepper and mix gently. Adjust vinegar and salt to taste.

5. Add the mayonnaise if you insist, but I like it without mayonnaise myself.

Serves 4–6

Learn to Cook

AND DON'T FORGET ABOUT:

From Chapter 7: Breakfast

From Chapter 8: Lunch

From Chapter 9: Dinner

From Chapter 10: June Cleaver Cooking

CHAPTER 12

Easy Breads

Everyone should have some easy breads under their belt. Here are a few to get you started.

Garlic Bread

Kind of cheating, since you start with bread already made, but it's just such an easy and fast thing to make to go along with any soup that makes it seem more fancy and meal-like.

- » Bread (you can use sliced sandwich bread, dinner rolls, or a French loaf, cut open)
- » Butter
- » Garlic powder
- » Salt

1. Preheat the oven or toaster oven to 350º F.
2. Smear one side of the bread with butter. Sprinkle with garlic powder and salt.
3. Pop that bread into the oven for 5-10 minutes until the butter is melty and the bread is toasty. Mmm.

Cornbread

Without cornbread, chili would just be a big bowl of nothin'. Okay, not exactly, but try this with your chili next time and see if you don't kind of agree a tiny bit? A cast iron skillet here will really make it, too. By preheating the skillet with the butter melted in it before adding the batter, you end up with a super-crisp crust, which is a delight.

- » 1 cup corn meal
- » 1 cup whole wheat flour (or white flour)
- » 2 teaspoons baking powder
- » ½ teaspoon baking soda
- » 1 egg
- » ½ cup yogurt + ½ cup milk (or 1 cup buttermilk)
- » ¼ cup molasses, honey, or maple syrup
- » 2 tablespoons butter

1. Preheat oven to 425° F.

2. Whisk together dry ingredients in a bowl. Mix together wet ingredients in another bowl or large measuring cup.

3. Melt the butter in a cast iron skillet (or square cake pan) by putting it in the oven while it heats.

4. Mix the wet ingredients into the dry ones.

5. Remove the pan from the oven (with oven mitts! It's hot in there!) and pour the batter in.

6. Bake for 20 minutes.

Cut into 6–8 wedges.

Vegan Carrot Muffins

Came up with this little wiz of a recipe myself. Make these to go with any soup or stew.

- » 1 cup cornmeal
- » 1 cup whole wheat or white flour
- » ½ teaspoon baking soda
- » 1 teaspoon dried parsley, dill, basil, or oregano
- » ½ teaspoon garlic powder
- » 1 cup tomato sauce or juice
- » 2 cups grated carrots
- » ¼ cup oil
- » ½ cup non dairy milk
- » 1 tablespoon cider vinegar

1. Grease a muffin tin or use paper liners. Preheat the oven to 425° F.

2. Combine the dry ingredients in one bowl, the wet in another.

3. Add the wet mixture to the dry and mix quickly. Lumps are inevitable, but make sure all the flour is moist. Spoon into muffin tins, filling ¾ of the way up.

4. Bake 20 minutes.

Makes 12.

Chapatis

I was truly mystified by these babies before an Indian lady told me how to make them. You should try them. Only two ingredients combine to make your generic "Indian curry" suddenly seem fit for Ganesh. Chapatis are thinner and denser than flour tortillas, but very similar. For new bakers, I recommend starting with these, then moving on to make flour tortillas.

- » 1 cup whole wheat flour (plus more later)
- » ½ cup water
- » More flour for rolling
- » 1 tablespoon oil

1. Combine flour and water in a bowl to make a stiff dough. Cover with a damp towel or plastic wrap. Set aside for 30 minutes to an hour to rest. If you skip this step, it will be almost impossible to roll out the dough because it will spring back like a rubber band and frustrate the shizz out of you.

2. When it is time, divide the dough into 6 equal portions.

3. Sprinkle your countertop with flour and roll each dough ball out very thin, ⅛" or less. Set aside.

4. Heat a cast iron skillet over high heat and put just a smear of oil down, ½ teaspoon or less.

5. When it begins to smoke, cook the chapattis one or two at a time (however they fit), for 30 seconds on each side.

6. Set the cooked chapatis on a plate.

7. When they are all done, toast them over the open flame of a gas stove or on the electric stove for a few seconds on each side.

8. Serve right away or spread with butter and wrap in foil to hold.

Makes 6

Flour Tortillas

hilahcooking.com/
how-to-make-tortillas

Homemade flour tortillas are mind-blowingly good. Don't kid yourself like I did the first time; there is a definite learning curve with these, but you'll get the hang of it after rolling out a few of them. And even the ugly ones taste delicious. I hope you try this. It's really rewarding when you finally get it.

- » 2 cups all-purpose flour (plus ½ to ¾ cup more for kneading)
- » 1 ½ teaspoons baking powder
- » ½ teaspoon salt
- » 2 tablespoons oil
- » ¾ cup milk or water, room temperature

1. Combine dry ingredients. Add oil and milk and mix into a soft dough. Turn dough out onto a floured surface and knead for two minutes.

2. You will need to add more flour a little at a time as you knead. After about a minute, the dough will change from very soft and squishy and easily torn to slightly firmer and stretchier. At the end of two minutes, it will be a smooth dough ball, no longer sticky, but elastic.

3. Cover the dough ball with a damp cloth and let rest for 30 minutes. This resting step should not be omitted—the resting allows the gluten molecules in the flour to align themselves perfectly to create a tender, chewy tortilla and makes it much easier to roll the dough into a circle.

4. After thirty minutes, come back and divide the dough into 12 equally sized balls. Easiest way is to divide in half, then divide each half again, etc. Put the balls on a plate and let them rest another ten minutes.

5. On a lightly floured surface, pat each ball out flat to start it, then with your floured rolling pin, roll into a circle (or as close as you can get it) 6 to 8 inches in diameter. Remember when rolling stuff out: start at the middle of the circle and push out to the edge. Keep going around until you have a circlish thing that looks like a tortilla.

6. Preheat a heavy skillet on high (cast iron only please).

7. When it's super hot, cook each tortilla one at a time, a minute on each side until it's speckled with brown spots. Eat as soon as possible!

Makes 12

Baking Powder vs. Baking Soda

There is much confusion around these two terms and rightly so. It really seems to me that someone should have come up with a more different name for baking powder. I still get them confused occasionally.

Baking Soda is pure sodium bicarbonate, which is a naturally occurring compound that not only is used to make baked goods rise, but also as an antacid to relieve heartburn, as well as a lightly abrasive cleaner and deodorizer. When in contact with a liquid plus acid it releases carbon dioxide, creating bubbles and making the dough rise. Baking soda, then, is called for in recipes which also contain an acidic ingredient (molasses, cocoa, juice, vinegar, etc.) with which it can react.

Baking powder is a mixture of baking soda, some acid, and some starch and was created for recipes which do not have acidic ingredients. Because it's got an acidic compound already in it, baking powder will still produce carbon dioxide when mixed into your batter. Double-acting baking powder reacts twice: once when it's moistened while mixing the dough and again when it's heated in the oven. I recommend buying baking powder marked "aluminum-free." To replicate baking powder, combine ½ teaspoon cream of tartar + ¼ teaspoon baking soda to equal 1 teaspoon baking powder.

CHAPTER 13

Desserts

Everyone needs a couple easy things they can bust out when necessary and get the people salivatin'. Here are those things.

Cobbler

hilahcooking.com/
peach-cobbler

A Southern delicacy, you can make this with any soft, ripe fruit (peaches, pears, nectarines, apricots, plums) or berries of all sorts. Or mix it up with a fruity medley. If you want to use frozen fruit, you can thaw it first or throw it in there frozen and cook the cobbler an extra 10-15 minutes.

» 2 cups sliced fruit or whole berries

» ¼ cup sugar

» 4 tablespoons (¼ cup) butter, though my mama uses a ½ cup butter

» ¾ cup flour

» ¾ cup sugar (can be reduced to ½ cup)

» ¾ cup milk

» 1 teaspoon baking powder

1. Mix the fruit with the sugar and let it sit while you get the other stuff ready.

2. Turn the oven to 350º and put the butter in a two-quart baking dish. Put the dish in the oven while it's preheating to melt the butter.

3. Mix dry ingredients and add milk. Stir. It might be lumpy. That's okay.

4. When the butter is melted, take the pan out and pour in the batter.

5. Spoon the fruit and its juice on top.

6. Bake for 45–50 minutes. EAT IT. With … ice cream? You tell me.

Serves 4

Brownies

The best brownies you will ever eat, if you like chewy, fudgy brownies in your mouth. I've been making these since I was eight. They are impossible to "fudge" up; get it??! Frost them once cooled with the recipe below if you like frosted brownies. Personally, I think this recipe is rich enough without frosting.

- » 1 cup sugar
- » ½ cup butter (1 stick) softened at room temperature for an hour
- » 1 egg
- » 1 teaspoon vanilla extract
- » ½ cup flour
- » ½ cup cocoa
- » Optional: ½ cup chopped pecans or walnuts or chocolate chips

1. Preheat the oven to 350º. Grease an 8" x 8" baking pan.

2. Cream the butter and sugar together until light and fluffy looking.

3. Add the egg and vanilla and mix well.

4. Add the flour and cocoa and combine. Add any optional items now, too.

5. Spread into a greased 8" x 8" baking pan (the batter is very thick, do not be alarmed) and bake for 30 minutes.

6. Cut into 9 squares and serve warm or at room temperature.

Makes 9

Chocolate Frosting

This is a simple frosting that is just chocolate and cream. It's called a ganache.

- » ½ cup heavy cream
- » ½ cup semi-sweet chocolate chips

1. Heat the cream in the microwave or in a small pot until steaming.

2. Stir in the chocolate chips. Stir quickly until the chocolate is melted. Cool until it thickens enough to spread.

Makes about a cup, which is enough for a thick layer on an 8" x 8" cake.

Vegan Chocolate Cake

hilahcooking.com/
vegan-chocolate-cake

This cake is so moist and delicious, you won't even care that it's not giving you a heart attack. You can cut it into 4 or 6 pieces, but four people can easily eat the whole thing so you might just want to make another one.

- » 1 ½ cups flour
- » 1 cup sugar
- » 1/3 cup cocoa powder
- » 1 teaspoon baking soda
- » ½ teaspoon salt (optional)
- » 1 cup water
- » ¼ cup oil (or melted coconut oil for a coconutty flavor)
- » 1 tablespoon vinegar (cider, white, or wine vinegar)
- » 2 teaspoons vanilla

Glaze:
- » 2 cups sifted powdered sugar
- » 3-4 tablespoons orange juice, coffee, or water
- » 1 teaspoon orange zest, vanilla extract, or liqueur

1. Preheat oven to 375º. Grease an 8"x8" square pan and put some parchment paper on the bottom if you have it (if you don't, then plan on serving the cake directly out of the pan because it will be difficult to remove in one piece).
2. Sift the dry ingredients together. Whisk the wet ingredients together.
3. Add the wet to the dry and mix well.
4. Pour into the pan and bake 30 minutes or until a toothpick inserted in the center comes out clean. Cool.
5. Make the glaze by mixing the sifted sugar with 2 tablespoons of your liquid. Add the teaspoon of flavoring and mix well. Add up to another tablespoon of your liquid to make a smooth glaze.
6. Pour over cooled cake and serve right away or the next day.

Serves 4-6

FRUIT DESSERTS

These are classy as shit and healthy, too. People will think you just came back from Spain or somewhere fancy like that.

1. Bananas, peeled and sliced, sprinkle with fresh lime juice and powdered sugar. My dad made this when I was a kid, and his grandma made it for him when he was a kid. It tastes all tropical.

2. Strawberries, hulled (de-stemmed) and halved, topped with orange liqueur or fresh orange juice and whipped cream. Or strawberries topped with sour cream and brown sugar. Decadent, dudes.

3. Thawed, frozen cherries or blackberries, drizzled with sweet red wine and sprinkled with brown sugar

Fruit Compote

Nice to serve in the wintertime with some fresh cream poured atop or alongside sugar cookies. Also really nice for breakfast, with or without oatmeal underneath.

> » 1 pound dried fruit (cherries, apricots, apples, pears, peaches, figs)
> » 3 cups water
> » 1 teaspoon minced ginger or lemon or orange zest
> » ½ cup sugar
> » Optional: 1 tablespoon brandy, rum, or whiskey

1. Cut any big fruit into bite-sized pieces.

2. Put the fruit, water, and ginger or zest in a saucepan and bring to a simmer over medium heat. Cover and simmer, stirring occasionally, 20 minutes until the fruit is soft. Depending on how dry the fruit is to begin with, you may need to add more water and cook a little longer.

3. Add the sugar and simmer another 5 minutes, stirring to dissolve.

4. Add the optional booze and simmer another 5 minutes. Serve warm or at room temperature.

Makes about 3 cups, which will serve about 6 people

Lemon Ginger Sugar Cookies

If you want plain sugar cookies, you can leave the lemon and ginger out, replacing them with 1 teaspoon vanilla extract. But it is good in there.

» ½ cup (1 stick) butter, softened

» ¾ cup sugar

» 1 egg

» 1⅓ cup flour

» ½ teaspoon baking soda

» ½ teaspoon ground ginger

» 1 teaspoon lemon zest

» ½ cup chopped candied ginger

1. Preheat oven to 375º.

2. In a large bowl, cream butter, sugar, and egg until well combined.

3. Sift in the flour, baking soda, and ginger and stir together. Add the zest and candied ginger and combine.

4. Grease a cookie sheet and drop the dough on by teaspoons, about an inch apart from center-to-center. Bake for 10–12 minutes.

5. Cool on the sheet for a few minutes, then remove to a plate with a spatula.

Makes about 24 cookies.

Mexican Wedding Cookies

I make these at Christmas because they are easy and cute. They look like snowballs and since I live in Central Texas, they are about the closest we ever get to seeing snowballs.

- » ½ cup (1 stick) butter, softened
- » ¼ cup powdered sugar
- » 1 teaspoon vanilla extract
- » ½ cup pecans, minced
- » 1 cup flour
- » Extra powdered sugar, up to ½ cup (for rolling the cookies in after they are cooked)

1. Preheat oven to 350°. Grease a cookie sheet.

2. Cream butter and ¼ cup sugar together until well blended.

3. Add vanilla, pecans, and flour; blend. Use your hands if necessary to get the flour incorporated and the pecans distributed.

4. Roll the dough into small balls, about a tablespoon of dough each, making balls about an inch across. Set on the cookie sheet about an inch apart, center-to-center.

5. Bake 12–15 minutes until the bottoms are just light brown. The tops should still be white.

6. Cool on a rack for 10–15 minutes.

7. Roll in the extra powdered sugar and store in an airtight container.

Makes about 30 cookies.

Learn to Cook

Baking with Butter

Soft (or "softened") butter is what you'll use in most cookie, cake, quick bread recipes, some frostings, and pretty much any recipe which directs you to cream the butter or "cream the butter and sugar together." The reason for creaming the softened butter is to incorporate air into it, and therefore into the batter, to create a light and tender final product with a good rise.

Softened butter means room temperature butter, and it is best gotten to that temperature slowly. If you have the time and forethought, leave your butter out on the counter at room temperature for 30–60 minutes before you begin your recipe. If you forget, place the still wrapped stick of butter in a bowl of warm water for 5 minutes. When it's soft enough, it will be easy to cut with a butter knife. Once your butter is softened, place it in a mixing bowl and use a hand mixer (with the standard beaters) or stand mixer (with the paddle attachment) on medium-high speed to beat it until it looks creamy, slightly paler in color, and slightly more voluminous; it will take 1–2 minutes. This can also be done by hand with a wooden spoon and a lot of elbow grease.

Now you can add in the sugar if the recipe directs and continue to beat until it's even paler and fluffier. Cake and cookie recipes will usually call for granulated or superfine (caster) sugar whose microscopic crystalline edges serve to further break the butterfats up and help incorporate even more air to make a light cake.

CHAPTER 14

Food to Impress People

Here are some things you can make to take to a potluck or a picnic or a pool party. We've got side salads and appetizers—all of them are party-friendly meaning they travel well and can be made ahead of time in some respect or sit out perfectly well on a buffet table. People will go ape-shit over these, even though it hardly took you any effort. There may be some new ingredients to buy, but nothing too foreign or fancy.

Quinoa Salad

hilahcooking.com/
quinoa-salad

This uses quinoa, which is a high-protein grain that cooks quickly and has the added benefit of looking like teeny-weeny sea shells. It's really cute! If you can't find quinoa substitute bulgur wheat or cooked brown rice. If you want to make this ahead of time, cook the quinoa, make the dressing, and cut up the vegetables but wait until serving to mix all together, otherwise the vegetables will lose their crunch.

Salad:

» ¾ cup quinoa

» ½ cup thinly sliced green onions (about 6 onions)

» 1 cup sliced radishes

» 1 stalk celery, thinly sliced

» 1 cup cucumber chunks, ½" cubes (about 1 small cucumber)

» ½ cup chopped cilantro leaves

Ginger Dressing:

» 4 tablespoons oil

» 2 tablespoons lime juice

» 1 tablespoon rice wine vinegar (unseasoned) or cider vinegar

» 1 teaspoon minced grated ginger (a ½" chunk, peeled and grated)

» 1 teaspoon minced garlic (1 clove)

» ½ teaspoon honey

» ¼ teaspoon salt

1. Soak the quinoa in water to cover for 15 minutes. Drain in a fine sieve, or lacking that, lay a paper towel or some cheesecloth in the bottom of your colander. The grains are very small and will slip through the holes on most colanders.

2. Put the soaked quinoa in a pot with 1 ¼ cups water. Cover, bring to a boil, then immediately reduce heat to simmer. Simmer for 20 minutes. Remove from heat and cool.

3. While it is cooking, mix your dressing ingredients together in a jar. Shake well.

4. Cut up the vegetables and put them in a bowl.

5. Add the cooled quinoa and dressing and mix gently. Taste and adjust salt if needed.

Serves 4–6 people.

Confetti Corn Salad

This salad is gorgeous, especially when compared to all the white foods on the potluck table. It's also free of mayonnaise, so it's lighter and less likely to go off when sitting in the sun for 3 hours. This version has an Asian angle, but if you'd like to keep it more traditional, leave out the ginger and sesame oil.

- » 2 cups corn kernels (canned or frozen for this)
- » 1 can black beans, rinsed and drained (1 ½ cups cooked)
- » ½ cup sliced green onions
- » ½ cup diced red bell pepper or orange or green (red is prettiest)
- » 1 cup diced cucumber
- » 1 clove garlic, minced (1 teaspoon)
- » ¼ cup minced cilantro
- » 1 jalapeño, minced (and seeded for less heat)
- » ¼ teaspoon ground ginger
- » 1 tablespoon sesame oil
- » 2 tablespoons olive oil or vegetable oil
- » 2 tablespoons rice vinegar, cider vinegar, red wine vinegar, or white vinegar
- » 2 tablespoons lime juice

1. Mix everything together and stick it in the fridge for 2 hours or up to 8 hours.

Serves about 8 people.

Learn to Cook

Baked Beans

If you have some time around the house before a potluck thing, make some slow-cooked beans and find out what the big deal is. You could make these a day or two before, and they will get even better. See page 161 for tips on cooking dried beans.

» 1 cup dry navy beans (½ pound)

» 3 cloves garlic, minced

» 1 chipotle pepper, minced (or use ½ for less heat)

» 2–3 tablespoons molasses or maple syrup

» ½ cup diced onion

» ½ cup diced bell pepper

» 1 tablespoon ketchup

» 1 tablespoon mustard

» 1 teaspoon vinegar

» 1 teaspoon ground ginger

» 1 teaspoon salt

1. Rinse beans in cold water and inspect carefully, removing any old, shriveled or funky beans and checking for small rocks. In a 5 quart pot, heat 8 cups of water and the beans over high heat until boiling. Cook 3 minutes. Remove from heat and cover. Let stand 1 hour. (Alternately, soak them in lots of water over night.)

2. Drain and rinse beans. Combine with all other ingredients plus enough water to cover.

3. Bring to a boil, reduce heat, cover and simmer one hour or until the beans are tender, adding water if necessary.

4. Taste and adjust for salt and sweetness. These keep well and even get better after a day or two in the refrigerator, just reheat before serving.

Serves 6

Learn to Cook

Mother-Hugging Guacamole

If you haven't ever had guacamole the way my real Mexican friends make it, meaning without a bunch of tomatoes and onions mucking things up, you are in for a real treat. You DO NOT need to put the pits into the bowl to prevent browning. That doesn't do anything except make it look unappetizing. "Who put this compost in my guacamole?" The browning happens for the same reason apples and pears turn brown: oxidation. The acid in the lime juice slows that process, but the only way to prevent it completely is to remove all air. You could slap some plastic wrap over the top, so it touches the guacamole and seals it, and that will keep it fresh in the refrigerator for up to 6 hours. Or just eat it all real quick.

- » 4 ripe avocados
- » 4 tablespoons lime juice (about 1 lime)
- » ¼ teaspoon salt
- » ¼ cup minced cilantro
- » 1–2 tablespoons minced jalapeño or serrano peppers
- » 1 clove garlic, minced (1 teaspoon)
- » Optional, if you insist on breaking my heart: ½ cup seeded, diced tomato and/or ¼ cup sliced green onions

1. Cut open the avocados and remove the pits. Scoop the meat out and into a bowl. Mash it up with a fork until it's pretty smooth.

2. Add everything else and mix well.

Makes about 3-4 cups, depending on the size of your 'cados. That would serve 12–16 people by US RDA serving size standards, but in real life maybe 8 people. I'm telling you, everybody loves guacamole. Except the people who really hate it.

Learn to Cook

Salsa!

Take homemade salsa to your next party and buy yourself free reign of the beer cooler. Bring some tortillas chips to serve with it, demonstrating to the world your marvelous thinking-ahead-and-preparing-for-everything skills! Turn this into Salsa de Fuego in a jiff by blackening the tomatoes and peppers under the broiler for a few minutes (like we did the poblanos in the stuffed peppers recipe) before blending. Be careful when blending hot things, as always.

hilahcooking.com/
how-to-make-salsa

- » 5 Roma tomatoes, chopped (seeded for a more refined salsa)
- » ¼ cup chopped onion
- » 1 clove garlic
- » 1–2 jalapeño or serrano peppers
- » 2–4 tablespoons lime juice
- » ½ teaspoon salt
- » ¼ cup cilantro, chopped

1. Chop everything coarsely. Seed the jalapeños for less heat.
2. Combine everything except cilantro in a blender. Whizz around until smooth. (If you want a chunkier salsa, you can mince everything by hand or use a food processor.)
3. Add a little more salt or lime juice, if necessary. Add cilantro.
4. Set aside for an hour to let the flavors blend. This well keep in a tightly closed jar in the refrigerator for up to a week.

Makes about 2 cups

248

Spinach Dip

This is pretty danged healthy and tasty as all get-out on some Triscuits. They didn't even pay me to say that! It gets better with time so if you can make it a day before, do. If not, don't sweat it too much.

- » 10 ounce box frozen chopped spinach
- » 1 cup sour cream or yogurt (full fat, low fat, or fat free Greek style yogurt)
- » 1 can water chestnuts
- » 1 teaspoon lemon pepper
- » ½ teaspoon garlic powder
- » ½ teaspoon dill
- » ½ teaspoon salt

1. Defrost the spinach by unwrapping it and microwaving it in a bowl for a couple of minutes. It should be soft enough then to break up into chunks. Get it all broken apart and put it into a colander.

2. Let it drain while you open and drain the water chestnuts. Finely chop the water chestnuts and put 'em in a bowl with the sour cream.

3. Mash the water out of the spinach as good as you can. Mash it hard.

4. Chop it up some more now. Add that and the seasonings to the sour cream. Mix it up good.

5. Refrigerate until serving time. Pass it with some crackers or chips or celery sticks.

Makes about 2 ½ cups, enough for 8–10 people to get their snack and munch on

Learn to Cook

SAUCES MAKE A DIFFERENCE

Sauces serve many purposes. They might add a complementary flavor or texture to the main dish to balance it out. Think about the classic pairing of a fat, succulent bratwurst with a sharp mustard that cuts the richness. Texturally, you might consider the combination of a sweet, sticky fruit chutney alongside salty, charred meats or a slick garlic olive oil on a crunchy crostini.

Sauces might also enhance a dish by matching its flavor, rather than contrasting. This is a little trickier to do; it works best when the main dish is mildly seasoned—think of baked chicken and chicken gravy or broiled white fish with anchovy butter melted over top.

Sauces are also a lifesaver to overcooked meats. A dry chicken breast or fish fillet becomes edible again with a pat of compound butter melted on top or covered in a cream sauce. That's not to say we should aim for overcooked as an excuse to make a buttery sauce, but it's a good trick to remember.

And of course, sauces also add visual appeal, as in shiny powdered sugar glaze on chocolate cake.

Basically what I'm saying is:

Sauces make things fancier than they were before. Learn to use them to your advantage.

Chimichurri

I'll start with a super simple, uncooked sauce that goes great over grilled, roasted, or baked meats and seafood and also goes well with boiled or roasted potatoes, steamed green beans and summer squash, and fresh sliced tomatoes. And, omigaw, it's stupendous on a simple cheese omelet. It's a spicy Argentinian sauce called Chimichurri and there are endless variations. The basic recipe is this:

- » ½ cup minced, packed cilantro or parsley (or a mix of both)
- » 6 tablespoons red wine vinegar
- » 2 tablespoons olive oil
- » 2 cloves garlic, minced (2 teaspoons)
- » ½ teaspoon dried oregano
- » ¼ teaspoon salt
- » ¼ – ½ teaspoon crushed red pepper flakes, depending on your taste
- » Optional: ¼ cup minced onion (white, yellow, red, or shallots)

1. Combine all ingredients and let stand at room temperature for at least 30 minutes and up to 2 hours before serving. This will keep refrigerated up to 48 hours.

Makes about ¾ cup of sauce

Some variations:

- » Substitute lemon, lime, or orange juice for the vinegar to make a citrusy sauce for seafood
- » With parsley, add a teaspoon of fresh thyme or mint for a sauce well-suited to chicken and lamb
- » Add a ½ teaspoon toasted cumin seeds for an earthy touch that goes even better with beef

Learn to Cook

Persillade

If you vary chimichurri far enough, you'll come to the land of persillade and gremolata, which are chopped herb condiments of the French and Italian persuasions, respectively. To turn this into gremolata, add a tablespoon of lemon zest.

- » ½ cup chopped parsley (flat leaf if you can get it; it looks prettier in this sauce)
- » 2 cloves minced garlic
- » 2–3 tablespoons extra virgin olive oil
- » ¼ teaspoon salt
- » Optional, if you like this sort of thing: 1 anchovy fillet, mashed

1. Combine the above and serve immediately atop cooked meats and fish or stir into bean or seafood soups just before serving to add a bright, clean flavor and a shot of color.

Makes about ½ cup

Compound Butter

You can flavor this with any herbs your heart desires and it keeps almost forever in the refrigerator. Throw a pat of this over any cooked meat to liven it up and add mouth-appeal. Also a great way to preserve fresh herbs.

- » 4 tablespoons (¼ cup) softened butter
- » 1 tablespoon minced fresh herbs or 1 teaspoon dried herbs
- » ⅛ teaspoon ground black pepper
- » ⅛ teaspoon salt, only if you're using unsalted butter
- » ½ teaspoon lemon zest (optional)

1. Mash all ingredients together in a small bowl.
2. Scrape mixture out onto a small sheet of waxed paper or plastic wrap. Form into a cylinder and wrap it up tightly.
3. Refrigerate until hardened and store wrapped in refrigerator until ready to use.

Makes about ¼ cup

Learn to Cook

Lemon Butter Sauce with Capers

This is what you would use to dip steamed lobster and boiled shrimp, but it has also been shown to make steamed vegetables two to three times more interesting that they were before. It would also compliment pan fried chicken breasts very well.

- » 4 tablespoons unsalted butter
- » 1 clove garlic, minced (1 teaspoon)
- » Grind of black pepper
- » Pinch of salt
- » 1 tablespoon fresh lemon juice (½ a lemon)
- » 1 teaspoon dijon mustard
- » 1 teaspoon capers, drained and chopped
- » Optional: ½ teaspoon minced fresh dill or parsley

1. Melt the butter over low heat and add the garlic. Allow it to sizzle gently for about 30 seconds (you don't want it to brown).

2. Remove from heat and whisk in the lemon juice and mustard until combined.

3. Add capers and optional herbs and serve.

Makes about ⅓ cup

Barbecue Sauce

Make your own barbecue sauce! Put it in a mason jar and fool people into thinking you are an accomplished cook out artist. This also makes a great, cheap "hostess gift" to bring when someone has invited you over for a barbecue. Just put it into a pretty jar and label it with a ribbon or something.

» 1 cup chopped onion

» 1 tablespoon oil

» 8 ounces tomato sauce

» 2 tablespoons light brown sugar

» ¼ cup cider vinegar

» ½ teaspoon ginger

» ¼ teaspoon allspice and black pepper, each

» ¾ teaspoon salt

1. Saute the onion in oil until translucent, about 10 minutes over medium heat.

2. Add everything else.

3. Cover and simmer 20 minutes. This keeps refrigerated up to two weeks. Store in a tightly closed jar.

Makes about 2 cups

Cranberry Sauce

hilahcooking.com/
homemade-cranberry-sauce

Way yummier than canned sauce. And prettier. And almost as quick. Volunteer to make this for Thanksgiving and it's all anyone will ever ask you to bring again. You're getting off easy.

- » 1 cup sugar
- » 1 cup water
- » ½ cup dried apricots or apples, chopped
- » ½ teaspoon ground cardamom or ginger
- » 2 tablespoons lemon juice
- » 12 ounces fresh or frozen cranberries

1. Combine sugar, water, dried fruit, spice, and lemon juice in a saucepan and bring to a boil over high heat.

2. Add the cranberries and simmer about 10 minutes until cranberries have 'sploded and spilled their guts out.

3. Remove from heat, cool, and refrigerate a couple of hours or overnight before serving.

Makes about 3 cups of sauce, serving 8–12 people

Variation: Cranberry Relish

An uncooked version of the recipe above, all you gotta do is put all those same ingredients (minus the water!) into a blender and whizz it around until finely chopped. Stick it in the fridge overnight. Serve.

Learn to Cook

CHAPTER 15

Snackies!

Snackies are a very important part of my life. I love snackies. Some people are not really snackers, and to them I say, how can you not love salty sweet popcorn and cheesy tostadas? That hurts my feelings. The best part about snackies is that they can also be your lunch. Or breakfast.

Popcorn

Please take the 5 minutes it requires to learn to make popcorn outside of a micro-wave. It's better tasting, better textured, and better for you. Plus, it makes you look like a badass. If you have a 4 quart or larger stock pot with a lid, use that and ½ cup kernels to make about 16 cups of popcorn. If you have a 2 quart sauce pot, use ¼ cup kernels to make 8 cups of popcorn. Some people will tell you that you have to shake it the whole time, but a nice South African lady told me once that shaking is unnecessary because the motion of the kernels popping keeps everything moving, and I think she was right. Mostly. I still shake it towards the end when the popping slows down.

> » ¼–½ cup popcorn kernels
> » 1–2 tablespoons oil (depending on the amount of popcorn popping. I almost wrote "pooping" — hehe!)
> » Sprinkle of salt
> » Optional: Tabasco sauce, 1–2 tablespoon melted butter, nutritional yeast, lemon juice

1. Heat the oil in your pot (one with a lid!) over high heat. Drop in 3 kernels of corn and put the lid on the pot.

2. When you hear the first kernel pop, pour in the rest of your popcorn and put the lid on. Let if go for a minute or so until you start to hear furious popping going on in there.

3. When the popping starts to slow down just a little, reduce the heat to medium-high to prevent to already-cooked corn from burning until it's all popped. Now is a good time to shake the pot a few times, too. Make sure to hold the lid on while you shake it.

4. Turn the heat off when the popping sounds have slowed to less than once per second. It should take 2–3 minutes before the popping stops.

5. Pour into a large bowl, sprinkle with salt, toss around and drizzle on the butter, yeast, lemon juice, or Tabasco (try it!).

Kettle Corn

This is like sweet, crispy clouds of heaven. You really should have a stock pot for this. The sugar gets sticky and burns easily in a small pot. You'll also need to shake it the whole time to keep the sugar moving.

- » ½ cup popcorn
- » 2 tablespoons oil
- » 2–4 tablespoons sugar (I prefer 2 tablespoons, but 4 makes it more like what you get at the mall)
- » Salt

1. Just like the popcorn recipe, heat the oil with 3 kernels to test.
2. Pour in the popcorn and immediately afterwards sprinkle the sugar over. Shake this time! You must shake or the sugar will stick to the bottom and burn and not be all over the popcorn like it's supposed to. Shake a lot.
3. It's done when it stops popping.
4. Sprinkle with a little salt for that sweet-n-savory thing.

Learn to Cook

Tostadas

You don't need to buy the premade, fried tostada shells if you have an oven or a toaster oven. Imagine that. Did I blow your mind just then?

» 2 corn tortillas

» ½ cup canned beans (whole or refried; of course you can cook your own beans, too)

» ½ cup grated cheese

» Assorted cold things: lettuce, tomato, onion, salsa, avocado, figure it out

1. Heat the oven to 350º and put the tortillas in there, right on the rack. Toast for about 3 minutes and check them.

2. Once they are fairly stiff, but not crispy yet, pull them out (Cuidado! They're hot!) and spread with beans and cheese and put them back in for about 2 more minutes.

3. They should be crispy and melty. Top with whatever and eat.

Quesadillas

These are what Tex-Mex restaurants call quesadillas. They go well with hangovers.

» 2 flour or corn tortillas

» ¼ cup grated cheese

» Other things: diced onion, bell pepper, cilantro, salsa, cooked sweet potatoes, beans, leftover meat

1. Put half the cheese on half of each tortilla along with anything else you want in there and fold it over to make a half-circle.

2. Cook in a dry skillet over medium heat until the cheese is melty. Flip it and cook more until toasted. Cut it into triangles, eat it and go back to bed. You could also use a microwave or toaster oven if you're feeling extra lazy.

Old White Lady Nachos

I invented this one night when I was ... how shall I say? Under the influence. The name made me laugh so hard and the "nutritional value" makes me laugh even harder. The measurements went out the window along with my pride as I scarfed this down, so just do what you think looks right. They always fucking rule.

» Potato chips (thick-cut, kettle chip types work best)

» Leftover pot roast or roast chicken, diced

» Grated cheese (American, pepper jack, mozzarella. Who cares!)

» Pickled jalapeño slices (Holy fuck. Or sweet pickles!? Yes.)

1. Lay out an even layer of potato chips on a baking sheet (Great time to use that toaster oven!).

2. Evenly distribute meat over the chips. Sprinkle with cheese and jalapenos.

3. Toast in the toaster oven until cheese melts or bake in the oven at 400º.

Learn to Cook

CHAPTER 16

Drinks

Here's a smattering of some alcoholic and non-alcoholic drinks. When mixing any cold drinks, please make them very cold. Chill all juices and boozes in the fridge or freezer first, and you won't have to water it down with a bunch of damn ice.

CLASSY DAY TIME DRINKING

For the obvious reason of "try every day not to get smashed before lunch" I keep my day-drinking limited to wines and beers, and I think that's the way the rest of the civilized world does it, too.

Champagne Drinks

Champagne (or, more common 'round these parts, "sparkling wine") makes for great light drinking before and after noon o'clock. These would be great to serve at a brunch or bridal shower. Make sure everything is well chilled beforehand and I find it works best to put the juice in the glass first, then pour the wine in gently. Don't stir or you'll ruin the bubbles.

Mimosa — Equal parts good orange juice and cheap champagne

Poinsettia — Equal parts cranberry juice and cheap champagne

Champagne Cocktail — 1 teaspoon sugar plus a dash of bitters in a champagne flute; slowly pour in cold champagne

Champagne "Plus" — Honestly I just made this name up. Anyway, try adding a half-ounce of cherry, currant, or elderflower liqueur to a glass of champagne and see what happens. (Good things, I promise.)

Michelada

The absolute best hangover cure in existence. Note: Since the first publication of this book, I've simplified my michelada recipe, and I like it better. The original version had ½ teaspoon Worcestershire sauce and ½ teaspoon liquid aminos (or soy sauce or Maggi sauce) instead of salt. Try it both ways and see what you like!

- » Equal parts salt and chili powder, mixed, for rimming the glass
- » ½ teaspoon Tabasco (or a similar hot pepper sauce)
- » ⅛ teaspoon salt
- » half a lime (2 teaspoons lime juice)
- » 12 ounces cold beer (lager or other light beer)

1. Rub the lip of a pint glass with the cut lime and then dip into the salt/chili powder mixture.
2. Put your flavorings in the glass and stir up.
3. Add ice if you like that (I do) and then slowly pour in the beer. It will foam up a LOT so have patience. Pour a little, let it settle, and repeat.
4. Adjust the seasoning with more lime or Tabasco as you see fit. Refresh

Sangria

Here's a delicious way to make cheap wine seem like fancy wine and a shitty party seem like a goddamn Caribbean cruise. It's pretty hard to screw this up so try experimenting and, if it turns out great, then you will have invented your signature sangria. Don't forget to write down what you put in it before you get drunk.

- » 750 milliliter bottle wine (red, white, pink—doesn't matter)
- » ½ cup juice (orange, apple, cranberry, grapefruit, or a combo)
- » ¼ cup fruit liqueur (limoncello, triple sec, anything) or brandy
- » 1 cup chopped fresh or frozen fruit (whatever you have around)
- » Optional: to stretch it, add up to a liter of club soda or Sprite

1. Mix everything in a large pitcher, chill and serve over ice.

NIGHTTIME DRINKING

Nighttime drinking differs from daytime drinking because it usually involves more hard liquor, karaoke machines, and a sudden drop in standards across the board. But your taste in drinking doesn't have to suffer.

Here are some basic guidelines for mixing cocktails:

1. Put the ice in the shaker first to chill it and chill the liquid as you pour it in; use about 5 ice cubes per drink.

2. Cocktails made with pure booze such as Martinis, Manhattans, and Gimlets are supposedly better if you stir rather than shake them. Use the shaker jar with ice to mix in and stir briskly.

3. Cocktails made with cream, eggs, sugar, or other ingredients besides booze should be shaken with ice. Shake as hard as you can for a count of ten.

4. Pour into a glass through a strainer; try not to spill it all over the place.

Martini

I'm talking about a real martini here, folks. It's not sweet, it's not pink, there's no syrups or sugar rims; it's just booze. You may use vodka or gin. "Dry" means use very little vermouth (less than this recipe even); "Sweet" means use sweet vermouth in place of dry vermouth; "Dirty" means put some olive juice in it. Personally, I like a dry, dirty gin martini.

> » 2 ounces gin or vodka
>
> » ½ ounce dry vermouth
>
> » Fat green olives (plus some of their juice for a dirty martini)
>
> » Ice cubes

1. Stir or shake the gin and vermouth (and olive juice) with ice.

2. Strain into a chilled glass and garnish with a big fat olive or two.

Mint Julep

Good golly, is this drink phenomenal! And not for the faint of heart. I hope you have a hammer and canvas bag in which to crush the ice properly. And a fresh mint patch just begging to be plundered. And a big white porch to drink this on.

- » Sprig fresh mint (5–6 leaves)
- » 1 teaspoon sugar
- » 2 ounces bourbon
- » Finely crushed ice

1. Crush the mint and sugar together in the bottom of a squatty 8 ounce glass with a spoon or a muddler or a souvenir baseball bat. Get the mint very bruised to release its mintyness.

2. Put some ice in a clean canvas bag or, lacking that, wrap a few cubes in a sturdy dish towel. Smash the holy living shit out of it with a hammer to pulverize the ice. Probably want to do this outside on concrete. Keep smashing. You're not done yet, smash some more. Does it look like snow yet? Keep smashing!

3. Finally, pack your glass with the crushed ice. Pack it hard.

4. Top with bourbon and stir well.

5. Add more ice if needed to fill up the glass.

6. Sip it until you magically know how to play the ukulele.

Cosmopolitan

The drink those chicks drank in that one TV show all the time. Chicks dig this drink.

- » 2 ounces vodka citron
- » 1 ounce Cointreau or Triple Sec
- » 1 ounce cranberry juice
- » 1 ounce lime juice

1. Shake well over ice. Strain into a martini glass and garnish with a lime slice to really knock the pants off somebody.

Pina Colada

On a trip to Puerto Rico a few years back, we held an informal contest to see who among us could drink 50 piña coladas in a week. It was pathetic. I think the most anyone got to was 12. They are incredibly rich. And incredibly delicious. So delicious in fact, this would make a fabulous dessert drink to serve after a meal. You can mix it in a blender or just shake it really well and pour over crushed ice.

- » 1 ounce white rum
- » 1 ounce cream of coconut (this is a sweetened coconut cream; Coco Lopez is the only brand I've ever seen)
- » 3 ounces pineapple juice

1. Combine in a blender with 1 cup of ice. Whizz around until it's smooth.
2. Serve with a big-ass straw and a nude beach.

NON-ALCOHOLIC DRINKS

I'm not going to go crazy here, but there are certain drinks you need to know how to make in order to be considered a Real Grownup. And some certain other drinks that you should have around in case the kids start crying that mommy and daddy are drinking fancy drinks and they only get hose water.

Coffee

Don't give me that crap about not knowing how to make coffee just so that you don't have to be the one to make coffee. That's not going to fly with me. Just learn how to make coffee, okay?

You can buy whole beans if you have a grinder. If you drink coffee everyday, though, it's unlikely you'll notice a difference between pre-ground and fresh ground because you're using it so quickly. I don't notice a difference anyway. Shade-grown organic beans are the nicest to the planet and the most likely to impress girls and sensitive types. Dark and French roasts make a darker, deeper-flavored brew. P.S. PLEASE don't assume that everyone loves flavored coffee as much as you do. We don't. When in doubt, just make plain old coffee and put some cinnamon in your own cup.

The rule is 2 tablespoons of ground coffee per 8 ounces of water equals 1 cup of coffee. Be sure to start with cold water because sometimes there's gross tastes and mineral deposits in the hot water heater, especially if your house is old and crotchety. Cold-brewed coffee is a neat trick for when the hurricanes come and the electricity is out.

Learn to Cook

For an electric coffee pot: measure ground coffee into a filter and put the filter in the basket. Measure the water with the clean coffee pot and pour it into the machine. Put the pot in place. Turn the machine on. Wait.

For a French press: Measure ground coffee and put it in the bottom of the pitcher. Add boiling water. Put the lid on, leaving the plunger up. After 5 minutes, press the plunger down slowly, dragging with it all the floating coffee particles, leaving fresh brewed coffee.

For cold-brewed coffee: The standard coffee/water ratio gets screwy without the benefit of heat. Combine 1½ cups water with ⅓ cup ground coffee in a container with a lid. Let sit about 12 hours at room temperature. Put a paper filter or towel in a sieve and strain it through that into a pitcher. Drink it iced when you feel bad in the morning, and you will feel better.

Tea

Someday it will happen that your dear old auntie or that sexy yoga teacher is at your house and wants some G.D. tea. Black, green, herbal? If you don't drink tea yourself, you could be on thin ice in this situation. What's the difference anyway? Well, here's the deal with tea.

Black and green tea both come from the same plant, but black tea has been oxidized, giving it a stronger tea flavor, more caffeine, and darker color. If you're not going to be drinking a lot of tea, get some black tea because it keeps its flavor longer. Black tea also makes the best iced tea, in my opinion.

Green tea is thought have more health benefits, but some people don't like the flavor as much; then again, some people do.

Herbal teas (really just an herb infusion) can be made of anything except actual tea leaves and are caffeine free by nature. Popular herbal teas are chamomile, mint, hibiscus, rose hip, and ginger.

Tea bags are pre-measured little sacks, portioned for one cup.

Loose tea is generally of a higher quality and to use it you will need either a tea-ball (small, metal, perforated ball) or a strainer to get the leaves out after steeping. Or just drink it wild-style and get leaves all in your teeth.

For green and black tea, use 1 teaspoon (or one bag) to 1 cup of water. For herbal tea, use up to 2 teaspoons. And as with coffee, always begin with clean, cool water.

Black Tea: Boil some water and pour it over the tea. Let it steep for 3–5 minutes, until the color is fairly dark and it smells strongly of tea. Add milk if you like and sugar or honey to taste.

Green Tea: Bring some water to just below the boiling point. Pour it over the tea. Let it steep for 1–2 minutes, until the color turns dark yellow to light green color. If you steep it too long, it will be unpleasantly bitter. Serve with honey or sugar; milk and cream don't really go here.

Herbal Tea: Bring some water to boil. Pour it over your tea or 1 to 2 teaspoons of dried herbs or spices to make your own herbal tea. Add honey or sugar.

Iced Tea: The best way to do this is to make a batch of hot tea and let it cool (sweeten now if you want sweet tea). Then ice it. If you don't have that much time, make a batch of hot tea using double the amount of tea, then sweeten to taste and add ice to chill it fast!

Sun Tea: A fun way to make iced tea! Get a large clear glass pitcher and fill with cold water. Add 4 teabags, cover with plastic wrap or a towel and a rubber band to keep dem bugs out, and put it in a sunny spot for a few hours until it's tea-colored. Drink the power of the sun.

Yogi Tea

Coffee shops call this chai tea, but I know the truth. Mama made this when we were sick, and I make it when my loved ones are sick now. Make some for your sicky baby and be like Florence Nightingale. If you are missing one of the spices, just don't tell anyone. This is to make two cups because you will probably want one for yourself, too, after you smell it.

- » 2½ cups water
- » 6 whole cloves
- » 8 cracked whole cardamom pods (¼ teaspoon seeds)
- » 8 black peppercorns
- » 1 stick cinnamon
- » 1 teaspoon green or black tea (one teabag)
- » 1 cup milk (or almond milk)
- » Honey
- » Optional: fresh ginger slices (for congestion)

1. Boil water with spices, not including tea, for 10-15 minutes, covered.
2. Remove from heat, add tea and steep 2 minutes.
3. Strain into two mugs and top with milk. Add honey to taste.

Hot Cocoa

Might as well make two cups of this while you're making one. It's just as easy. And then you can share. If you add the cinnamon, you can call it Mexican Hot Cocoa, and it will make more sense when you wear your sombrero to bed.

- » 1 tablespoon cocoa powder
- » 1 tablespoon sugar
- » 1 cup water
- » 1 cup milk or half-and-half
- » ½ teaspoon vanilla or dash cinnamon

1. Combine cocoa, sugar, and water in a small saucepan and bring to boil. Stir and boil 1 minute.
2. Add milk and vanilla and gently heat over low until it's very warm.

Agua Fresca

Mexico did it again, amigos. Agua fresca is like a refreshing fruit breeze that blew in from a sweet mountaintop of pleasure. You can make it with many different fruits. You can mix it with vodka or gin if you like that sort of thing. One of the best accidental cocktails I ever created was with some gin and guava agua fresca.

- » 3 cups fresh or frozen fruit (melons, berries, peaches, guava, mango)
- » 1½–2 cups cold water
- » ¼ cup sugar
- » ¼ cup lime juice

1. Pit, peel, and chop the fruit as needed. Throw it all in a blender and puree it.
2. Strain through a fine colander or mesh strainer into a large pitcher. If you have some cheesecloth handy, lay that in the colander first to strain finer particles and leave you with a clear juice.
3. Serve very cold. Garnish with fresh mint if you like.

Makes about 4 cups.

Lemonade

America's answer to agua fresca. You can make it with limes, too. And mix it with booze!

> » ¾ cup sugar
>
> » 1 cup fresh lemon or lime juice (about 6 lemons)
>
> » 6 cups cold water

1. Combine the sugar and juice in a pitcher and stir rapidly to dissolve. Add the water.

2. Serve over ice.

Makes about 7 cups.

Applejack

My aunt used to make this for my cousins and me when we were kids. I loved it and felt very special when we were served this in a fancy glass-glass with a straw.

> » 1 part ginger ale
>
> » 1 part apple juice

1. Stir together in a pitcher or glass and serve over ice.

Appendices

Abbreviations

c = cup

C = Celsius degrees

F = Fahrenheit degrees

fl oz = fluid ounce

g = gr = gram

gal = gallon

kg = kilogram

L = liter

ml = mL = milliliter

oz = ounce

pound = # = pound

pt = pint

qt = quart

t = tsp = teaspoon

T = tbl = tbsp = tablespoon

Equivalencies by Volume

Gallon	4 quarts	16 cups	3.785 liters
Quart	2 pints	4 cups	946 milliliters
Pint	2 cups	16 ounces	473 milliliters
Cup		8 ounces	236 milliliters
Ounce	2 tablespoons		30 milliliters
Tablespoon	3 teaspoons		15 milliliters
Teaspoon			5 milliliters

Equivalencies by Weight

Pounds	454 grams	.454 kilograms
Ounce	28 grams	4 cups
Kilogram	2.3 pounds	1000 grams
Gram	0.35 ounces	

Temperature Equivalents

Fahrenheit to Celsius. All temperatures assume you are at sea level.

Water Freezes	32° F	0° C
Water Simmers	115° F	45° C
Water Boils	212° F	100° C
Very Low Oven	250°–275° F	121°–135° C
Low Oven	300°–325° F	149°–163° C
Moderate Oven	350°–375° F	177°–191° C
Hot Oven	400°–425° F	204°–218° C
Very Hot Oven	450°–475° F	232°–246° C

Ingredient Equivalents

For ease of list-making and ingredient-prepping, here are some common ingredients and their approximate equivalent weights and volumes after prepping (and after cooking, when applicable).

Beans, canned, 15 ounce can = 1½ cups drained

Beans, dried, 1 pound = 2 cups dry, yields 5 cups cooked

Butter, 1 pound = 2 cups

Cheese, hard, 1 pound = 4 cups grated

Chocolate chips, 12 ounces = 1 cup

Cracker crumbs, 1 cup = 15 graham crackers, 30 saltines

Eggs, 1 large or x-large, cracked = ¼ cup

Flour, all-purpose, 1 pound = 4 cups

Honey, 1 pound = 1 ⅓ cups

Meat, ground, 1 pound = 2 cups uncooked

Nuts, 1 pound in shell = ½ pound shelled = 2 cups

Onions, 1 pound = 2 ½ cups chopped

Pasta, small, 1 pound = 4 cups uncooked, 8 cups cooked

Peanut butter, 18 ounce jar = 2 cups

Potatoes, 1 pound raw = 4 cups chopped, yields 2 cups cooked

Rice, 1 pound raw = 2 cups, yields 6 cups cooked

Sugar, white, 1 pound = 2 cups

Sugar, brown, 1 pound = 2 ¼ cups packed

Sugar, powdered, 1 pound = 3 ½–4 cups

Tomatoes, fresh, 1 pound = 2 cups chopped

Yeast, dry, 1 package = 1 ¼ teaspoons

Ingredient Substitutions

Sometimes you will find that you are out of something just as it is time to put that something in. Drat! Here's a list of some common ingredients and some alternatives to use in a pinch.

Baking powder (1 teaspoon) =
½ teaspoon cream of tartar + ¼ teaspoon baking soda

Buttermilk (1 cup) =
1 cup milk + 1 tablespoon lemon juice or vinegar
½ cup milk + ½ cup yogurt or sour cream

Chocolate, unsweetened baking (1 ounce) =
3 tablespoons cocoa powder + 1 tablespoon butter or oil

Cream, light, for baking or sauces (1 cup) =
¾ cup plus 2 tablespoons milk + 3 tablespoons butter

Flour, cake (1 cup) =
¾ cup plus 2 tablespoons sifted, all-purpose flour

Flour, self-rising (1 cup) =
1 cup all-purpose flour + 1½ t baking powder + ½ t salt

Flour, for thickening sauces (1 tablespoon) =
1½ teaspoon cornstarch for equivalent thickening power

Lemon juice (1 teaspoon) =
½ teaspoon vinegar for equivalent sour power

Sugar, brown (1 cup) =
1 cup white sugar + 1 tablespoon molasses

Learn to Cook

Troubleshooting in the Kitchen

I Burned The Beans!

Fix it: *Stop stirring.* Leave the burned stuff at the bottom of the pot and put the nonburned portion of beans (or rice or soup or whatever) into a new pot. Taste it; if the burny taste has permeated the dish, congratulations. You have just ruined your first pot of beans.

Prevent it: Make sure your stove is on the lowest heat possible and don't forget to stir soups and beans and liquid things occasionally (at least twice an hour). For rice, measure the water and rice exactly, make sure to turn it to simmer after the initial boil and turn it off when the timer dings at you. Use a heavy-bottomed pot for foods that will simmer a long time. Aluminum pots or cheap non-stick cookware have more problems with burning than Richard Pryor.

I Oversalted the Beans!

Fix it: There's no easy way. Basically the only thing you can do is make more beans or soup or whatever. Add more water or tomatoes, more onion, a grated potato—whatever seems appropriate. Don't add any more salt, obviously. Now you have a lot more soup than you bargained for, but at least it's edible. Freeze what you don't eat in containers and take them for lunch next week.

Prevent it: Measure the salt! Make sure you read that right: teaspoon, not tablespoon. Measure it away from the pot so that your elbow doesn't get jostled and you end up accidentally pouring way too much salt in. When tasting for salt, taste the broth of the beans or soup. If you taste the beans themselves for salt you will end up adding far too much.

My Gravy Is Lumpy!

Fix it: Pour the sauce or gravy through a mesh strainer to remove lumps. If the lumps are many and large, pour the sauce into the blender and whiz it around. Be careful when blending hot things! To prevent the lid from popping off, hold the lid down with a towel over it.

Prevent it: Add liquid slowly (start with ½ cup) and whisk after each addition to get it fully incorporated and smooth before adding more liquid.

My Chili Is Too Spicy!

Fix it: This works for any kind of stew or curry, too. Add a teaspoon of sugar at a time and taste after each addition. Don't add more than a few teaspoons or it will just taste sweet. Or you could add more tomatoes (or coconut milk or yogurt to a curry) to dilute the spiciness. Or you could serve it over rice. Or you could grow a pair.

Prevent it: Remember, the smaller the pepper, the spicier. Remove seeds and membranes to reduce the heat. If you can handle it, taste the peppers before adding them since spiciness varies from pepper to pepper, even in the same species (jalapeños are notoriously unpredictable.)

My Mashed Potatoes Are Too Thin!

Fix it: Add some instant potato flakes or dry milk by the tablespoon until the potatoes thicken up.

Prevent it: Drain the potatoes well and put them back in the hot pot for a few minutes before adding cream and butter. The heat from the pan will force the excess water to evaporate.

My Cake Looks Ugly!

Fix it: Trim off any weird lumps or an uneven top. Cover it with icing or glaze. Or cube it and make parfaits or a trifle instead.

Prevent it: Make sure you measure accurately and that the oven is fully pre-heated to the proper temperature. Check the expiration dates on your baking powder and soda.

My Brown Sugar Is Too Hard!

Fix it: Put the lump in the microwave for a few seconds. It will soften enough to measure.

Prevent it: Seal tightly before storing. But really, with a fix that easy, it's no big deal anyway.

My Pan Is the Wrong Damn Size!

Fix it: Check out the next chart to find the requisite pan size and its volume. Find another pan that you do have that has the same volume. OR, split your batter up into two smaller pans. You'll have to adjust the cooking time either way.

Prevent it: Prepare your cake pans before you start cooking! Get 'em out, grease 'em, flour 'em, make sure they are the right size. Geez!

Pan Sizes and Volumes

INCHES	CENTIMETERS	VOLUME
ROUND		
6x2 tall	15 x 5	4 cups
8 x 1.5 tall	20 x 4	4 cups
8 x 2 tall	20 x 5	6 cups
9 x 1.5 tall	23 x 4	6 cups
9 x 2 tall	23 x 5	8 cups
SQUARE		
8 x 8 x 1.5 tall	20 x 20 x 4	6 cups
8 x 8 x 2 tall	20 x 20 x 5	8 cups
9 x 9 x 1.5 tall	23 x 23 x 4	8 ciups
9 x 9 x 2 tall	23 x 23 x 5	10 cups
RECTANGULAR		
11 x 7 x 2 tall	28 x 18 x 5	6 cups
9 x 13 x 2 tall	33 x 23 x 5	14 cups
LOAF		
8 x 4 x 2.5 tall	20 x 10 x 6	4 cups
9 x 5 x 3 tall	23 x 13 x 8	8 cups
BUNDT/TUBE		
9 x 3 tall	23 x 8	9–10cups

Meat Cooking Temperatures

These are the temerpatures recommended by the USDA for safe meat-eating. When testing whole poultry, insert the thermometer into the thigh meat, not touching the bone for an accurate reading.

Ground Poultry	165° F/74° C
Ground Beef, Pork	160° F/71° C
Beef, Veal, Lamb	
Medium-rare	145° F/ 63° C
Medium	160° F/ 60° C
Well-done	170° F/ 77° C
Pork	
Medium	160° F/ 60° C
Well-done	170° F/ 77° C
Poultry	
Whole Chicken/Turkey	180° F/ 82° C
Poultry Breasts	170° F/ 77° C
Poultry Thighs	180° F/ 82° C
Whole Duck/Goose	180° F/ 82° C
Fish	
Well-done	145° F/ 63° C
Casseroles of Eggs or Meat	165° F/ 74° C

Learn to Cook

Recommended Cookbooks

As a new cook, you may not even own a cookbook. (Except this one, obviously.) Once you get a little more interested in cooking, you may start looking around some bookstores, poking around for something new. Here's what I look for in a cookbook. Maybe it will help.

1. Descriptions of each recipe. I like to know where it comes from, where it's going, what's it like, and what's it good with. Photos of the finished dish are pretty, but usually not very helpful unless it's something really complicated.

2. Clear font. It sounds dumb, but you'd be surprised how many publishers use a script font to make a book seem "homey," and all it really does is make it irritating to look at.

3. Drawings or photos of unusual ingredients. It's helpful to have pictures of the exciting new produce you've never heard of so you can find it in the store.

4. Well organized index. Take a look at it. Are there a billion categories and subcategories? Good. That means they didn't leave any out. Is everything alphabetical? It oughta be. If it's a cookbook from foreign lands, make sure the index offers the English and the native recipe names.

6. Community cookbooks. These are fun. I pick them up for a dollar and have a ball flipping through them on the couch, laughing, "Ew! Cheese candy!" and then getting hungry. I rarely make recipes from this type of cookbook, but I do find it interesting to know what the ladies of the First Lutheran Church of Westlake were cooking in 1972. (*Note: these cookbooks almost always fail my above requirements. I like them for a different reason, obviously.)

Finally, I feel I would be doing you a disservice if I didn't mention my favorite, most-used cookbook: *The Joy of Cooking* by Rombauer and Becker. It is the one of the best cookbooks in print. There are chapters on nutrition, menu planning, food storage, cocktails, as well as a few thousand recipes. Highly recommended.

And In Conclusion

Gosh, I don't really know what to say here. I feel like I've been talking for days. My voice is hoarse. I'm pale and shaking. Do you know how to cook yet? I sincerely hope so. At the very least I hope you have endeavored to try and have had enough successes to keep trying.

Come visit me at hilahcooking.com. I welcome comments, questions, and suggestions that I get a new hobby. I know. I keep telling myself. I love you. Thanks for reading. Bye.

Index

Learn to Cook

C

Learn to Cook

D

E

F

Learn to Cook

M

N

O

Learn to Cook

293

Learn to Cook

Learn to Cook

Made in the USA
Middletown, DE
20 December 2014